The Conifers And Taxads Of Japan

Ernest Henry Wilson

In the interest of creating a more extensive selection of rare historical book reprints, we have chosen to reproduce this title even though it may possibly have occasional imperfections such as missing and blurred pages, missing text, poor pictures, markings, dark backgrounds and other reproduction issues beyond our control. Because this work is culturally important, we have made it available as a part of our commitment to protecting, preserving and promoting the world's literature. Thank you for your understanding.

INTRODUCTION

THE Conifers and Taxads of Japan are of especial interest to us as many of them are of ornamental value in Western gardens. All that are known are now in cultivation in this country and nearly all of them are also in Europe. Many of these plants are perfectly hardy in the northern United States and in Europe, and one or two promise to be of economic value as forest trees in Great Britain and other countries. The importance and value of these trees warrant the publication of all available information concerning them. Much has been written about them since the appearance of Siebold & Zuccarini's *Flora Japonica*, new species have been discovered and much has been added to our knowledge of these plants. Some problems, however, have remained unsolved in regard to the habitat, the range of distribution and the validity of certain species and varieties. To investigate these problems, to collect specimens and take photographs of the trees was one of the principal objects of the Arnold Arboretum Expedition to Japan in 1914. From Professor Sargent I received very definite instructions and these I did my best to fulfill. In these days, thanks to a good railway service it is possible to travel quickly and with ease through the whole length of Japan, otherwise it would have been impossible to cover the ground I did in one year. On the island of Yaku-shima, the most southern point of Japan proper, the work began in wonderful and impressive forests in which the Cryptomeria is the dominant tree. From there I travelled northward through Kyushu, Shikoku, Hondo and Hokkaido to Japanese Saghalien. I saw growing, with the exception of *Juniperus communis* L. and its var. *montana* Ait., every conifer and taxad known from Japan and with the exception of these Junipers and of *Juniperus procumbens* Sieb., *J. chinensis* L., *Pinus Armandi* Franch. and *Podocarpus nagi* Zoll. & Moritz., I saw them all, growing wild. There is no record of anyone — foreigner or native — having previously enjoyed such opportunity to study these plants. I owe much to the aid and advice of Dr. H. Shirasawa and Dr. K. Miyabe through whose efforts the Government Forestry Officers everywhere gave me great assistance. It is with pleasure that I recall the meetings and talks with these gentlemen and I acknowledge with sincerest thanks their invaluable services to the Arnold Arboretum Expedition to Japan. Since my return, and under the direction of Professor Sargent, I have elaborated my field notes, and these with a full synonymy of the different species and varieties and references to the principal literature appear in the following pages.

Japan is singularly rich in coniferous trees and they range from the extreme south to the northern limit of the empire and from sea-level to the summits of the highest mountains. They are more numerous than other trees and impart much character to the scenery. Indeed, in Japan one is never out of sight of conifers. In Pinaceae with 12 genera Japan compares favorably with North America where 13 genera occur, but naturally in the larger territory of North America more species are found. In Japan three genera are endemic and of the 32 species and 8 varieties of Pinaceae only 12 species and 2 varieties are known to grow spontaneously outside of that country. Neither of the two Hard Pines reaches the mainland, but of the four Soft Pines the Korean *Pinus koraiensis* S. & Z. is really a continental species which just reaches Japan and this is true of the Chinese White Pine (*P. Armandi* Franch.) now known to grow spontaneously on the southern islands of Tanega-shima and Yaku-shima. This species also grows in Formosa. The dwarf *P. pumila* Regel has a wide range of distribution in northeastern Asia as well as on the mountains of Japan from central Hondo northward. Of the Spruces only *Picea jezoënsis* Carr. is actually known to grow on the mainland of eastern Asia, although it is probable that the species growing in Korea and now referred to *P. Schrenkiana* Fisch. & Mey. is not that species but is the same as the newly discovered *P. Koyamai* Shiras. *Larix dahurica*, var. *japonica* Maxim. apparently reaches the continent and it is doubtful if this is really different from the type species. The other Japanese members of the subfamily Abieteae are endemic.

The subfamily Taxodieae is represented by the endemic *Sciadopitys verticillata* S. & Z. and by *Cryptomeria japonica* D. Don. The latter tree was discovered on the Chusan Islands in China by James Cunningham in 1701, but it is doubtful if it is really indigenous anywhere outside of Japan. Of the subfamily Cupresseae, *Chamaecyparis obtusa* S. & Z. also grows in Formosa and *Thuja Standishii* Carr. in Korea. Except *Juniperus conferta* Parl. and the little known *J. procumbens* Sieb. no species of Juniper is peculiar to Japan, although the var. *nipponica* of *J. communis* L. and var. *Sargentii* of *J. chinensis* L. must be so considered in the present state of our knowledge of these plants. Of the Japanese Taxaceae none is endemic. *Torreya nucifera* S. & Z. grows on the island of Quelpaert off the coast of southern Korea but is otherwise confined to Japan. *Taxus cuspidata* S. & Z. grows in Korea and in eastern Siberia and is represented in China and Formosa by the var. *chinensis* Rehd. & Wils. *Cephalotaxus drupacea* S. & Z. reaches central China but is more generally represented there by the var. *sinensis* Rehd. & Wils. The two species of Podocarpus also grow in the Liukiu Islands and in Formosa. The Ginkgo is planted in Japan as in China and is probably unknown in the wild state. Three Chinese trees (*Cunninghamia lanceolata* Hook., *Cupressus funebris* Endl. and *Thuja orientalis* L.) are sparingly planted in temple grounds and gardens in Japan but are uncommon and since they are not indigenous all further reference to them in these pages will be omitted.

In Japan the distribution of many conifers is clearly defined and often limited. Of the Abieteae only *Picea jezoënsis* Carr., *Pinus parviflora* S. & Z. and *Pinus pumila* Regel are common to Hondo and Hokkaido though it is possible that *Pinus densiflora* S. & Z. may grow on these two islands. Of the other Pinaceae which grow in Hondo only *Juniperus conferta* Parl. and *J. chinensis*, var. *Sargentii* Henry grow also in Hokkaido. The two species of Podocarpus are confined to the warm parts of Shikoku and Kyushu in the south; the Torreya is only questionably wild north of latitude 36°, but the Cephalotaxus is common as far north as central Hokkaido and *Taxus cuspidata* S. & Z. is also found in the Kuriles and in Saghalien. The circumpolar *Juniperus communis* L. just reaches northern Hokkaido and is found also in the Kuriles and in Saghalien; the var. *montana* Ait. is found in Saghalien. These two Junipers are the only American and European conifers found within the limits of the Japanese Empire.

In the case of many species it is clearly demonstrated that climate is the all-important factor in limiting the distribution of conifers in Japan, yet it cannot be claimed that this has anything to do with the absence of such hardy trees as *Picea jezoënsis* Carr. and *Larix Kaempferi* Sarg. from Hondo north of the Nikko region. Again, it is curious that no Larch is indigenous in Hokkaido, yet *Larix*

INTRODUCTION

dahurica, var. *japonica* Maxim. reaches Shikotan in the southern Kuriles only a few miles from northeast Hokkaido and is abundant in Saghalien where grow in great plenty *Abies sachalinensis* Mast. and *Picea jezoënsis* Carr. which are the dominant conifers of the Hokkaido forests.

It has been stated and the statement is rather widely accepted that the Tsugaru Straits which separate northern Hondo and Hokkaido form a well-marked phytogeographical and zoögeographical boundary — the so-called Blakiston line — but so far as plants are concerned this has no foundation in fact. The warm current which flows up the east coast of Japan and is deflected out to sea about the latitude of Tokyo exercises a strong influence over the climate and consequently also over the flora. South of Tokyo broad-leaved evergreens are a feature of the vegetation and north of that latitude they rapidly disappear and the general appearance of the forests is markedly different. No hard and fast phytogeographical boundary exists, but such as it is it is found about latitude 36°.

The whole flora of Japan is largely endemic but is an integral part of the great flora which includes that of southern Korea, has its headquarters in China and extends westward to the border of the Thibetan highlands and along the Himalayas to eastern Nepal. In northern Hondo and in Hokkaido are many elements of the flora of continental northeast Asia which extends eastward from the region of Lake Baikal. And in the same region of Japan grow a number of circumpolar plants, especially members of the Ericaceae. There is some affinity between the flora of Japan and that of eastern North America, but it is much less strong than between the floras of the latter region and of central China. As far as the conifers and taxads of Japan are concerned the affinity is certainly more with western North America than with the region east of the Mississippi River. Indeed, only the Hemlocks, the two Hard Pines and *Picea Glehnii* Mast. can be said to be more nearly related to species of eastern North America than to those of the Pacific slope.

Japan is composed fundamentally of Archean rocks much overlaid with volcanic ejectamenta during different geological epochs. It is very mountainous and is mainly made up of a backbone of volcanic ranges, of which many peaks are still active, and narrow flanks of sedimentary rocks. In western Shinano and Hida provinces in central Hondo there are granite mountains and the southern island of Yaku-shima is a gigantic upthrust of the same igneous rock. There is extremely little limestone in Japan and this may have much to do with its richness in coniferous trees. The rainfall varies according to latitude from about twenty-six inches to one hundred and nineteen inches in a year and the number of rainy days averages about one hundred and fifty. The annual average amount of moisture in the air is given as 80 per cent. The high humidity and abundant precipitation are very favorable to the growth of coniferous plants. The climate of the greater part of Japan is mild and equable; in the extreme south it is warm-temperate and in the extreme north the summers are short and hot and the winters long and almost arctic in severity. But in the north snow lies deep and undisturbed upon the ground from December to the approach of spring in April and is an effectual protection to the numerous low-growing, broad-leaved Bamboos (*Sasa spp.*) and such evergreen shrubs as *Skimmia japonica* Thunb., *Daphniphyllum humile* Maxim., *Ilex rugosa* Schmidt and others which form the characteristic undergrowth in the forests.

The formation of the islands, with their high central ranges and short precipitous swift-flowing rivers, make floods particularly prevalent and dangerous, and the necessity of preserving the forest-covering of the upper mountain-slopes proportionately great and it is mainly these slopes that are clothed with conifers. In few other countries are the forests of such supreme importance to the prosperity of the nation and no other people are such consumers of forest products as the Japanese, as nearly all their buildings and most of their articles of domestic use are entirely made of wood. The coniferous trees are the principal source of the timber supply and the government forests now controlled by a good and increasingly efficient forestry service are a source of very considerable revenue. As timber trees the most valuable conifers are *Chamaecyparis obtusa* S. & Z., *C. pisifera* S. & Z., *Cryptomeria japonica* D. Don, *Tsuga Sieboldii* Carr., *Thujopsis dolabrata*, var. *Hondai* Mak., *Sciadopitys verticillata* S. & Z., *Larix Kaempferi* Sarg., *Pinus densiflora* S. & Z., *P. parviflora* S. & Z., *Picea jezoënsis* Carr. and *Abies sachalinensis* Mast.

Tree planting has been practised in Japan from time immemorial and planted avenues and groves of *Cryptomeria japonica* D. Don and *Pinus Thunbergii* Parl. are to-day common and impressive features of many popular and sacred places in the land. In reafforestation the conifers which are now planted in quantity in Japan are *Cryptomeria japonica* D. Don, *Chamaecyparis obtusa* S. & Z. and *Larix Kaempferi* Sarg. In northern Hondo *Thujopsis dolabrata*, var. *Hondai* Mak. is planted rather freely. For covering bare hills *Pinus densiflora* S. & Z. and by the sea *P. Thunbergii* Parl. are extensively grown. On the Nemuro peninsula in Hokkaido *Larix dahurica*, var. *japonica* Maxim. has been experimentally planted, and in many parts of Hokkaido similar plantings of Norway Spruce (*Picea Abies* Karst.) have been made. Near Aomori, in extreme northern Hondo, the Austrian Pine (*Pinus nigra* Arn.) is being experimented with, but in its place the forestry officials might well try *P. resinosa* Ait., the Red Pine of northeastern North America.

In North America experiments with Japanese conifers in forest planting have scarcely commenced, but in parts of Europe they have been in progress for a number of years. In Great Britain the Japanese Larch (*Larix Kaempferi* Sarg.) is by some planters regarded as a promising tree and with others *Picea jezoënsis* Carr. is in favor. I think that *Chamaecyparis obtusa* S. & Z. is worthy of extensive trial in the wetter parts of Great Britain.

In this country the conifers and taxads of Japan are valued for their ornamental qualities and no other country has contributed so many exotic plants of this class to the gardens of eastern North America. In the Hunnewell Pinetum at Wellesley, Massachusetts, founded in 1853 by Horatio Hollis Hunnewell, and on the estate of the late Dr. George R. Hall at Bristol Neck, near Warren, Rhode Island, there are growing some of the oldest and finest Japanese conifers in the Eastern States. In the former are particularly good specimens of *Torreya nucifera* S. & Z., *Picea bicolor* Mayr, *Abies homolepis* S. & Z., *A. Veitchii* Lindl., *Thuja Standishii* Carr., *Chamaecyparis pisifera*, var. *plumosa* Beissn. and *C. pisifera*, var. *squarrosa* Beissn. On the Hall estate there is a very large bush of *Taxus cuspidata* S. & Z., and tall, handsome trees of *Pinus koraiensis* S. & Z., *P. densiflora* S. & Z., *Picea polita* Carr., *P. jezoënsis* Carr., *Abies firma* S. & Z. and *Chamaecyparis obtusa* S. & Z. Dr. Hall planted these trees about 1870, and most if not all of them had been brought from Japan by him to the nursery of Samuel Parsons at Flushing, Long Island, in March 1862.

ILLUSTRATIONS

PLATE
- I. PODOCARPUS NAGI ZOLL. & MORITZ.
  Tree 21 m. tall, trunk 2 m. in girth. Nara Park, Nara, Yamato province, Hondo.
- II. PODOCARPUS NAGI ZOLL. & MORITZ.
  Trunk 2 m. in girth. Nara Park, Nara, Yamato province, Hondo.
- III. TORREYA NUCIFERA S. & Z.
  Tree 15 m. tall, trunk 2 m. in girth. Imperial Botanic Garden, Tokyo, Hondo.
- IV. TORREYA NUCIFERA S. & Z.
  Trunk 6 m. in girth. Hachiman Shrine, Kamo, Satsuma province, Kyushu.
- V. TAXUS CUSPIDATA S. & Z.
  Tree 11.5 m. tall, trunk 2 m. in girth. Yatsuga-dake, alt. 1300 m., Shinano province, Hondo.
- VI. PINUS KORAIENSIS S. & Z.
  Tree 21 m. tall, trunk 1.8 m. in girth. Imperial Botanic Garden, Tokyo, Hondo.
- VII. PINUS KORAIENSIS S. & Z.
  Trunk 1.5 m. in girth. Mt. Ontake, alt. 2100 m., Shinano province, Hondo.
- VIII. PINUS PUMILA REGEL
  Shrub 1 m. high, *Abies Mariesii* Mast. in the rear. Mt. Ontake, alt. 2800 m., Shinano province, Hondo.
- IX. PINUS PARVIFLORA S. & Z.
  Tree 16–20 m. tall, trunk 1.3–1.6 m. in girth. Adzuma-san, alt. 1200 m., Uzen province, Hondo.
- X. PINUS PARVIFLORA S. & Z.
  Trunk 3.75 m. in girth. Shiraga-yama, alt. 1600 m., Tosa province, Shikoku.
- XI. PINUS DENSIFLORA S. & Z.
  Tree 30–33 m. tall, trunk 2.6–3.3 m. in girth. Fuji-san, alt. 750 m., Suruga province, Hondo.
- XII. PINUS DENSIFLORA, VAR. UMBRACULIFERA MAYR
  Tree 3 m. tall. Imperial Botanic Garden, Tokyo, Hondo.
- XIII. PINUS THUNBERGII PARL.
  Tree 20–25 m. tall, trunk 2–2.3 m. in girth. Mt. Kirishima, Osumi province, Kyushu.
- XIV. PINUS THUNBERGII PARL.
  Yaku-shima, alt. 150 m., Osumi province, Kyushu.
- XV. LARIX KAEMPFERI SARG.
  Tree 20–25 m. tall, trunk 1.6–2.3 m. in girth. Senjo-ga-hara, Nikko region, Shimotsuke province, Hondo.
- XVI. LARIX KAEMPFERI SARG.
  Trunk 3.75 m. in girth. Yumoto, Nikko region, Shimotsuke province, Hondo.
- XVII. LARIX DAHURICA, VAR. JAPONICA MAXIM.
  Tree 25 m. tall, trunk 2–2.6 m. in girth. Konuma, near Toyohara, Saghalien.
- XVIII. LARIX DAHURICA, VAR. JAPONICA MAXIM.
  Trunk 2.6 m. in girth. Konuma, near Toyohara, Saghalien.
- XIX. PICEA POLITA CARR.
  Tree 20–25 m. tall, trunk 2–3.3 m. in girth. Lake Yamanaka, base of Fuji-san, Suruga province, Hondo.

ILLUSTRATIONS

PLATE

XX. PICEA POLITA CARR.
    Trunk 2.6 m. in girth. Lake Yamanaka, base of Fuji-san, Suruga province, Hondo.

XXI. PICEA MAXIMOWICZII REGEL
    Tree 8 m. tall, trunk 0.75 m. in girth. Yatsuga-dake, alt. 1600 m., Shinano province. Hondo.

XXII. PICEA MAXIMOWICZII REGEL
    Trunk 2 m. in girth. Tsushima Temple, Yatsuga-dake, Shinano province, Hondo.

XXIII. PICEA KOYAMAI SHIRAS.
    Tree 18 m. tall, trunk 1 m. in girth. Yatsuga-dake, alt. 1750 m., Shinano province, Hondo.

XXIV. PICEA KOYAMAI SHIRAS.
    Tree 13–18 m. tall, with *Larix Kaempferi* Sarg. Yatsuga-dake, 1750 m., Shinano province, Hondo.

XXV. PICEA GLEHNII MAST.
    Tree 26 m. tall, trunk 2.3 m. in girth. Rubeshibe, Kitami province, Hokkaido.

XXVI. PICEA GLEHNII MAST.
    Trunk 3.3 m. in girth, with *Abies sachalinensis* Mast. in the rear. Oketo, Kitami province, Hokkaido.

XXVII. PICEA JEZOËNSIS CARR.
    Tree 33 m. tall, trunk 3.75 m. in girth, with *Betula Maximowicziana* Regel. Noboribetsu, Iburi province, Hokkaido.

XXVIII. PICEA JEZOENSIS CARR.
    Trunk 3.75 m. in girth. Noboribetsu, Iburi province, Hokkaido.

XXIX. TSUGA SIEBOLDII CARR.
    Tree 25 m. tall, trunk 6 m. in girth, *Abies firma* S. & Z. in the rear. Yaku-shima, alt. 780 m., Osumi province, Kyushu.

XXX. TSUGA SIEBOLDII CARR.
    To the left *Cryptomeria japonica* D. Don. Yaku-shima, alt. 700 m., Osumi province, Kyushu.

XXXI. TSUGA DIVERSIFOLIA MAST.
    Tree 26 m. tall, trunk 2.75 m. in girth, to the left *Abies Veitchii* Lindl. Yumoto, Nikko region, Shimotsuke province, Hondo.

XXXII. TSUGA DIVERSIFOLIA MAST.
    Trunk 3.75 m. in girth. Nakabusa-onsen, alt. 1300 m., Shinano province, Hondo.

XXXIII. PSEUDOTSUGA JAPONICA BEISSN.
    Tree 20 m. tall, trunk 2.6 m. in girth. Nishinogawa, Tosa province, Shikoku.

XXXIV. PSEUDOTSUGA JAPONICA, BEISSN.
    Trunk 2.25 m. in girth. Nishinogawa, Tosa province, Shikoku.

XXXV. ABIES FIRMA S. & Z.
    Tree 20–23 m. tall, trunk 2.6–3.3 m. in girth, to the left a Cryptomeria tree 27 m. tall. Yaku-shima, alt. 780 m., Osumi province, Kyushu.

XXXVI. ABIES FIRMA S. & Z.
    Trunk 6 m. in girth. Mt. Kirishima, Osumi province, Kyushu.

XXXVII. ABIES HOMOLEPIS S. & Z.
    Tree 20 m. tall, trunk 2 m. in girth, *Larix Kaempferi* Sarg. in the rear. Fuji-san, 1500 m., Suruga province, Hondo.

XXXVIII. ABIES HOMOLEPIS S. & Z.
    Trunk 5.5 m. in girth. Lake Chuzenji, Nikko region, Shimotsuke province, Hondo.

XXXIX. ABIES HOMOLEPIS, VAR. UMBELLATA WILS.
    Tree 18 m. tall, trunk 2 m. in girth. Lake Chuzenji, Nikko region, Shimotsuke province, Hondo.

ILLUSTRATIONS

PLATE

XL. ABIES MARIESII MAST.
    Tree 5–8 m. tall, *Rhododendron brachycarpum* G. Don in foreground. Adzuma-san, alt. 2000 m., Uzen province, Hondo.

XLI. ABIES MARIESII MAST.
    Tree 13–16 m. tall, trunk 1–2 m. in girth. Onsenga-dake, Nikko region, Shimotsuke province, Hondo.

XLII. ABIES VEITCHII LINDL.
    Tree 25 m. tall, trunk 2 m. in girth, *Picea jezoënsis* Carr. in rear with an undergrowth of *Sasa nipponica* Mak. & Shibata. Mt. Ontake, alt. 2000 m., Shinano province, Hondo.

XLIII. ABIES VEITCHII LINDL.
    Trunk 2.25 m. in girth. Yumoto, Nikko region, Shimotsuke province, Hondo.

XLIV. ABIES SACHALINENSIS MAST.
    Tree 23–25 m. tall, trunk 1–1.6 m. in girth, with *Hydrangea petiolaris* S. & Z. clothing trunks. Nopporo, Ishikari province, Hokkaido.

XLV. ABIES SACHALINENSIS MAST.
    Trunk 2.25 m. in girth. Konuma, near Toyohara, Saghalien.

XLVI. SCIADOPITYS VERTICILLATA S. & Z.
    Tree 18–25 m. tall, trunk 1–2 m. in girth. Koya-san, alt. 1300 m., Kii province, Hondo.

XLVII. SCIADOPITYS VERTICILLATA S. & Z.
    Trunk 4 m. in girth. Koya-san, Kii province, Hondo.

XLVIII. CRYPTOMERIA JAPONICA D. DON
    Tree 37 m. tall, trunk 3.3 m. in girth. Jimba, Ugo province, Hondo.

XLIX. CRYPTOMERIA JAPONICA D. DON
    Trunk 11 m. in girth. Kasuga-yama, Nara, Yamato province, Hondo.

L. THUJOPSIS DOLABRATA, VAR. HONDAI MAK.
    Tree 21 m. tall, trunk 2.25 m. in girth. Aomori, Mutsu province, Hondo.

LI. THUJOPSIS DOLABRATA, VAR. HONDAI MAK.
    Trunk 2.5 m. in girth. Aomori, Mutsu province, Hondo.

LII. THUJA STANDISHII CARR.
    Tree 15 m. tall, trunk 3.6 m. in girth. Yumoto, Nikko region, Shimotsuke province, Hondo.

LIII. THUJA STANDISHII CARR.
    Trunk 3.6 m. in girth, *Sasa paniculata* Mak. & Shibata as an undergrowth. Yumoto, Nikko region, Shimotsuke province, Hondo.

LIV. CHAMAECYPARIS OBTUSA S. & Z.
    Tree 25–30 m. tall, trunk 2.5–3.3 m. in girth. Koya-san, Kii province, Hondo.

LV. CHAMAECYPARIS OBTUSA S. & Z.
    Trunk 4.75 m. in girth. Koya-san, Kii province, Hondo.

LVI. CHAMAECYPARIS PISIFERA S. & Z.
    Tree 33–46 m. tall, trunk 3.3–5 m. in girth. Mt. Ontake, alt. 1600 m., Shinano province, Hondo.

LVII. CHAMAECYPARIS PISIFERA S. & Z.
    Trunk 4.75 m. in girth. Kurosawa, Mt. Ontake, Shinano province, Hondo.

LVIII. JUNIPERUS RIGIDA S. & Z.
    Tree 5 m. tall, with scrub growth of *Pinus densiflora* S. & Z. Yatsuga-dake, Shinano province, Hondo.

LIX. JUNIPERUS CONFERTA PARL.
    Covering sand dunes on shores of Okhotsk Sea, Sakaihama, Saghalien.

CONIFERS AND TAXADS OF JAPAN

GINKGOACEAE

GINKGO L.

GINKGO BILOBA Linnaeus, *Mant. Alt.* 313 (1771). — Thunberg, *Fl. Jap.* 358 (1784). — Miquel in Siebold & Zuccarini, *Fl. Jap.* II. 73, t. 136 (1870. — Franchet & Savatier, *Enum. Pl. Jap.* I. 474 (1875). — Masters in *Jour. Linn. Soc.* XVIII. 500 (1881); XXVI. 546 (1902). — Sargent, *Forest Fl. Jap.* 75 (1894). — Fujii in *Tokyo Bot. Mag.* IX. 444, t. 8 (1895). — Shirasawa, *Icon. Ess. For. Jap.* I. 10, t. 8, fig. 1-14 (1900). — Matsumura, *Ind. Pl. Jap.* II. pt. 1, 3 (1905). — Elwes & Henry, *Trees Gr. Brit. & Irel.* I. 56, t. 21-23 (1906). — Silva Tarouca, *Uns. Freiland-Nadelh.* 79, fig. 73 (1913). — Rehder & Wilson in Sargent, *Pl. Wilson.* II. 1 (1914).

Salisburia adiantifolia Smith in *Trans. Linn. Soc.* III. 330 (1797).
Pterophyllus Salisburiensis Nelson, *Pinac.* 163 (1866).
Ginkgo macrophylla Jackson in *Index Kew.* I. 1028 (as a synonym) (1898).

The Ginkgo which is the only representative of its family is a commonly planted tree, especially in the grounds of Buddhist temples, but is nowhere spontaneous in Japan and, indeed, has not yet been discovered in a wild state in any country.[1] Here and there in Japan are magnificent specimens of this interesting tree from 26 to 30 m. tall and from 5 to 8 metres in girth of trunk with broad wide-spreading crowns. In the city of Tokyo there are many fine Ginkgo trees; and one of the largest grows in the courtyard of Koyenji Temple and measures fully 26 m. tall with a trunk 8.5 m. in girth at 1.5 m. from the ground. In front of the Bodoiin Temple at Nara there is growing a Ginkgo tree and within it a large Keaki tree (*Zelkova serrata* Makino). The trunk of the Ginkgo encloses the Keaki on three sides and the whole measures nearly 5 m. in girth. Presumably a bird or the wind deposited a seed of the Keaki in a crack or hollow in the Ginkgo, where it germinated and has grown into a large tree. On many old Ginkgo trees " chi-chi," or nipples, are freely developed. These stout aërial root-like protuberances are often from 1.5 to 2 m. long. When they reach the ground they develop roots from the apex and leafy branches above. This phenomenon is common in Japan.

The Ginkgo is too well known to need description. It is a survival of prehistoric forests and one of the handsomest of all trees. In the autumn the leaves change to clear yellow and the tree becomes as conspicuous as it is beautiful. The yellow plum-like fruit has a very rancid smell, but the nut-like kernel when roasted is eaten; it is, however, much less esteemed in Japan than in China. The wood is light yellow in color, soft and brittle and has no economic value.

[1] According to Frank N. Meyer, botanical explorer for the U. S. Department of Agriculture, "the Ginkgo grows spontaneously in rich valleys over some ten square miles near Changhua Hsien, about 70 miles west of Hangchou in the Chekiang province, China." There "the trees are so common that they are cut for firewood." It is, however, by no means certain that this is the original home of the Ginkgo as these trees may all have descended from a planted tree. Meyer's discovery, however, is interesting, for there is no other evidence of the Ginkgo growing spontaneously or that it is cut for any purpose.

Japanese names for this tree are Ichō or Ichō-no-ki and Ginnan-no-ki. The name Ginkgo is Kaempfer's (*Amoen.* fasc. V, 811, t. [1712]) rendering of the Chinese character for Yin-kuo, i. e. Silver-nut. It was found by Kaempfer in Japan and was introduced into cultivation in Europe at the Botanic Garden at Utrecht about 1730. It was introduced into this country in 1784 by William Hamilton, who planted it in his garden at Woodlawn, near Philadelphia. It grows well and is perfectly hardy in New England. In Washington it is used as a street tree.

TAXACEAE

KEY TO THE JAPANESE GENERA

Subfam. PODOCARPEAE

Leaves strap-shaped, linear, or lance-shaped to ovate; male aments cylindrical, in threes; fruit peduncled, drupaceous; seed inverted . . . . PODOCARPUS.

Subfam. TAXEAE

Leaves linear; male aments globose; seed erect.
    Fruit drupe-like, maturing in two seasons.
        Leaves not pungent, midrib prominent on upper side; fruit long-peduncled.
                CEPHALOTAXUS.
        Leaves pungent, midrib not showing on upper side; fruit sessile or subsessile.
                TORREYA.
    Fruit nut-like, maturing in one season, seated within a fleshy, scarlet aril . . TAXUS.

Subfam. PODOCARPEAE Reichb.

PODOCARPUS L'Herit.

A genus of about 60 species confined mainly to the Southern Hemisphere and especially to Malaysia, Australia and New Zealand. Some 13 species are found in South America and the West Indies; eight are known from Africa and two from India. In Japan two species are indigenous and are also found in the Liukiu Islands and in Formosa.

KEY TO THE JAPANESE SPECIES

Leaves alternate or subopposite, strap-shaped or linear, with a prominent midrib; fruit seated on a fleshy purple-colored receptacle . . . . P. MACROPHYLLUS.
Leaves opposite or subopposite, lanceolate to ovate, without a midrib; fruit globose, subtended by a few scaly bracteoles . . . . P. NAGI

PODOCARPUS MACROPHYLLUS D. Don

PODOCARPUS MACROPHYLLUS D. Don in Lambert, *Descr. Pinus*, II. 22 (1824); ed. minor, II. 143 (1832). — Siebold & Zuccarini in *Abh. Akad. Münch.* IV. pt. 3, 232 (*Fl. Jap. Fam. Nat.* 108) (1846). — Endlicher, *Syn. Conif.* 216 (1847). — Miquel in *Ann. Mus. Lugd.-Bat.* III. 168 (1867); *Prol. Fl. Jap.* 332 (1867); in Siebold & Zuccarini, *Fl. Jap.* II. 70, t. 133 (1870). — Franchet & Savatier, *Enum. Pl. Jap.* I. 475 (1875). — Masters in *Jour. Linn. Soc.* XVIII. 501 (1881). — Sargent, *Forest Fl. Jap.* 77 (1894).—Shirasawa, *Icon. Ess. For. Jap.* I. 31, t. 13, fig. 13–25 (1900). — Kent in Veitch, *Man. Conif.* ed. 2, 150 (1900). — Matsumura in *Tokyo Bot. Mag.* XV. 139 (1901); *Ind. Pl. Jap.* II. pt. 1, 15 (1905). — Pilger in Engler, *Pflanzenr.* IV.-5, 79 (*Taxaceae*) (1903). — Silva Tarouca, *Uns. Freiland-Nadelh.* 260, fig. 271 (1913).

    Taxus macrophylla Thunberg, *Fl. Jap.* 276 (1784). — Banks, *Icon. Kaempfer*, t. 24 (1791).

I saw this tree growing wild in the forests at the base of the active volcano Higashi-Kirishima, near the hamlet of Arasho in Osumi province, Kyushu. These forests are evergreen and composed largely of Oaks such as *Quercus gilva* Bl., *Q. glauca* Thunb., *Q. acuta* Thunb., *Q. myrsinaefolia* Bl., and various members of Lauraceae, among which *Machilus Thunbergii* S. & Z. is dominant; *Distylium racemosum* S. & Z. and such conifers and taxads as *Abies firma* S. & Z., *Pinus densiflora* S. & Z., *P. Thunbergii* Parl., *Tsuga Sieboldii* Carr., *Cephalotaxus drupacea* S. & Z. and *Torreya nucifera* S. & Z. are also common. The undergrowth is chiefly *Aucuba japonica* Thunb. and *Skimmia japonica* Thunb. The Podocarpus trees are not large, being from 16 to 20 m. tall and in girth of trunk from 1 to 1.5 m. The trunk is straight and is clothed with gray, shallowly fissured, shreddy bark. The branches are short, thin, very numerous and spreading, and the aspect of the tree is decidedly sombre. The leaves are narrow-oblong to oblong-lanceolate, very dark green, and occasionally somewhat glaucous beneath. The fruit is about the size of a garden pea, greenish and pruinose or sometimes purplish and is seated upon a fleshy purple-colored receptacle. The wood is yellowish brown and very durable in water, but the tree is so rare that the wood has no recognized market value.

Japanese names for this Podocarpus are Kusa-maki, Inu-maki, Hon-maki or simply Maki. It is a great favorite in gardens, cemeteries and temple grounds everywhere in the warmer parts of Japan, and is in general use as a hedge plant and in topiary work. The leaves vary in size and are sometimes variegated, and in cultivation several varieties are recognized. A form with large leaves is f. *grandifolius* Pilger (in Engler, *Pflanzenr.* IV.-5, 80 [*Taxaceae*] [1903]) and another with narrow leaves is f. *angustifolius* Pilger (l. c.).

I have seen specimens of this tree from the Liukiu Islands and from Formosa, but I do not know if they were from wild or cultivated trees. The species is very closely related to the Indian *P. neriifolius* D. Don and it is doubtful if the two are really distinct. Like a number of other Japanese plants, *P. macrophyllus* was first made known in the West by Kaempfer under its vernacular name of Maki (*Amoen. fasc.* V. 78 [1712]), and his specimen is figured by Banks under Thunberg's name of *Taxus macrophylla*. According to Aiton (*Hort. Kew.* ed. 2, V. 416 [1813]) it was introduced from China, by William Kerr, to Kew in 1804. It was taken to Java by the Dutch probably from Japan at an early date and Siebold says it was introduced into Holland in 1830. On subsequent dates it has been sent or brought to Europe and it is one of the many plants which Dr. George R. Hall brought from Japan to this country in March, 1862. The Maki is too tender for cultivation in the Northern States, but it thrives in California and in the Southern States. In Great Britain and in Europe generally it can only be grown in the open ground in the mildest regions. A variety of this species is

PODOCARPUS MACROPHYLLUS, var. MAKI Siebold in *Jaarb. Nederl. Maatsch. Aanmoed. Tuinb.* 1844, 35 (*Naaml.*). — Endlicher, *Syn. Conif.* 216 (1847). — Miquel in Siebold & Zuccarini, *Fl. Jap.* II. 71, t. 134 (1870). — Maximowicz in *Bull. Acad. Sci. St. Pétersbourg*, sér. 3, XV. 380 (1871); in Mél. Biol. VII. 562 (1871).

Taxus chinensis Roxburgh, *Hort. Bengal.* 73 (1814).
Podocarpus chinensis Sweet, *Hort. Brit.* 371 (1827). — Tanaka, *Useful Pl. Jap.* 66, fig. 578 (1891).
Juniperus chinensis Roxburgh, *Fl. Ind.* ed. 2, III. 840 (not Linnaeus) (1832).
Taxus Makoya Forbes, *Pinet. Woburn.* 218 (1839).

Podocarpus japonica Siebold in *Jaarb. Nederl. Maatsch. Aanmoed. Tuinb.* 1844, 85 (*Naaml.*).
Podocarpus Makoyi Blume, *Rumph.* III. 215 (1847).
Podocarpus Vrieseana Hort. ex Parlatore in De Candolle, *Prodr.* XVI. pt. 2, 516 (as a synonym) (1868).
Podocarpus Miquelia Hort. ex Parlatore l. c. (as a synonym) (1868).
Podocarpus macrophyllus, subsp. *maki* Pilger in Engler, *Pflanzenr.* IV.-5, 80 (*Taxaceae*) (1903). — Matsumura, *Ind. Pl. Jap.* II. pt. 1, 16 (1905).

This variety is distinguished by its small, densely crowded, linear-lanceolate leaves and by its erect or ascending-spreading branches. As usually seen in gardens and temple grounds in Japan it is a low bush, but when allowed to grow freely it forms a small bushy tree and in appearance is not so distinct from the type species. This Maki is known only as a cultivated plant, but as such is plentiful in the warmer parts of Japan and in China. According to Siebold it was brought to Europe in 1800, and as we know from Forbes, it was introduced about 1830 into the Woburn Pinetum. According to Roxburgh it was sent from China by William Kerr to Calcutta in 1812. Roxburgh cites Lo-hon-tsong as the Chinese name for this plant. In central and western China this name (Lo-han-sung, i. e. Lo-han's Pine) is applied to *Cephalotaxus Fortunei* Hook. The variety *maki* is no more hardy than the type and its real origin is unknown. The Japanese cultivate variegated forms of this variety. Another variety of this species (var. *appressus* Matsumura, *Ind. Pl. Jap.* II. pt. 1, 16 [1905]), known as the Sekkwa-maki, is also cultivated in Japan. This plant has even smaller leaves than has the var. *maki*, and the branches spread horizontally and are often subpendulous. It is a low shrub and was first described by Maximowicz as a species under the name of *P. appressa* (in *Bull. Acad. Sci. St. Pétersbourg*, sér. 3, XV. 379 [1871]; in *Mél. Biol.* VII. 561 [1871]).

PODOCARPUS NAGI Zoll. & Moritz.

Plates I and II

Podocarpus nagi Zollinger & Moritzi apud Zollinger, *Syst. Verz. Ind. Arch.* II. 82 (as a synonym) (1854). — Makino in *Tokyo Bot. Mag.* XVII. 113 (1903). — Pilger in Engler, *Pflanzenr.* IV.-5, 60, t. 9, fig. c–e (*Taxaceae*) (1903).

Myrica nagi Thunberg, *Fl. Jap.* 76 (1784).
Nageia japonica Gaertner, *Fruct.* I. 191, t. 39, fig. 8 (1788).
Podocarpus Nageia R. Brown apud Mirbel in *Mém. Mus. Paris*, XIII. 75 (1825). — Siebold & Zuccarini in *Abh. Akad. M¨nch.* IV. pt. 3, 233 (*Fl. Jap. Fam. Nat.* 109) (1846). — Endlicher, *Syn. Conif.* 207 (1847). — Zollinger, *Syst. Verz. Ind. Arch.* II. 82 (1854). — Miquel in *Ann. Mus. Lugd.-Bat.* III. 168 (1867); *Prol. Fl. Jap.* 332 (1867); in Siebold & Zuccarini, *Fl. Jap.* II. 71, t. 135 (1870). — Franchet & Savatier, *Enum. Pl. Jap.* I. 474 (1875). — Masters in *Jour. Linn. Soc.* XVIII. 501 (1881). — Sargent, *Forest Fl. Jap.* 77 (1894). — Henry in *Trans. Asiat. Soc. Jap.* XXIV. suppl. 91 (*List Pl. Formos.*) (1896). — Shirasawa, *Icon. Ess. For. Jap.* I. 30, t. 13, fig. 1-12 (1900). — Kent in Veitch, *Man. Conif.* ed. 2, 151 (1900). — Matsumura in *Tokyo Bot. Mag.* XV. 139 (1901); *Ind. Pl. Jap.* II. pt. 1, 16 (1905).
Dammara Veitchii Henkel & Hochstetter, *Syn. Nadelh.* 216 (1865).
Podocarpus Japonica Nelson, *Pinac.* 155 (not Siebold) (1866).
Agathis Dammara Engler in *Bot. Jahrb.* VI. 49 (not Richard) (1885).
Nageia Nagi Kuntze, *Rev. Gen. Pl.* II. 798 (1891).

I did not see wild trees of this species in my travels in Japan, but Shirasawa and Matsumura both state that it is indigenous in Shikoku and in Kyushu. The first tree I saw was at Kagoshima, where it grows in the famous garden of Prince Shimazu and is about 16 m. tall, with a trunk 1.3 m. in girth. The tree is rather crowded and the branches somewhat sparse. At Nara, the old eighth-century capital, there are several groves and many scattered trees in the park and in the woods about Kasuga-yama. In all probability these or their parents were planted in early times, but from the many seedling and young trees it is evident that they have long perpetuated themselves. As seen at Nara the Nagi, as the Japanese call it, is one of the most strikingly beautiful of all evergreen trees. It is of medium size, growing from 16 to 23 m. tall and from 1.3 to 2.5 m. in girth of trunk, which is straight, and if tapped with the knuckle sounds hollow. The bark is nearly smooth, brownish purple and on old trees scales off in thin gray flakes. The branches are numerous, ascending-spreading and spreading, moderately long and not very thick and the crown is more or less oval. The leaves are lance- or elliptic-lance-shaped, lustrous dark green and are often slightly glaucous, more especially on the under side. The fruit is globose and plum-like, from 1.3 to 1.6 cm. wide, bluish black and pruinose and the foot-stalk is not thickened. The wood is pale yellowish brown, soft and compact, with a wavy grain.

Matsumura reports this tree from the Liukiu Islands and Henry says that in Formosa it is known as the Sha-shan or Shan-sha, and that it is a valuable timber tree. Probably it is indigenous there. In gardens in the warmer parts of Japan the Nagi is cultivated and varieties with narrow, broad, and variegated leaves are recognized.

Like *P. macrophyllus* D. Don, this species was first made known to us by Kaempfer (*Amoen.* fasc. V. 773, 874 [1712]), who describes it as *Laurus Julifera, folio specioso enervi* and gives an excellent figure of it under its vernacular name of Nagi. According to Siebold (*Jaarb. Nederl. Maatsch. Aanmoed. Tuinb.* 1844, 35 [*Naaml.*]) it was introduced by him to Ghent in 1830. It is less hardy than *P. macrophyllus* D. Don, but grows very well in California.

Subfam. TAXEAE Reichb.

CEPHALOTAXUS S. & Z.

A small genus of low trees or shrubs consisting of seven species all indigenous in the Orient; two grow on the Khasia and Mishmi Hills in northern Assam, one in Formosa and four with two varieties are found in China. One of these species is also indigenous in Japan.

CEPHALOTAXUS DRUPACEA S. & Z.

CEPHALOTAXUS DRUPACEA Siebold & Zuccarini in *Abh. Akad. Münch.* IV. pt. 3, 232 (*Fl. Jap. Fam. Nat.* II. 108) (1846). — Endlicher, *Syn. Conif.* 239 (1847). — Miquel in *Ann. Mus. Lugd.-Bat.* III. 169 (1867); *Prol. Fl. Jap.* 333 (1867); in Siebold & Zuccarini, *Fl. Jap.* II. 66, t. 130, 131 (1870). — Franchet & Savatier, *Enum. Pl. Jap.* I. 473 (1875). — Masters in *Jour. Linn. Soc.* XVIII. 499 (1881); in *Gard. Chron.* ser. 3, XXXIII. 228, fig. 94 (1903). — Sargent, *Forest Fl. Jap.* 75 (1894). — Shirasawa, *Icon. Ess. For. Jap.* I. 31, t. 14 (1900). — Kent in Veitch, *Man. Conif.*

ed. 2, 112 (1900). — Palibin in *Act. Hort. Petrop.* XIX. 136 (*Consp. Fl. Kor.*) (1901). — Pilger in Engler, *Pflanzenr.* IV.-5, 100, fig. 19, 20 (*Taxaceae*) (1903). — Matsumura, *Ind. Pl. Jap.* II. pt. 1, 6 (1905). — Hemsley in *Bot. Mag.* CXXXV. t. 8285 (1909). — Hayata, *Veget. Mt. Fuji*, 46 (1911). — Elwes & Henry, *Trees Gr. Brit. & Irel.* VI. 1469 (1912). — Rehder & Wilson in Sargent, *Pl. Wilson.* II. 3 (1914). — Bean, *Trees & Shrubs Brit. Isl.* I. 330, fig. (1914).

Taxus coriacea Hort. ex Knight & Perry, *Syn. Conif.* 51 (as a synonym) (1850?).
Cephalotaxus coriacea Hort. ex Knight & Perry l. c. (as a synonym) (1850?).
Podocarpus drupacea Hort. ex Knight & Perry l. c. (as a synonym) (1850?).
Podocarpus coriacea Hort. ex Knight & Perry l. c. (as a synonym) (1850?).
Cephalotaxus Fortunei foemina Hort. apud Carrière, *Traité Conif.* 509 (1855).
Taxus Japonica Hooker ex Gordon, *Pinet.* suppl. 21 (as a synonym) (1862).
Cephalotaxus foemina Hort. ex Carrière, *Traité Conif.* ed. 2, 720 (as a synonym) (1867).

This is the only species of Cephalotaxus indigenous in Japan, where as a bush or low bushy tree it is more or less common in woods and thickets from Satsuma province northward through Kyushu, Shikoku, and Hondo to Hokkaido, where it is a common undergrowth in forests of *Abies sachalinensis* Mast. at Nopporo in Ishikari province beyond Sapporo. It has also been reported from the mainland of Korea and from Hupeh province in central China. In the forests at Nopporo and elsewhere in the colder parts of Japan it is a shrub from 1 to 2.5 m. tall and of no particular shape, but in the milder regions it is usually a small tree. At Gotemba, in Suruga province, on the lower slopes of Fuji-san between 600 and 800 m. in open moorland, it is common as a bushy tree from 5 to 8 m. tall with a trunk from 0.75 to 1 m. in girth. The largest trees I saw grow in the rich forests at the foot of Higashi-Kirishima, near Araso in Usumi province, Kyushu, where *Podocarpus macrophyllus* D. Don also grows wild. In these forests I saw many trees from 8 to 10 m. tall with trunks from 1 to 1.3 m. in girth and wide-spreading branches forming broad rounded crowns.[1] Such trees, with their dark-green leaves pale or glaucescent on the under side, are very beautiful. The bark is gray and fissured into narrow strips which are easily detached. The leaves are from 2 to 4.5 cm. long, straight or slightly curved, abruptly contracted to a mucronate apex and pectinately arranged; on flat lateral branches they are strictly in one plane or slightly irregular, on ascending branches the arrangement is more or less irregular and they are ascending-spreading. The fruit is obovoid to ellipsoid, from 1.6 to 2.5 cm. long, purplish in color, and ripens the second year. It is rich in oil, which is or was formerly expressed and used as an illuminant. The wood is whitish brown, firm and straight-grained and is employed for making small household utensils. This Cephalotaxus has several Japanese names, but in Hondo and southward it is usually called the Inu-gaya or Abura-gaya and in Hokkaido by the Ainu name of Anatni.

Cephalotaxus drupacea was introduced into cultivation in the Botanic Garden at Ghent, by von Siebold in 1830. It is scarcely hardy in this country as far north as Boston, Massachusetts, although in this Arboretum it is growing well in a moist shady place. At Wodenethe in Beacon on the Hudson River, New York, there are fine plants of this Cephalotaxus. In Japan I secured seeds from its

---

[1] Mayr (*Fremdl. Wald- u. Parkb.* 269 [1906]) says that in the warmer parts of Japan it grows 20 m. tall. I neither saw nor heard of such large trees and suspect that he confused it with *Torreya nucifera* S. & Z.

northern limits at Nopporo and also from Hayachine-san in northern Hondo, and it will be interesting to see if these produce a hardier race than that in general cultivation. A variety of this species is

CEPHALOTAXUS DRUPACEA, var. PEDUNCULATA Miquel in *Ann. Mus. Lugd.-Bat.* III. 169 (1867); *Prol. Fl. Jap.* 333 (1867).

>   *Taxus Harringtonia* Knight apud Forbes, *Pinet. Woburn.* 217, t. 66 (1839).
>   *Taxus Inukaja* Knight apud Loudon, *Encycl. Trees*, 943 (1842). — Knight & Perry, *Syn. Conif.* 51 (as a synonym) (1850?).
>   *Cephalotaxus pedunculata* Siebold & Zuccarini in *Abh. Akad. Münch.* IV. pt. 3, 232 (*Fl. Jap. Fam. Nat.* II. 108) (1846). — Endlicher, *Syn. Conif.* 238 (1847). — Miquel in Siebold & Zuccarini, *Fl. Jap.* II. 67, t. 132 (1870). — Franchet & Savatier, *Enum. Pl. Jap.* I. 473 (1875). — Masters in *Jour. Linn. Soc.* XVIII. 499 (1881); in *Gard. Chron.* n. ser. XXI. 113 (1884). — Elwes & Henry, *Trees Gr. Brit. & Irel.* VI. 1471 (1912).
>   *Taxus Sinensis* Knight ex Gordon, *Pinet.* suppl. 21 (as a synonym) (1862).
>   *Cephalotaxus drupacea*, var. β Miquel in Siebold & Zuccarini, *Fl. Jap.* II. 68 (as a synonym) (1870).
>   *Cephalotaxus Harringtonia* K. Koch, *Dendr.* II. pt. 2, 102 (1873). — Silva Tarouca, *Uns. Freiland-Nadelh.* 160, fig. 159 (1913).
>   *Cephalotaxus drupacea*, var. *Harringtonia* Pilger in Engler, *Pflanzenr.* IV.-5, 102 (*Taxaceae*) (1903). — Matsumura, *Ind. Pl. Jap.* II. pt. 1, 7 (1905).

In the woods and thickets of Japan I searched diligently for a specimen of this curious plant, but failed to discover one. Male specimens collected on Shiragayama in Tosa province, Shikoku, approach it closely in length of peduncle; they have acuminate bracts, but the flower clusters are simple as in the type. In Siebold & Zuccarini, *Flora Japonica*, it is stated that *C. pedunculata* and *C. drupacea* grow in the same regions and are both wild and cultivated. Apart from material cultivated in Europe I have seen one specimen only and that from a garden in Tokyo which represents the true *C. pedunculata* S. & Z. The male plant only is known and I can see no reason for regarding it other than an abnormal variant of the common wild *C. drupacea* S. & Z., and this is the view taken by Japanese botanists and horticulturists. This variety was introduced by von Siebold into the Botanic Gardens at Leyden in 1829. Another variety of this species is

CEPHALOTAXUS DRUPACEA, f. FASTIGIATA Pilger in Engler, *Pflanzenr.* IV.-5, 103 (*Taxaceae*) (1903). — Matsumura, *Ind. Pl. Jap.* II. pt. 1, 7 (1905).

>   *Podocarpus coraianus* Siebold in *Jaarb. Nederl. Maatsch. Aanmoed. Tuinb.* 1844, 35 (name only) (*Naaml.*).
>   *Podocarpus koraiana* Endlicher, *Syn. Conif.* 217 (1847). — Carrière in *Rev. Hort.* 1863, 349, fig. 36.
>   *Cephalotaxus koraiana* Hort. ex Gordon, *Pinet.* 275 (as a synonym) (1858).
>   *Taxus Japonica* Loddiges ex Gordon l. c. (as a synonym, not Hooker) (1858).
>   *Cephalotaxus pedunculata fastigiata* Carrière, *Prod. Fix. Vars.* 44, fig. 1 (1865); *Traité Conif.* ed. 2, 717 (1867).
>   *Cephalotaxus ? Buergeri* Miquel in *Ann. Mus. Lugd.-Bat.* III. 169 (1867); *Prol. Fl. Jap.* 333 (1867).
>   *Podocarpus Sciadopitys* Hort. ex Beissner, *Handb. Nadelh.* 181 (as a synonym) (1891).

This fastigiate form is common in Japanese gardens and is known as the Chosenmaki (i. e. Korean Podocarpus). It was introduced into the Botanic Garden at more long and from 0.3 to 0.45 m. in girth. The living plants make such a dense thicket that it is nearly impossible to ascertain their manner of growth, but the summit of Shiribeshi-san was burnt over a few years ago and at the time of my visit the stark dead growth of this Pine could be easily examined. Where this Pine grows scattered with dwarf Bamboo or other aggressive shrubs the prostrate branches are either very short or turn upward and the lateral branches are all ascending and the result is a dense more or less pyramidal or oval bush from 2 to 3 m. tall. Such bushes may be seen on Teine-yama near Sapporo. A small specimen brought from this mountain by Dr. K. Miyabe and planted in the Botanic Garden at Sapporo has grown into a shapely small tree about 2.5 m. tall with a distinct leading shoot, but branched from the base; all the branches are ascending-spreading and the leaves are from 6 to 10 cm. long. The shoot of *Pinus pumila* is stout and is clothed with short, dense gray-brown or fulvous tomentum; the winter-bud is reddish, cylindric-conic, acute and resinous, with the tips of the bud-scales free. The leaves are in fascicles of five, crowded and point forward, from 4 to 7 cm. (occasionally up to 10 cm.) long, slightly curved, triquetrous, with stomata on the ventral surface only and external resin-ducts. On all my specimens, whether from Saghalien, Hokkaido or Hondo, the leaves are nearly all obscurely and remotely serrulate, and on some two or three year old seedlings collected on Hakkoda-yama the leaves are sharply serrulate. The cones are subterminal, clustered, short-peduncled and spreading, violet-purple when young, changing the second season to green with purple about the umbos and when ripe to dull reddish or yellowish brown. In shape the cone is ovoid, from 3 to 4.5 cm. long, and when ripe falls to the ground, carrying its short peduncle with it. The cones ripen early in September and on falling to the ground are quickly carried off by squirrels and other rodents and hidden away, and so rapidly do they disappear that it is a difficult matter to find a ripe cone. The cone is not properly dehiscent, neither can it be called indehiscent, for after falling the cone-scales shrink and open sufficiently to shed the seeds. The cone itself disintegrates rapidly and is even more fragile than that of *P. cembra* L., of which many botanists have considered it to be merely a variety. It is certainly closely related to that species, but it occupies a distinct geographical area, is totally different in habit, and from what I saw of it wild it appears to me to be fully entitled to specific rank. Certainly it could never be mistaken for any other species of Pinus. It is in cultivation in this Arboretum from seeds I secured in Japan, but it is too early to tell anything of their behavior. In Japan this dwarf Pine is generally known as the Hai-matsu.

This dwarf Pine is first mentioned from Kamtchatka by Abbé Chappe d'Auteroche in his *Voyage en Sibérie*, I. 360 (1768), and later by Pallas. It was early introduced to Petrograd from eastern Siberia and Loudon mentions a plant in the gardens at Dropmore, England, which was planted in 1817 and "was not more than 6 inches high." From Japan, according to Jackson, two living plants were sent (in 1909?) to the garden of H. Clinton-Baker, at Bayfordbury, England, from Nyoho-san in the Nikko region by his brother, Captain L. Clinton-Baker, R.N. It was received at this Arboretum in November, 1903, from Messrs. Regel & Kesselring of Petrograd, but the plants afterwards died.

Ghent by von Siebold in 1830. As a wild plant it is unknown and appears to be a seminal variant analogous to the Irish Yew (*Taxus baccata*, f. *fastigiata* Loud.). It is commonly cultivated in the warmer parts of this country, but is not hardy in eastern Massachusetts.

TORREYA Arn.

A genus of Yew-like trees of which four species are known, two in North America and two in eastern Asia. Of the American species one (*T. taxifolia* Arn.) grows in western Florida, the other (*T. californica* Torr.) in California. One of the Asiatic species (*T. grandis* Fort.) is widely distributed and endemic in China and the other is common in Japan, but does not reach the mainland.

TORREYA NUCIFERA S. & Z.

Plates III and IV

TORREYA NUCIFERA Siebold & Zuccarini in *Abh. Akad. Münch.* IV. pt. 3, 232 (*Fl. Jap. Fam. Nat.* 108) (1846). — Endlicher, *Syn. Conif.* 240 (1847). — Miquel in *Ann. Mus. Lugd.-Bat.* III. 169 (1867); *Prol. Fl. Jap.* 333 (1867); in Siebold & Zuccarini, *Fl. Jap.* II. 64, t. 129 (1870). — Franchet & Savatier, *Enum. Pl. Jap.* I. 473 (1875). — Masters in *Jour. Linn. Soc.* XVIII. 500 (1881). — Shirasawa, *Icon. Ess. For. Jap.* I. 32, t. 15, fig. 19–34 (1900).—Kent in Veitch, *Man. Conif.* ed. 2, 119 (1900). — F. W. Oliver in *Ann. Bot.* XVII. 468 (1903). — Pilger in Engler, *Pflanzenr.* IV.-5, 105, fig. 21 (*Taxaceae*) (1903). — Matsumura, *Ind. Pl. Jap.* II. pt. 1, 19 (1905). — Hayata, *Veget. Mt. Fuji*, 46 (1911). — Elwes & Henry, *Trees Gr. Brit. & Irel.* VI. 1463 (1912).—Silva Tarouca, *Uns. Freiland-Nadelh.* 132, fig. 130 (1913). — Bean, *Trees & Shrubs Brit. Isl.* II. 558 (1914).

> *Taxus nucifera* Linnaeus, *Spec.* 1040 (1753). — Thunberg, *Fl. Jap.* 275 (1784). — Gaertner, *Fruct.* II. 66, t. 91 (1791). — Richard, *Comm. Bot. Conif.* 21, t. 2 (1826).
> *Podocarpus nucifera* Persoon apud Loudon, *Arb. Brit.* IV. 2100 (1838).
> *Caryotaxus nucifera* Zuccarini ex Endlicher, *Syn. Conif.* 241 (as a synonym) (1847).
> *Fœtataxus nucifera* Nelson, *Pinac.* 168 (1866).
> *Tumion nuciferum* Greene in *Pittonia*, II. 194 (1891).—Sargent, *Forest Fl. Jap.* 76 (1894); *Silva N. Am.* X. 56 (1896).

I met with this Torreya, or Kaya as the Japanese call it, as a scattered tree growing among broad-leaved and coniferous trees in nearly every wood and forest visited from Yaku-shima, in the extreme south of Kyushu, to the latitude of Tokyo, in central Hondo. But in one place only is it common, and that is on Takao-san, a hill some 500 m. high, about 27 miles southwest of Tokyo and in Musashi province. Here it is remarkably plentiful and is associated with *Abies firma* S. & Z., on steep slopes composed of shale rocks. I have a specimen collected at Sendai, in Rikuzen province, and Matsumura records it from Hirosaki, in Mutsu, the most northern province of Hondo, but I did not see it wild north of Musashi province, not even in the Nikko region, and strongly suspect that the trees in northern Hondo are cultivated and not wild. Outside of Japan it is known with certainty to be wild only on Quelpaert Island, where it has been collected by Taquet. On the mainland of Korea, Nakai thinks that it is cultivated and escaped.

On Yaku-shima I measured a tree 16 m. tall with a trunk 2.3 m. in girth; on Takao-san the trees average from 16 to 20 m. tall and from 1.3 to 2 m. in girth.

Of wild trees these are the largest I saw, but Sargent records some on the banks of the Kiso-gawa, near Agematsu, 26 m. tall with trunks from 4 to 5 m. in girth. At Hachiman Shrine, Kamo, in Satsuma province, Kyushu, there are several magnificent planted trees of Torreya. Of these the finest is 28 m. in height and has a slightly buttressed trunk which measures 5.5 m. in girth at 1.6 m. from the ground. This is the largest tree of *Torreya nucifera* I saw in Japan, but here and there in temple grounds were others nearly as large. The bark is nearly smooth, pale gray to grayish brown and on old trees shallowly fissured into narrow strips which flake off. The branches are numerous, stout, horizontally wide-spreading and form a more or less oval crown; the branchlets are green and change to red-brown or reddish purple the second and third seasons. This change of color in the shoot is constant and by this character alone this Torreya may be at once distinguished from the Chinese *T. grandis* Fort., in which the shoots do not change color, but remain yellowish green until they finally become gray. The leaves of *T. nucifera* are lustrous, blackish green and very pungent. The flowers are axillary: the male on the shoot of the previous year, the female on that of the current season and near the base. The male and female flowers open simultaneously. After fertilization the ovule grows only slightly during that season. The fruit is sessile, ripens the second season and is obovoid to ellipsoid, from 2 to 2.5 cm. long; when ripe it is green, faintly tinged and striped with purple more especially on the apex, splitting and exposing the seed rich in an oil which is extracted for culinary purposes. The kernels are a favorite article of food. The wood is yellowish to pale brown, firm and lustrous and durable in water. It is used for making water-pails and for cabinet-work and for the pieces used in the Japanese game of chess. Old trees of the Kaya sometimes have few branches and are ragged in appearance, but usually the trees are clad with branches to near the ground and are strikingly ornamental. In the gardens of western lands this tree is not so well known as its distinctive beauty warrants. In those of eastern North America it is rare. It is quite hardy and ripens fruit in this Arboretum where it starts to grow very late, although its rate of growth is as rapid as is that of any other hardy taxad. In the Hunnewell Pinetum there is a specimen 6 m. tall.

The Japanese Torreya was first described and figured by Kaempfer (*Amoen.* fasc. V. 814, fig. [1712]) under the name of *Taxus nucifera*, the name which was later adopted by Linnaeus. Kaempfer's description and figures are excellent and one of the figures shows the splitting of the fruit. According to Aiton (*Hort. Kew.* V. 416 [1813]) it was in cultivation in England with Captain Thomas Cornwall in 1764. In 1830 it was introduced to the Botanic Gardens at Ghent by von Siebold.

TAXUS L.

In his monograph Pilger considers all the Yews subspecies, varieties and forms of the European *T. baccata* L., but types which occupy well-defined geographical areas behave quite differently in cultivation and have characters by which they can be distinguished in herbaria and in the field are best considered distinct species. From this point of view seven species of Taxus are recognized. Four are found in North America, two in eastern Asia and one (*T. baccata* L.) in Europe and Asia Minor to northern Persia and Afghanistan. Of the four American species *T. canadensis* Marsh. is monoecious and is distributed from Newfoundland to the northern shores of Lake Superior and Lake Winnipeg and southward to New Jersey and Minnesota; *T. floridana* Chapm. is confined to a limited area in western Florida;

T. brevifolia Nutt. is found from Queen Charlotte Islands in western North America southward through the coast ranges to the Bay of Monterey in California and west to the slopes of the Rocky Mountains in Montana; the fourth species, *T. globosa* Schlechtend., grows in southern Mexico. In southeastern Asia *T. Wallichiana* Zucc. is distributed from Nepal and Sikkim eastward along the Himalayas to the Khasia Hills and through Upper Burmah and Malaya to Sumatra and the Philippine Islands. In China *T. cuspidata*, var. *chinensis* Rehd. & Wils. is widely spread and grows also in Formosa. In northeastern Asia *T. cuspidata* S. & Z. has a wide range of distribution and is the only Yew found in Japan.

TAXUS CUSPIDATA S. & Z.

Plate V

Taxus cuspidata Siebold & Zuccarini in *Abh. Akad. Münch.* IV. pt. 3, 232 (*Fl. Jap. Fam. Nat.* II. 108 (1846). — Endlicher, *Syn. Conif.* 243 (1847). — Miquel in *Ann. Mus. Lugd.-Bat.* III. 169 (1867); *Prol. Fl. Jap.* 333 (1867); in Siebold & Zuccarini, *Fl. Jap.* II. 61, t. 128 (1870). — Franchet & Savatier, *Enum. Pl. Jap.* I. 472 (1875). — Masters in *Jour. Linn. Soc.* XVIII. 499 (1881). — Miyabe in *Mem. Boston Soc. Nat. Hist.* IV. 261 (*Fl. Kurile Isl.*) (1890). — Sargent, *Forest. Fl. Jap.* 76 (1894). — Shirasawa, *Icon. Ess. For. Jap.* I. 33, t. 15, fig. 1–18 (1900). — Kent in Veitch, *Man. Conif.* ed. 2, 143 (1900). — Komarov in *Act. Hort. Petrop.* XX. 210 (*Fl. Mandsh.* I.) (1901). — Rehder & Wilson in Sargent, *Pl. Wilson.* II. 8 (1914). — Bean, *Trees & Shrubs Brit. Isl.* II. 582 (1914). — Takeda in *Jour. Linn. Soc.* XLII. 486 (1914). — Miyabe & Miyake, *Fl. Saghal.* 590 (1915).

> *Taxus baccata* Thunberg, *Fl. Jap.* 275 (not Linnaeus, according to Siebold & Zuccarini) (1784). — Ruprecht & Maximowicz in *Bull. Phys.-Math. Acad. Sci. St. Pétersbourg*, XV. 142 (not Linnaeus) (1857). — Ruprecht & Maack in *Bull. Phys.-Math. Acad. Sci. St. Pétersbourg*, XV. 383 (1857).
> *Cephalotaxus umbraculifera* Siebold apud Endlicher, *Syn. Conif.* 239 (1847). — Franchet & Savatier, *Enum. Pl. Jap.* I. 473 (1875).
> *Taxus baccata*, var. *microcarpa* Trautvetter in *Mém. Sav. Étr. Acad. Sci. St. Pétersbourg*, IX. 259 (Maximowicz, *Prim. Fl. Amur.*) (1859). — Fr. Schmidt in *Mém. Acad. Sci. St. Pétersbourg*, sér. 7, XII. no. 2, 175 (*Reis. Amur. Sachal.*) (1868).
> *Taxus baccata cuspidata* Carrière, *Traité Conif.* ed. 2, 733 (1867). — Elwes & Henry, *Trees Gr. Brit. & Irel.* I. 100, t. 31 (1906). — Beissner, *Handb. Nadelh.* ed. 2, 51 (1909).
> *Taxus baccata*, subsp. 2. *cuspidata* Pilger in Engler, *Pflanzenr.* IV.–5, 112 (*Taxaceae*) (1903). — Matsumura, *Ind. Pl. Jap.* II. pt. 1, 17 (1905). — Hayata, *Veget. Mt. Fuji*, 46 (1911).
> *Taxus baccata*, subsp. 2. *cuspidata*, var. a. *latifolia* Pilger l. c. (1903) — Matsumura l. c. 18 (1905).

The Japanese Yew is widely distributed in Japan from about latitude 34° northward through Hondo and Hokkaido to the Kurile Islands and Japanese Saghalien. On the mainland it grows in the Amur region and southward through Korea to Quelpaert in the Korean Archipelago. It has not been reported from Mandshuria, and in China proper and in Formosa it is represented by the variety *chinensis* Rehd. & Wils. As a wild tree *T. cuspidata* cannot be said to be common anywhere in Japan that I visited except, perhaps, in Kitami province, Hokkaido. On the lower slopes of Fuji-san in Suruga province, Hondo, and more especially round the villages of Gotemba and Yamanaka, there are many fine trees of this Yew, but it is impossible to decide whether they are wild or planted. The most southern place in Japan that I have seen wild specimens from is Mt. Daisen in Hoki province, Hondo, which is about 2000 m. high and is the loftiest mountain on the west coast. The Rev. Arthur Stanford of the American Board Mission gave me the material and told me that the plant forms a dense scrub from 1 to 2 m. high covering large areas on the wind-swept middle and upper slopes. I have seen material from Takayama in Hida province, but whether wild or cultivated I do not know. On the lower middle slopes of Yatsuga-dake on the borders of Shinano and Kai provinces I saw this Yew wild in moist woods, and in the village of Naka-shinden it is the common hedge plant. It grows on Nantai-san in the Nikko region, but is rare, although in the temple grounds and gardens in this region it is a very common shrub or tree. On the wind-swept upper slopes of Hakkoda-yama in Mutsu province, between 1600 and 2000 m. high this Yew grows sparingly as a low, broad shrub from 1 to 1.5 m. tall. I met with it occasionally elsewhere in Hondo within the limits here sketched, but except in and near villages where it is questionably wild this tree is rare on the main island of Japan. In the moist forests of northern Hokkaido, especially in those of Kitami province round Rube-shibe and Oketo, it is fairly common, growing mixed with *Picea jezoënsis* Carr., *P. Glehnii* Mast., *Abies sachalinensis* Mast., *Populus Maximowiczii* Henry, *Acanthopanax ricinifolius* Seem., *Ulmus japonica* Sarg. and *Acer pictum* Thunb. On the slopes of Shiribeshi-san in Shiribeshi province I found it growing between 1300 and 2000 m. altitude either prostrate on the ground or as a broad shrub from 1 to 2 m. high. I did not meet with it in Saghalien nor in Shikoku, but Shirasawa reports it from the latter island.

The largest trees I saw were from 15 to 16 m. tall and about 2 m. in girth of trunk. The branches are usually very numerous, horizontally spreading or ascending-spreading and form a flattened round and broad crown; occasionally the branches are comparatively sparse and relatively short and the crown narrow and irregular in outline. The bark is red-brown, sometimes grayish brown, and shallowly fissured. When this Yew fruits it appears to bear very large crops and many trees which I saw presented a wonderful sight with their wealth of scarlet fruits. The wood is red or reddish brown, very hard, tough and durable. It is very lasting in wet soil and on this account is valued for piles in the foundations of houses and buildings generally. It is also highly esteemed for cabinet-work, for carving and for indoor-decorations of better-class houses. Formerly the Japanese used it for making bows, as do the Ainu people to the present day. In Hondo the common name for this tree is Ichii and in Hokkaido it is Onko; less frequently the Japanese term it Araragi and Sūo-no-ki.

The Ichii is very generally cultivated in Japan as a hedge plant, for topiary work, as a tree or shrub or as a closely cut low bush. For the gardens of eastern Massachusetts it is the most valuable evergreen that eastern Asia has supplied. It is perfectly hardy and in full exposure to the sun its leaves retain their dark-green color throughout the year, while those of most of the forms of the European Yew under the same conditions brown very badly.

The Japanese Yew was discovered by Thunberg; it was introduced into England by Robert Fortune between 1854 and 1856, and sent by him to Mr. R. Glendinning of Chiswick Nursery, Turnham Green. In his own words (in *Gard. Chron.* 1860, 170) Fortune says of its introduction: "This species was brought from Japan to Shanghai and presented to me by the late Mr. Beale. I believe it is distinct from anything formerly introduced." In Great Britain this Yew never appears to have attracted much attention, probably because *T. baccata* L. and its forms are so common, quite hardy and thrive so well. It was introduced into America by Dr. George R. Hall in 1862, who gave it to Parsons & Co., Nurserymen, Flushing, Long Island, New York. It appears to have made slow headway for many years in gardens here, but it is now becoming well known and its merits as the hardiest of all the Yews properly appreciated. On the estate of the late Dr. Hall there is growing a specimen which is 7 m. high and 40 m. round. It was planted about 1870 and is probably one that he brought from Japan.

In cultivation here are two forms besides the type: one, a low wide-spreading shrub with short leaves, is f. *nana* Rehder (in Bailey, *Cycl. Am. Hort.* IV. 1773 [1902]) and the other, a low compact shrub, is f. *densa* Rehder (in Bailey, *Stand. Cycl. Hort.* VI. 3316 [1916]) (syn. *T. baccata*, subsp. *globosa*, f. *tardiva* Matsumura, *Ind. Pl. Jap.* II. pt. 1, 18 [1905], not *T. baccata*, f. *tardiva* Pilger).[1]

[1] These are the only Yews known from Japan, but in books reference is frequently made to another, erroneously supposed to be of Japanese origin and known variously as *Taxus brevifolia* Hort., *Cephalotaxus tardiva* Siebold apud Endlicher, *Taxus tardiva* Hort., *T. adpressa* Hort. Endlicher (*Syn. Conif.* 239 [1847]) apparently started the story that it came from Japan. Pilger names it *T. baccata*, f. *tardiva* (in Engler, *Pflanzenr.* IV.-5, 114 [*Taxaceae*] [1903]), following the much copied error that Knight had named it *T. sinensis tardiva*. Knight's name (*Syn. Conif.* 52 [1850?]) is *T. ? tardiva*. The proper name for this plant is *T. baccata*, var. *adpressa* Carrière (in Jacques & Herincq, *Man. Pl.* IV. 380 [1857]). This plant originated as a chance seedling from *T. baccata* L. in the nurseries of Messrs. Dickson at Chester, England, about 1826. Its history is given in *The Garden*, XXIX. 149, 221, 268 (1886) under the names of *T. adpressa* Hort. and *T. brevifolia* Hort.

PINACEAE

KEY TO THE JAPANESE GENERA

Subfam. ABIETEAE

Fruit maturing in two seasons; leaves fascicled, needle-shaped, enclosed at the base in a membranous sheath . . . . PINUS.
Fruit maturing in one season.
    Leaves scattered on leading shoots and in rosettes on short spur-like branchlets, deciduous . . . . LARIX.
    Leaves scattered, linear, persistent.
        Cones pendulous, the scales persistent on the axis.
            Branchlets roughened by the persistent leaf-bases; leaves falling off in drying; bracts shorter than the cone-scales.
                Leaves sessile, 4-sided, or flattened and stomatiferous above . . . . PICEA.
                Leaves stalked, flattened and stomatiferous below . . . . TSUGA.
            Branchlets not roughened by leaf-bases; leaves stalked, flattened, not falling off in drying; bracts longer than the cone-scales . . . . PSEUDOTSUGA.
        Cones erect, their scales deciduous from the axis, longer or shorter than the bracts.
        Leaves sessile, flat . . . . ABIES.

Subfam. TAXODIEAE

Fruit maturing in two seasons; leaves crowded, scale-like, with long, narrow, strap-shaped cladodes arising from their axils and arranged in whorls of from 20 to 30 like the ribs of an umbrella . . . . SCIADOPITYS.
Fruit maturing in one season; leaves spirally arranged in 5 rows, short, linear-subulate, irregularly 4-sided, falcately incurved, rarely straight and spreading, keeled on the lower side, sessile . . . . CRYPTOMERIA.

Subfam. CUPRESSEAE

Fruit a cone, maturing in one season; leaves usually scale-like, often dimorphic.
    Cones broadly ovoid or globose, the scales rhomboidal, imbricated; seeds five at the base of each scale . . . . THUJOPSIS.
    Cones oblong, the scales oblong, in four decussate pairs, the middle ones only fertile; seeds two at the base of each scale . . . . THUJA.
    Cones globose or nearly so, the scales peltate, from 8 to 12; seeds from 2 to 6 on each scale . . . . CHAMAECYPARIS.
Fruit a berry, maturing in two or three seasons; flowers dioecious; leaves decussate or in threes, subulate or scale-like, often of two forms . . . . JUNIPERUS.

Subfam. ABIETEAE Spach

PINUS L.

The genus Pinus is widely distributed through the Northern Hemisphere from the Arctic Circle southward to the Bahamas, the West Indies and the mountains of Central America in the New World; to the Canary Islands, northern Africa, Sumatra and to the Philippine Islands in the Old World. The genus has its greatest development in western North America, where 28 species are found. The latest monographer, Shaw (*Genus Pinus*, 24 [1914]), recognizes 66 species, of which 43 belong to the New and 23 to the Old World. Sargent (*Silva N. Am.* XI. 2 [1897]) gives the total number of species as about 70; Elwes & Henry (*Trees Gr. Brit. & Irel.* V. 1003 [1910]) estimate the number at 80. In Japan six species are indigenous, of which three also grow on the mainland of eastern Asia.

KEY TO THE JAPANESE SPECIES

Wood soft, close-grained; bark thin, smooth, as a rule scaly on the trunks of old trees; leaves normally five in each fascicle with one fibro-vascular bundle, sheaths deciduous . . . . SOFT PINES.
  Seeds wingless.
    Cone indehiscent, subsessile, deciduous; shoots densely hairy.
      Leaves serrate; resin-ducts medial, confined to the angles; cone from 7 to 15 cm. long . . . . P. KORAIENSIS.
      Leaves remotely serrulate; resin-ducts usually external; cone from 3 to 5 cm. long . . . . P. PUMILA.
    Cone dehiscent, long-peduncled; shoots glabrous; leaves serrulate; resin-ducts external, external and medial, or medial; cone from 4.5 to 20 cm. long.
                                                       P. ARMANDI.
  Seeds winged.
    Cone dehiscent, persistent, subsessile; shoots pubescent or glabrous; leaves with resin-ducts external and dorsal . . . . P. PARVIFLORA.
Wood heavy, coarse-grained; bark thin and scaly on upper parts, deeply furrowed on the trunk; leaves normally two in each fascicle, with two fibro-vascular bundles, sheaths persistent. . . . . HARD PINES.
  Bark on upper parts of the trunk reddish, terminal buds reddish; shoots more or less pruinose; leaves slender, gray-green; resin-ducts external . . P. DENSIFLORA.
  Bark blackish gray; terminal buds long, very white; shoot yellow-brown; leaves stout, dark green; resin-ducts medial . . . . P. THUNBERGII.

PINUS KORAIENSIS S. & Z.

PLATES VI AND VII

PINUS KORAIENSIS Siebold & Zuccarini. *Fl. Jap.* II. 28, t. 116 exclude fig. 1–4 (1844). — Endlicher, *Syn. Conif.* 172 (1847). — Lindley in *Gard. Chron.* 1861, 1114. — J. G. Veitch in *Gard. Chron.* 1862, 309. — Murray in *Proc. Hort. Soc. Lond.* II. 266, fig. 1–12 (1862); *Pines & Firs Jap.* 5, fig. 1–12 (1863). — Miquel in *Ann. Mus. Lugd.-Bat.* III. 166 (1867); *Prol. Fl. Jap.* 330 (1867). — Franchet & Savatier, *Enum. Pl. Jap.* I. 465 (1875). — Masters in *Jour. Linn. Soc.* XVIII. 504 (1881). — Veitch, *Man. Conif.* 178, fig. 40 (1881). — Mayr, *Monog. Abiet. Jap.* 73, t. 5–6, fig. 18 (1890); *Fremdl. Wald- u. Parkb.* 386 (1906). — Shirasawa, *Icon. Ess. For. Jap.* I. 12, t. 2, fig. 17–32 (1900). — Palibin in *Act. Hort. Petrop.* XIX. 135 (*Consp. Fl. Kor.*) (1901). — Komarov in *Act. Hort. Petrop.* XX. 183 (*Fl. Mandsh.* I.) (1901). — Matsumura, *Ind. Pl. Jap.* II. pt. 1, 14 (1905). — Clinton-Baker, *Ill. Conif.* I. 28, t. (1909). — Elwes & Henry, *Trees Gr. Brit. & Irel.* V. 1041 (1909). — Nakai in *Jour. Coll. Sci. Tokyo,* XXXI. 379 (*Fl. Kor.* pt. 2) (1911). — Shaw, *Gen. Pinus,* 26, t. 8, fig. 85, 86 (1914).

  ?*Pinus Strobus* Thunberg, *Fl. Jap.* 275 (not Linnaeus) (1784).
  Pinus Cembra, β *excelsa* Maximowicz in *Bull. Phys.-Math. Acad. Sci. St. Pétersbourg,* XV. 141 (1857).
  Pinus mandshurica Ruprecht in *Bull. Phys.-Math. Acad. Sci. St. Pétersbourg,* XV.

382 (1857); in *Mél. Biol.* II. 567 (1857). — Maximowicz in *Mém. Sav. Étr. Acad. Sci. St. Pétersbourg*, IX. 263 (*Prim. Fl. Amur.* (1859); in *Bull. Acad. Sci. St. Pétersbourg*, sér. 3, XXVII. 559 (1881); in *Mél. Biol.* XI. 349 (1881).

Pinus cembra, var. *Manchurica* Masters in *Bull. Herb. Boiss.* VI. 271 (1896). — Matsumura, *Ind. Pl. Jap.* II. pt. 1, 13 (1905).

In Japan the Korean Nut Pine is native on several mountains in central Hondo, but is very local. Mayr, who first discovered this Pine wild in Japan, found it on the mountains of Kozuke province. I met with it in a wild state on the slopes of Mt. Ontake in Shinano province between 2000 and 2500 m. altitude, scattered in forests mainly composed of *Picea jezoënsis* Carr., *Abies Veitchii* Lindl., *Tsuga diversifolia* Mast. and occasional Birches. The undergrowth is almost impenetrable and consists of dwarf Bamboos (*Sasa spp.*). Further to the northwest in the same province I found it to be fairly common on Tsubakura-dake between 2150 and 2600 m. altitude, growing with *Pinus parviflora* S. & Z. and the other conifers named above. These are the only places where I saw spontaneous trees. Mr. M. Koyama told me that he had collected it on the west slopes of Fuji-san in Kai province and on Yatsuga-dake on the borders of Kai and Shinano provinces. Very probably it grows on other mountains in these parts of Hondo, but elsewhere in Japan it is known only as a planted tree. On the mainland this Pine is distributed from the Amur region southward into Korea and westward into Mandshuria, but its exact geographical range and its abundance north and west are not properly known. Dr. Nakai informed me that in Korea this tree is found where granitic and Archean schistose rocks occur. It is abundant in north-central Korea and is said to be especially so in the adjoining region in Mandshuria and to the northward. In the extreme northeast of Korea it is rare, but in the contiguous region in Mandshuria, and particularly in the valley of the Konchung River, it is plentiful. In western Korea, where formerly it was common, it has nearly all been felled. In east-central Korea, along the main mountain chain from Kumgan-san down to Sho-Paik-san, this Pine is seldom found wild below 600 m. altitude and its higher limit is about 1200 m. altitude. The southernmost range of the species is the Chiri-san chain, which runs east and west, and there it grows between 1100 and 1500 m. above the sea.

The largest spontaneous trees I saw were from 26 to 30 m. tall and in girth of trunk from 3 to 3.5 m., but these were exceptional, and the average was from 20 to 25 m. by 2 to 2.5 m. in height and girth respectively. The branches are rather short and slender, spread horizontally and form a narrow more or less pyramidal crown. The branches are not dense and light shows clearly through the crown; generally the trunk divides in its upper part into two or three ascending stems. The shoots are stout and densely clothed with rufous-brown tomentum. The winter-buds are reddish brown, cylindric-ovoid, acuminate and slightly resinous. The bark is thin and scaly, gray-brown to gray and easily peels off in irregularly shaped flakes and shows red-brown beneath. The leaves are usually in fives, but often only in fours or even in threes in each fascicle, stout, triquetrous and sharply serrulate, from 6 to 10 cm. long, with stomata on the ventral side only and with medial resin-ducts confined to the angles. The cone is normally subterminal, erect and peduncled, solitary or in clusters round the leading shoot. When ripe they are pale nut-brown, from 9 to 14 cm. long, ovoid-cylindrical in shape, resinous and indehiscent, and fall to the ground with the peduncle attached. Squirrels and a bird, a species of Nutcracker, attack the cones as they ripen and devour the seeds. The cone is heavy and the cone-scales as they dry shrink and expose the wingless seeds, which are released only by the disintegration of the fallen cone. The wood is very resinous and is the most valuable produced by any species of Pine of eastern Asia, although in Japan it is too rare to have any value as a timber-tree.

In Shinano province this Pine is known as the Oba-goyō-matsu (Large Five-leaved Pine), but everywhere in the gardens of Japan it is called the Chosen-matsu (i. e. Korean Pine). This latter name doubtless denotes the early place of origin of these cultivated trees, for it is only quite recently that it has been discovered wild in Japan, and there only in remote places difficult of access and very sparsely peopled. The Chosen-matsu, though a favorite tree, is not common in Japanese gardens. At Nikko I saw only young trees and overlooked the fine specimens Mayr tells of. In the Imperial Botanic Garden, Tokyo, there is a good specimen some 21 m. tall, with a trunk 1.75 m. in girth, which was planted before the Meiji era. But the finest specimens and the greatest number of these planted trees I saw grow in the park at Morioka in Rikuchu province, northern Hondo, which was formerly the seat of the Daimyō of Nambu. In Japanese gardens I saw occasional plants of the var. *variegata* Mayr, which has yellowish white splashes and stripes down the leaves. It is propagated by grafting on *P. Thunbergii* Parl.

Pinus koraiensis was first discovered wild in the Amur region by C. Maximowicz in June 1855, and by R. Maack in July of the same year. In Japan it was known as a planted tree only until about 1889, when H. Mayr discovered it growing wild on the mountains of the Kozuke province. It was introduced from Japan in 1861 by John Gould Veitch into England, and from there it was later sent to this country. It is perfectly hardy in eastern North America at least as far north as Boston, Massachusetts, where there are trees from 12 to 13 m. tall which bear cones annually. In this Arboretum it grows faster and is a more satisfactory tree than *P. cembra* L.

It is generally believed that Thunberg's *P. Strobus* is the same as *P. koraiensis* S. & Z., and his brief description fits it very well. But the Korean Pine does not grow wild on the Hakone Mountains, as Thunberg says of his Pine. He may have seen a planted tree of *P. koraiensis*, but in his *Flora Japonica* Thunberg is very careful to distinguish between wild and cultivated plants. No specimen of Thunberg's exists to-day, so the point cannot be definitely settled, but I believe that *P. Strobus* Thunb. is really *P. parviflora* S. & Z.

PINUS PUMILA Regel

Plate VIII

PINUS PUMILA Regel in *Cat. Sem. Hort. Petrop.* 23 (1858); in *Bull. Soc. Nat. Mosc.* XXXII. pt. 1, 211 (1859). — Fr. Schmidt in *Mém. Acad. Sci. St. Pétersbourg,* sér. 7, XII. no. 2, 178 (*Reis. Amur. Sachal.*) (1868). — Mayr, *Monog. Abiet. Jap.* 80, t. 6, fig. 21 (1890). — Miyabe in *Mem. Boston Soc. Nat. Hist.* IV. 261 (*Fl. Kurile Isl.*) (1890). — Sargent, *Forest Fl. Jap.* 80 (1894). — Komarov in *Act. Hort. Petrop.* XX. 189 (*Fl. Mandsh.* I.) (1901). — Matsumura, *Ind. Pl. Jap.* II. pt. 1, 14 (1905). — Miyoshi, *Atlas Jap. Veget.* pt. VII. 4, t. 50 (1907); pt. IX. 3, t. 63 (1908); pt. XIV. 5, t. 99 (1909). — Shirasawa, *Icon. Ess. For. Jap.* II. t. 1, fig. 17–31 (1908). — Clinton-Baker, *Ill. Conif.* I. 46, t. (1909). — Jackson in *Gard. Chron.* ser. 3, XLVI. 93, fig. 41 (1909). — Elwes & Henry, *Trees Gr. Brit. & Irel.* V. 1045

(1909). — Nakai in *Jour. Coll. Sci. Tokyo*, XXXI. 379 (*Fl. Kor.* pt. 2) (1911). — Silva Tarouca, *Uns. Freiland-Nadelh.* 57, fig. 50 (1913). — Miyabe & Miyake, *Fl. Saghal.* 595 (1915).

    Pinus Cembra, B *pumila* Pallas, *Fl. Ross.* I. 5, t. 2, fig. f–h (1784). — Chamisso in Linnaea, VI. 534 (1831). — Endlicher, *Syn. Conif.* 142 (1847). — Ledebour, *Fl. Ross.* III. pt. 2, 674 (1851). — Trautvetter & Meyer in Middendorff, *Reis. Siber.* I. pt. 2, Bot. abt. 2, 88 (*Fl. Ochot.*) (1856). — Maximowicz in *Bull. Phys.-Math. Acad. Sci. St. Pétersbourg*, XV. 142 (1857); in *Mém. Sav. Étr. Acad. Sci. St. Pétersbourg*, IX. 262 (*Prim. Fl. Amur.*) (1859). — Regel & Tiling, *Fl. Ajan.* 120 (1858).
    Pinus Cembra, var. *pygmaea* Loudon, *Arb. Brit.* IV. 2276 (1838).
    Pinus pygmaea Fischer ex Endlicher, *Syn. Conif.* 142 (as a synonym) (1847).
    Pinus mandshurica Murray in Lawson, *Pinet. Brit.* I. 61 (not Ruprecht) (1866).
    Pinus parviflora Miyabe in *Mem. Boston Soc. Nat. Hist.* IV. 261 (*Fl. Kurile Isl.*) (not Siebold & Zuccarini) (1890).
    Pinus cembra Shaw, *Gen. Pinus*, 27 t. 8, fig. 89 (as to the synonyms *P. pumila* and *P. mandschurica*, not Linnaeus) (1914).

This dwarf Pine is abundant on the summits and upper slopes of most of the high mountains of Japan from the alps of Shinano province northward through Hondo and Hokkaido and descends to sea-level in Japanese Saghalien, at the shores of the Okhotsk Sea. It is said to be absent from Shikotan, but is common on most of the Kurile Islands. Masters' statement that it occurs in Arctic America has not been confirmed and is probably erroneous. In continental northeastern Asia it is widely distributed from Kamtchatka eastward to Yakutsk and southward through the Amur region to Mandshuria and northern Korea, where its southern limit is at about 1600 m. altitude on Kumgan-san (Diamond Mountain).

In Japan *Pinus pumila* grows on granite, and on old volcanic mountains and is absent from Fuji-san, Nantai-san and others of comparatively recent activity. I met with it first on Mt. Ontake in Shinano province, where between 2800 and 3250 m. it covers thousands of acres. At its lowest level on Mt. Ontake it grows with scrubby bushes of *Abies Mariesii* Mast., *Tsuga diversifolia* Mast., *Betula Ermanii* Cham., *Prunus nipponica* Mats. and with *Juniperus communis*, var. *nipponica* Wils., various Willows, Vacciniums and other alpine plants, but in its upper range it forms almost pure and impenetrable thickets from 0.3 to 2 m. high. On the summit and topmost slopes of Hakkoda-yama in Mutsu province this dwarf Pine covers great areas with *Pieris nana* Mak., *Vaccinium Vitis-idaea* L., *Phyllodoce aleutica* Mak., and other alpine plants. Between these two points in Hondo I met with it on most of the high mountains which I climbed and in all it must cover many hundreds of square miles. In Hokkaido I collected this Pine on Shiribeshi-san, where it covers most of the mountain top and upper slopes and is associated with *Rhododendron chrysanthum* Pall., *Phyllodoce caerulea* Mak., Willows and alpine plants; also on Teine-yama near Sapporo, where it grows with dwarf Bamboos (*Sasa spp.*) at 1100–1200 m. altitude. At Sakhaiyama in Saghalien I collected it at sea-level growing on sand dunes and in meadows with *Juniperus conferta* Parl., *Rosa rugosa* Thunb., *Empetrum nigrum* L., *Cornus suecica* L., *Lonicera Chamissoi* Bunge and scrubby growths of *Abies sachalinensis* Mast. and *Larix dahurica*, var. *japonica* Maxim. In habit this Pine is best described as creeping, for the main branch or branches are flat on the ground and emit roots freely throughout their entire length; the lateral branches are ascending, ascending-spreading or spreading and form a dense tangled mass from 0.3 to 2.5 m. high. There is no trunk and the prostrate main branches may be from 10 to 15 m. or

PINUS ARMANDI Franch.

PINUS ARMANDI Franchet in *Nouv. Arch. Mus. Paris*, sér. 2, VII. 95, t. 12 (*Pl. David.* I. 285) (1884); in *Jour. de Bot.* XIII. 254 (1899). — Beissner in *Nuov. Giorn. Bot. Ital.* n. ser. IV. 184 (1897). — Masters in *Jour. Linn. Soc.* XXVI. 549 (1902); XXXVII. 415 (1906). — Clinton-Baker, *Ill. Conif.* I. 6, t. (1909). — Elwes & Henry, *Trees Gr. Brit. & Irel.* V. 1043 (1909). — Stapf in *Bot. Mag.* CXXXVI. t. 8347 (1910). — Mottet in *Rev. Hort.* 1910, 423, fig. 177-188. — Shaw in Sargent, *Pl. Wilson.* I. 1 (1911); II. 12 (1914); *Gen. Pinus*, 30, t. 9, fig. 96-99 (1914).

Pinus quinquefolia David, *Voyage de Chin.* I. 192 (name only) (1875).
Pinus koraiensis Beissner in *Nuov. Giorn. Bot. Ital.* n. ser. IV. 184 (not Siebold & Zuccarini) (1897). — Masters in *Jour. Linn. Soc.* XXVI. 550 (1902); XXXVII. 415 (1906); in *Gard. Chron.* ser. 3, XXXIII. 34, fig. 18, 19 (1903).
Pinus scipioniformis Masters in *Bull. Herb. Boiss.* VI. 270 (1898).
Pinus mandshurica Masters in *Jour. Linn. Soc.* XXVI. 551 (not Ruprecht nor Murray) (1906).
Pinus Mastersiana Hayata in *Gard. Chron.* ser. 3, XLIII. 194 (1908).
Pinus Armandi, var. *Mastersiana* Hayata in *Jour. Coll. Sci. Tokyo*, XXV. art. 19, 215, fig. 8 (*Fl. Mont. Formos.*) (1908).
Pinus levis Lemée & Leveillé in Fedde, *Rep. Spec. Nov.* VIII. 60 (1910).
Pinus excelsa, var. *chinensis* Patschke in *Bot. Jahrb.* XLVIII. 657 (1912).

The specimens I have from wild trees of this interesting addition to the flora of Japan I owe to the kind services of Mr. T. Miyoshi and to the courtesy of his chief, Dr. Naito, head of the Government Forestry Bureau at Kagoshima, to whom Dr. H. Shirasawa wrote on my behalf. When at Yaku-shima the forestry officers told me that the Goyō-matsu (*P. parviflora* S. & Z.) grew there in limited numbers and also on the neighboring island of Tanega-shima. That this species should grow on the lofty, rocky Yaku-shima seemed to me quite natural, but that it also grew wild on the low narrow ridge which forms the backbone of Tanega-shima was quite another matter. I became rather sceptical as to the identity of this Pine and urged the officers to procure material for me, since I had not the time to visit the places myself. On my return to Kagoshima I saw growing in a garden a White Pine which looked to me like *P. Armandi*. It bore no cones, but I dried a vegetative shoot. Later, in Tokyo, Mr. T. Makino gave me cones and a branch, which he had collected in the garden of Prince Shimazu at Kagoshima. These most certainly belonged to *P. Armandi* and settled the question of this species being grown in gardens at Kagoshima. This suggested the idea that the Goyō-matsu of Tanega-shima and Yaku-shima might belong here, and on talking over the matter with Dr. Shirasawa he concurred in the probability.

In the autumn of 1914 I received from Mr. T. Miyoshi the promised specimens from the two southern islands. The material bore immature cones, of small size and superficially like those of *P. parviflora* S. & Z., and I was uncertain as to what species they belonged. On my return home I handed the specimens over to Mr. G. R. Shaw, the authority on the genus Pinus, and after a careful examination he pronounced them to be of *P. Armandi*. To satisfy myself I have now critically examined this Japanese material and find that the shoot, leaves, position of resin-ducts, the wingless seeds, with the spermoderm forming a narrow border and a rudimentary prolongation at the summit, agree exactly with the Chinese material, but the cones themselves appear different. The cones from Japan are from 4.5 to 11 cm. long and have a rounded apophysis with the umbo undeveloped and with the outer edge of the cone-scale recurved. Except for a slight inferiority in size the largest agree exactly with Hayata's excellent figure of his *P. Armandi*, var. *Mastersiana*. This herbarium is rich in Chinese material of *P. Armandi* and a careful examination shows that these cones are from 4.5 to 20 cm. long and that in many the outer edge of the cone-scale is recurved; in a number I find the development of the umbo arrested and in several the apophysis is broad and rounded. I have not found in any of the variants perfect seeds, and on re-examining the Japanese material I find the seeds empty. To make certain that the arrested development of the umbo and apophysis was correlated with infertile seeds I examined cones from the Arboretum living plants of *P. Armandi*, and found some indistinguishable from those from Japan in size and other characters mentioned and others approximately so, but none absolutely identical with perfect cones from China. In the perfect cone with fertile seeds the apophysis with fully developed umbo is obtuse and triangular in shape and the outer edge of the cone-scale is sometimes slightly reflexed. Between this and cones with infertile seeds, arrested umbo and short rounded apophysis as figured by Hayata I find every possible gradation. This variation in size and shape of the apophysis and in degree of development of the umbo in *P. Armandi* is interesting and probably occurs in many species of Soft Pines, but it is by no means so marked as in the cones of the Rocky Mountain *P. flexilis* James, its most closely related species.

As I did not see *P. Armandi* wild in Japan I can give no account of the trees, though they are evidently rare. Mr. Miyoshi, in his letter accompanying the specimens, says those from Yaku-shima "were collected from a wild tree in Hirase Government forest, Kamiyaka-mura, on October 19, 1914." Those from Tanega-shima "from a wild tree about 700 years old, 90 ft. tall, 20 ft. in perimeter of trunk, growing in Yakugawa Government forest, Kitatane-mura, at about 600 ft. above sea-level." The material was sent to me in a box made of the wood of this species. This wood is heavy, close-grained and darker brown than I remember seeing it in China, but this is a matter of no moment, for it is well known that soil, situation and climate strongly influence the character and quality of timber.

The discovery of this Pine wild in southern Japan adds remarkably to its distribution. It is indigenous on the mountains of Formosa and on those of the Chinese provinces of Kweichou, Hupeh, Shensi, Kansu, Szech'uan and Yunnan to the extreme western limits of China proper. Very probably it will yet be found on the higher mountains in the more eastern provinces of the Flowery Kingdom.

Plants of *P. Armandi* received from Monsieur Maurice L. de Vilmorin in 1902 and others raised from seeds sent from China on several occasions by myself are growing in this Arboretum. They are perfectly hardy, grow rapidly and are very ornamental; they produce cones at an early age, but unfortunately they suffer from attacks of boring insects and do not now promise to develop into good trees in this part of eastern North America.

Pinus Armandi was discovered in January 1873 on the Tsinling Mountains in Shensi province, China, by Père A. David and was introduced to the arboretum of Monsieur M. L. de Vilmorin at Les Barres, France, by Père P. Farges, who sent seeds from northeastern Szech'uan in 1895. Seeds of this Pine were sent to Kew by Augustine Henry in 1897, who collected them "ten miles north of Mengtsze," in Yunnan province. A portion of these seeds were received here in June 1897.

PINUS PARVIFLORA S. & Z.

Plates IX and X

PINUS PARVIFLORA Siebold & Zuccarini, *Fl. Jap.* II. 27, t. 115 (1842). — Endlicher, *Syn. Conif.* 138 (1847). — Carrière, *Traité Conif.* 292 (1855). — Lindley in *Gard. Chron.* 1861, 265. — J. G. Veitch in *Gard. Chron.* 1862, 309. — Murray in *Proc. Hort. Soc. Lond.* II. 272, fig. 13–27 (1862); *Pines & Firs Jap.* 11, fig. 13–29 (1863). — Miquel in *Ann. Mus. Lugd.-Bat.* III. 166 (1867); *Prol. Fl. Jap.* 330 (1867). — Franchet & Savatier, *Enum. Pl. Jap.* I. 465 (1875). — Syme in *Gard. Chron.* n. ser. X. 624, fig. 103 (1878). — Masters in *Jour. Linn. Soc.* XVIII. 504 (1881); XXXV. 578 (1904). — Mayr, *Monog. Abiet. Jap.* 76, t. 5, fig. 19 (1890); *Fremdl. Wald- u. Parkb.* 386 (1906). — Sargent, *Forest Fl. Jap.* 80 (1894). — Kent in Veitch, *Man. Conif.* ed. 2, 353 (1900). — Matsumura, *Ind. Pl. Jap.* II. pt. 1, 14 (1905). — Shirasawa, *Icon. Ess. For. Jap.* II. t. 2, fig. 30–42 (1908). — Clinton-Baker, *Ill. Conif.* I. 40, t. (1909). — Beissner, *Handb. Nadelh.* ed. 2, 357 (1909). — Elwes & Henry, *Trees Gr. Brit. & Irel.* V. 1033, t. 274 (1909). — Hayata, *Veget. Mt. Fuji*, 93 (1911). — Silva Tarouca, *Uns. Freiland-Nadelh.* 218, fig. 229 (1913). — Shaw, *Gen. Pinus*, 32, t. 11, fig. 114–116 (exclude the synonyms *P. morrisonicola* and *P. formosana*) (1914).

> *Pinus Cembra* Thunberg, *Fl. Jap.* 274 (not Linnaeus) (1784).
> *Pinus koraiensis* Siebold & Zuccarini, *Fl. Jap.* II. t. 116 as to fig. 1–4 (1844).
> *Pinus Cembra*, var. *Japonica* Nelson, *Pinac.* 107 (1866).
> *Pinus pentaphylla* Mayr, *Monog. Abiet. Jap.* 78, t. 6, fig. 20 (1890); *Fremdl. Wald- u. Parkb.* 377 (1906). — Sargent, *Forest Fl. Jap.* 80 (1894). — Kent in Veitch, *Man. Conif.* ed. 2, 356 (1900). — Masters in *Jour. Linn. Soc.* XXXV. 577 (1904). — Matsumura, *Ind. Pl. Jap.* II. pt. 1, 14 (1905). — Beissner, *Handb. Nadelh.* ed. 2, 356 (1909).
> *Pinus parviflora*, var. *pentaphylla* Henry in Elwes & Henry, *Trees Gr. Brit. & Irel.* V. 1033 (1909).

This is the Strobus Pine of Japan and the only species of the group known from that country. It is widely distributed from the mountains of Shikoku northward through Hondo to Hidaka province in southeastern Hokkaido, but Siebold's statement that it grows in the Kurile Islands, which has been so widely copied, is erroneous. According to information from Dr. Nakai this Pine grows on the island of Ooryöng off the east coast of Korea, and Matsumura reports it from the island of Tsushima, but it is apparently unknown in Kyushu. It delights in steep, rocky country and the only place I saw it really abundant was on Shiragayama in Tosa province, Shikoku. There it grows between 1300 and 1800 m. on schistose rocks with *Tsuga Sieboldii* Carr., *Chamaecyparis obtusa* S. & Z., *Abies firma* S. & Z., and such broad-leaved trees as *Stewartia monadelpha* S. & Z. and *Magnolia obovata* Thunb.; the undergrowth is of *Rhododendron Metternichii* S. & Z., *Skimmia japonica* Thunb., *Pieris japonica* D. Don, *Osmanthus Aquifolium* S. & Z., *Ilex rugosa* Schmidt and *Cephalotaxus drupacea* S. & Z. The Japanese White Pine is wild in Iga province, Hondo, and on most of the high mountains of central Japan, more especially on those of Shinano province, where on Tsubakuradake it is fairly plentiful on granite ridges between 1300 and 2600 m. altitude, growing with *Tsuga diversifolia* Mast., *Picea jezoënsis* S. & Z., *Abies Veitchii* Lindl., *Pinus koraiensis* S. & Z., Birches and several broad-leaved trees. In the

Nikko region it is rather rare, though on cliffs beyond Yumoto village there are quite a number of trees growing with *Tsuga diversifolia* Mast. On Adzumasan, on the borders of Iwashiro and Uzen province, in the ascent from the hot springs beyond Tōge, this Pine formerly was plentiful, but has been extensively felled, although on the wind-swept upper slopes it forms scrub with *Abies Mariesii* Mast. and *Juniperus communis*, var. *nipponica* Wils. It is more or less common also in woods near Kadoma at the base of Hayachine-san in Rikuchu province; round Lake Towada, in Mutsu province, it grows at water-level (alt. about 500 m.) with *Pinus densiflora* S. & Z.; on Hakkoda-yama this Pine occurs sparingly on cliffs. In Hokkaido *P. parviflora* grows in one or two localities in Oshima province, on the island of Okushiri in Shiribeshi province and in the southeast corner of Hidaka province. This is its most northern limit known, and there it grows in mixed forests with *Abies sachalinensis* Mast., *Picea Glehnii* Mast., *Cercidiphyllum japonicum* S. & Z., *Ulmus japonica* Sarg., *Betula Ermanii* Cham. and *Quercus mongolica*, var. *grosseserrata* Rehd. & Wils.

The Japanese White Pine is a tree averaging from 16 to 20 m. in height and in girth of trunk from 1.5 to 2.5 m. The largest tree I saw was in Shikoku; it measured 30 m. by 3.75 m. in girth. The bark on young trees is gray and smooth and resin pustules are prominent; with age it becomes fissured into thin scales of irregular shape. On trees growing in exposed places this scaly bark is fairly persistent, but on old trees, and especially on those growing in moist woods, it becomes loose and brittle, peels off in flakes and exposes a red-brown under surface. The branches are relatively few and short, horizontally spreading, often slightly upturned at the ends and form a narrow scrawny crown; the trunk is bare of branches from one-third to two-thirds the height of the tree. The shoots are more or less densely covered with a short pubescence or are quite glabrous, or the stout shoots are glabrous and the weaker ones pubescent. The winter-buds are short, ovoid, pale brown, and scarcely if at all resinous, with scales free at the tips. The leaves are slender and curved, serrulate, from 3 to 8 (usually from 4 to 6) cm. long, with stomata on the ventral surface only; the resin-ducts are external and dorsal. The cones are subterminal, short-peduncled or subsessile, in clusters of from three to several, when ripe yellow-brown, somewhat lustrous, ovoid to nearly cylindrical, from 4 to 10 (usually from 6 to 8) cm. long. They shed their seeds, turn nearly black and remain on the trees for years. The seed is relatively large and the prominent wing varies in size according to the shape and size of the cone. The wood is pale, brownish, resinous, close and straight grained, of good quality and makes durable boards and planks for general construction purposes. Since the tree is scarce it does not figure among the valuable timber-trees of Japan except in the island of Shikoku.

Since Mayr founded his *P. pentaphylla* there has been discussion whether it was really distinct from *P. parviflora*, and in order to try and settle this point I devoted much attention to this tree in Japan. I collected wild material in nineteen different localities from Shikoku to Mutsu province, north Hondo, and had material collected for me, through the kind help of Dr. K. Miyabe, in five localities in Hokkaido. In addition I have before me material from two other places in Hokkaido and from seven others in Hondo, including some collected by Mayr and by him named *P. pentaphylla*. The largest cones I have are from the Nikko region, but others from Shikoku and Hokkaido are scarcely smaller, and a great variation may occur in the size of the cones on the same tree. Mayr states that north of latitude 38° the wild Pine referred to *P. parviflora* is his *P. pentaphylla*, but specimens before me from Shikoku and from Hidaka province in Hokkaido are absolutely identical in every respect. They exhibit the same variation in size and shape of cone, size and shape of seed-wing, length of leaves and in the degree of pubescence on the shoots. After careful study in the field and a critical examination of much material I cannot discover any character by which two Japanese Strobus Pines, or a species with a variety or a form, can be distinguished. The slight differences in the bark mentioned by Mayr are due to age and the position in which the trees have grown. Everywhere in Japan this White Pine is common in gardens as a dwarfed tree in pots, or planted in the open ground. Usually it is kept clipped and is trained into various shapes. In the garden of the Kinkakuji Temple at Kyōto one of these Pines is fashioned to represent a native boat with all sails set. A picture of the curious specimen is given on page 384 of Veitch's *Manual of Coniferae* (ed. 2), but the author is wrong in considering it to be either *P. Thunbergii* Parl. or *P. densiflora* S. & Z. These stunted White Pines with short leaves and branches look very different from the free-growing trees and it is easy to imagine them belonging to a distinct species. The Japanese graft this Pine and others on *P. Thunbergii* Parl., and this fact, which does not appear to have been understood before, accounts for the difference in its appearance and rate of growth. It is well known that White Pines do not thrive when grafted on Hard Pines; in fact many propagators claim that such grafting cannot be done. In Japan I saw the whole process and made specimens of grafted *P. parviflora* which show clearly growths from the stock with the white winter-bud characteristic of *P. Thunbergii* Parl. In Europe and North America there are in cultivation both grafted and seedling plants of *P. parviflora*, and these are easily distinguished by their appearance. If the base of a plant with short needles and branches be examined the point of union of scion and stock can usually be seen, for the stock grows much more rapidly than the scion. On cultivated and grafted plants of the Japanese White Pine the cones vary much in size, and on Adzuma-san I found as much variation in the size of cones on the scrub growth as on tall trees.

Siebold & Zuccarini founded their *P. parviflora* on specimens from cultivated and probably grafted trees, and the cone in their plate is small but not abnormally so, and the one figured as the cone of *P. koraiensis*, which is that of *P. parviflora*, is typical. Mayr founded his *P. pentaphylla* on wild or seedling trees[1] and apparently selected for his type those with the largest cones he could find. My investigations and collections show conclusively that only one species of the Strobus group of Pinus grows wild in Japan. Shaw refers the Formosan *P. morrisonicola* Hayata (in *Gard. Chron.* ser. 3, XLIII. 194 [1908]) to *P. parviflora*, but this is an error. I have seen the type of Hayata's plant and it is certainly a distinct species.

The native names of *P. parviflora* are Goyō-matsu and Hime-komatsu and Japanese gardeners distinguish a number of forms, including one (f. *variegata* Mayr) with variegated leaves. In eastern North America this Pine is very satisfactory and is perfectly hardy. Trees raised from seeds grow freely, are densely branched and the branches are very long and straight. The appearance of these trees is very different from old wild trees in the forests of Japan, with their narrow, scraggy crowns. As it grows in this Arboretum the Japanese White Pine is an ornamental and valuable tree.

[1] Dr. Shirasawa told me that from conversation with Dr. Mayr he was of the opinion that the trees by the bronze tori in front of the Chuzenji Temple are those on which Mayr based his species. These are planted seedling trees and have large cones.

Pinus parvifolia was first noticed by Thunberg, who saw it near Tokyo. It was introduced into Great Britain in 1861 by John Gould Veitch, and the older plants in this country came from Veitch's stock.

PINUS DENSIFLORA S. & Z.

Plate XI

PINUS DENSIFLORA Siebold & Zuccarini, *Fl. Jap.* II. 22, t. 112 (1842). — Endlicher, *Syn. Conif.* 172 (1847). — Murray in *Proc. Hort. Soc. Lond.* II. 286, fig. 41–51 (1862); *Pines & Firs Jap.* 32, fig. 55–68 (1863). — Miquel in *Ann. Mus. Lugd.-Bat.* III. 165 (1867); *Prol. Fl. Jap.* 329 (1867). — Franchet & Savatier, *Enum. Pl. Jap.* I. 464 (1875). — Masters in *Jour. Linn. Soc.* XVIII. 503 (1881). — Mayr, *Monog. Abiet. Jap.* 72, t. 5, fig. 17 (1890). — Sargent, *Forest Fl. Jap.* 79 (1894). — Shirasawa, *Icon. Ess. For. Jap.* I. 10, t. 1, fig. 1–14 (1900). — Kent in Veitch, *Man. Conif.* ed. 2, 326, fig. 92 (1900). — Matsumura, *Ind. Pl. Jap.* II. pt. 1, 13 (1905). — Miyoshi, *Atlas Jap. Veget.* pt. VII. 2, t. 47 (1907). — Beissner, *Handb. Nadelh.* ed. 2, 437 (1909). — Clinton-Baker, *Ill. Conif.* I. 18, t. (1909). — Elwes & Henry, *Trees Gr. Brit. & Irel.* V. 1125 (1909). — Hayata, *Veget. Mt. Fuji*, 46 (1911). — Shaw, *Gen. Pinus*, 52, t. 20, fig. 179–181 (1914).

> *Pinus sylvestris* Thunberg, *Fl. Jap.* 274 (in part, not Linnaeus) (1784).
> *Pinus sylvestris*, b. *rubra?* Siebold in *Verh. Batav. Genoot.* XII. pt. 1, 12 (*Syn. Pl. Oecon. Jap.*) (name only) (1830).
> *Pinus scopifera* Miquel in Zollinger, *Syst. Verz. Ind. Arch.* II. 82 (1854).
> *Pinus Pinea* Gordon, *Pinet.* 179 (as to the synonym *P. densiflora*, not Linnaeus) (1858).
> *Pinus Massoniana* Hort. ex Masters in *Jour. Linn. Soc.* XVIII. 503 (as a synonym, not Lambert) (1881).

The Japanese Red Pine, or Aka-matsu, is very widely distributed in Kyushu, Shikoku and through Hondo to the northern province of Mutsu and has an altitudinal range from sea-level to 1600 m. It will grow on the poorest of soils and has been much planted in many parts of Japan. I was told by Japanese that this Pine was not indigenous in Hokkaido, but between Oshamambe and Mena on the main line from Hakodate to Otaru I saw from the railway-carriage window occasional trees which looked to me spontaneous. This species is not known to grow wild on the mainland of northeastern Asia, though there is a possibility that it occurs in Korea.

I first met with this Pine as a wild tree in the forests at the base of Higashi-Kirishima in Osumi province, Kyushu, growing with *Abies firma* S. & Z., evergreen Oaks, various Lauraceae and other broad-leaved trees. On the same mountain round Miya it forms woods either pure or mixed with *P. Thunbergii* Parl. On the slopes of Koya-san in Hondo, on the borders of Yamato and Kii provinces the Red Pine is abundant in pure stands or mixed with *Tsuga Sieboldii* Carr. and *Chamaecyparis obtusa* S. & Z. It also grows in the valley of the Kisogawa, in the Nikko region and elsewhere in central Hondo; round Lake Towada in Mutsu province it occurs at the water's edge with *Pinus parviflora* S. & Z. But the finest woods of this Pine I saw are at Yoshida on the northern slopes of Fuji-san in Suruga province. These woods are pure and though not extensive are probably the remains of great forests which once covered what is now wild moorland. As seen at Yoshida the Red Pine is strikingly picturesque, with its tall reddish trunk and thin mop-like crown. It grows from 30 to 35 m. tall and in girth of trunk from 3 to 4 m. The trunk is usually straight, sometimes somewhat leaning, and is bare of branches for one-half to three-fourths the height of the tree. The bark is orange-red, thin and scaly, but on old trees near the base of the trunk it is firmer, grayish and fissured in oblong and rectangular plates. The branches are rather short and horizontally disposed; sometimes they are slightly ascending, sometimes rather recurved and form a more or less flattened oval crown. The young shoots are more or less pruinose and the terminal buds are reddish brown, cylindrical, acute, and slightly resinous, with the scales free at the tips. The leaves are in pairs, dull, grayish green, slender, from 8 to 12 cm. long, twisted, finely serrulate, with stomata on both surfaces and marginal resin-ducts. The cone is subterminal, subsessile and spreading, symmetrical, ovoid-conic, from 3 to 5 cm. long, and dull pale tawny yellow in color, with a weak hold on the branch, though it often persists for two or three years. The wood is resinous, coarse-grained, but strong, and is used in quantity, since it is cheap, in all sorts of general construction work and for fuel. Though abundantly planted on barren soils for reafforestation from time immemorial the Red Pine is not much planted in the parks, temple grounds and gardens of Japan, where the favorite is *P. Thunbergii* Parl. There are, however, several dwarf, variegated and otherwise abnormal forms of *P. densiflora* which are great favorites with the Japanese and are perpetuated by grafting on *P. Thunbergii* Parl. The best of these is Tanyosho (*P. densiflora*, var. *umbraculifera* Mayr (Plate XII), which has a dense, rounded, umbrella-like crown and grows from 2 to 4 m. tall. This is one of the most useful and ornamental of low-growing Pines. Another dwarf form is that called Bandaisho (f. *globosa* Mayr). In all Mayr enumerates some 22 forms of the Japanese Red Pine, but the only others that need be mentioned here are the weeping form (f. *pendula* Mayr) and the golden form (f. *aurea* Mayr), often met with in gardens in this country and in Europe under the erroneous name of *Pinus Massoniana aurea*. This form is well distinguished by its name. It was introduced to this country by Dr. George R. Hall in 1862. In the garden of Mr. C. H. Tenney at Méthuen, Massachusetts, there is growing a fine specimen of this curious Pine which is 5 m. tall and 2.3 m. through the crown.

Pinus densiflora was discovered by Thunberg and introduced in 1854 by von Siebold into the Botanic Garden at Leyden; John Gould Veitch sent seeds of it to England in 1861. It was brought to this country by Dr. George R. Hall in 1862, who gave seeds to Parsons & Co., Flushing, Long Island. In gardens, both in this country and in Europe, it has been very generally known under the erroneous name of *P. Massoniana*.

The Japanese Red Pine is perfectly hardy in eastern North America as far north at least as Boston. It grows rapidly and on the Hall estate there are handsome trees from 16 to 19 m. tall and from 1.5 to 2 m. in girth of trunk. As a tree for parks and gardens here it promises to be valuable and ornamental. Another name for this tree in Japan is Me-matsu (Female Pine).

PINUS THUNBERGII Parl.

PLATES XIII AND XIV

PINUS THUNBERGII Parlatore in De Candolle, *Prodr.* XVI. pt. 2, 388 (not Lambert[1]) (1868). — Franchet & Savatier, *Enum. Pl. Jap.* I. 464 (1875). — Masters in *Jour. Linn. Soc.* XVIII. 504 (1881); in *Gard. Chron.* n. ser. XIX. 825, fig. 139 (1883); XXV. 344, fig. 63 (1885). — Mayr, *Monog. Abiet. Jap.* 69, t. 5, fig. 16, t. 7, fig. 1 (1890). — Sargent, *Forest Fl. Jap.* 79 (1894). — Shirasawa, *Icon. Ess. For. Jap.* I. 11, t. 1, fig. 15-29 (1900). — Kent in Veitch, *Man. Conif.* ed. 2, 383 (1900). — Matsumura, *Ind. Pl. Jap.* II. pt. 1, 15 (1905). — Miyoshi, *Atlas Jap. Veget.* pt. IV. 5, t. 29, 30 (1906); pt. XIII. 6, t. 91 (1909). — Beissner, *Handb. Nadelh.* ed. 2, 414 (1909). — Clinton-Baker, *Ill. Conif.* I. 55, t. (1909). — Elwes & Henry, *Trees Gr. Brit. & Irel.* V. 1143 (1909). — Shaw, *Gen. Pinus*, 56, t. 22, fig. 196, 197 (1914).

Pinus sylvestris Thunberg, *Fl. Jap.* 274 (in part, not Linnaeus) (1784). — Siebold in *Verh. Batav. Genoot.* XII. pt. 1, 12 (*Syn. Pl. Oecon. Jap.*) (1830).

Pinus Massoniana Siebold & Zuccarini, *Fl. Jap.* II. 24, t. 113, 114 (not Lambert) (1844). — Endlicher, *Syn. Conif.* 174 (1847). — J. G. Veitch in *Gard. Chron.* 1862, 309. — Murray in *Proc. Hort. Soc. Lond.* II. 278, fig. 28-40 (1862); *Pines & Firs Jap.* 23, fig. 39-54 (1863). — Gordon, *Pinet.* new ed. 241 (exclude synonyms *P. Cavendishiana* and *P. tabulaeformis*) (1880). — Veitch, *Man. Conif.* 148 (1881).

Pinus rubra Siebold & Zuccarini, *Fl. Jap.* II. 25 (as a synonym, not Miller) (1844).

This Black Pine, or Kuro-matsu, is found in Japan from southernmost Kyushu to the northern limits of Hondo, but it has been so much planted from the earliest days of Japanese history that it is impossible to-day to determine its original geographical range. It grows wild on the islands of Tanega-shima and Yaku-shima; on the first it forms very extensive forests and on the latter it occurs scattered through the coastal savannah and also in pure stands of small size. Around the base of Higashi-Kirishima in Osumi province, Kyushu, it is wild and forms pure woods or is mixed with *P. densiflora* S. & Z.; more rarely it grows in the forests of mixed trees. At Matsushima in Rikuzen province, northern Hondo, this Pine grows alone or with occasional trees of *P. densiflora* S. & Z. on the hundreds of sandstone islets for which that place is named. This is the most northern place I saw it wild; indeed these places, with the island of Miyajima in the Inland Sea, are the only ones where I saw this Black Pine truly indigenous. It is a maritime species and very probably at one time was widely distributed along the coastal regions of Japan. Outside of that country it is known to be indigenous only on the islands of Quelpaert and Ooryöng, two interesting outposts of the Japanese flora off the coast of Korea.

As usually seen this Black Pine is a most picturesque tree with a crooked trunk, ponderous, sprawling branches, dark green leaves, and a blackish-looking crown of no particular shape. Its odd habit, umbrageous withal, is probably what has so endeared it to the Japanese, by whom it has been more widely planted than any other tree except the Cryptomeria. It is certain that this Pine has in-

---

[1] *Pinus Thunbergii* Lambert (*Pinus*, ed. 2, preface, vi [1828]. — *Abies Thunbergii* Lindley in *Penny Cycl.* I. 34 [1833]), is based on *Pinus Abies* Thunberg (*Fl. Jap.* 275 [not Linnaeus] [1784]), an obscure plant of which no specimen exists. Some authors have referred it to *Picea polita* Carr., but with equal propriety it might be referred to *Abies firma* S. & Z.

fluenced Japanese art more than any other tree as it is a familiar subject on their paintings, wood-carvings and embroideries. The great highways of Old Japan, like the Tokaido, which stretched from Kyoto to Tokyo, and the Ōshū-kaidō, from Tokyo to Aomori, were lined with rows of this Pine, the remains of which may be seen to-day. In the grounds of the Daimyōs' palaces this tree was much planted and in those of Nagoya castle some fine trees are still growing. In Tokyo there is a picturesque group of this Pine outside the temples in Shiba Park, and in the grounds and on the inner wall of the moat which bounds the Emperor's palace there are many fine specimens. In many places in Japan are famous trees of this Pine which the people make long pilgrimages to see, one might say to worship. Such, for example, are the extraordinary tree at Karasaki on the shore of Lake Biwa, a description and picture of which appeared in the *Gardeners' Chronicle*, ser. 3, XV. 366, fig. 44 (1894), and the Ship Pine in front of the Kofukuji Temple at Nara. This latter is about 28 m. tall, 6 m. in girth of trunk and the lower branches, which form the prow and deck of the boat, are 50 m. long. The largest trees I saw were planted on the coast between Kochi and Aki in Tosa province, Shikoku, and are growing in sea-sand and gravel, and at flood tides and when high seas prevail the boles are washed by the waves. These trees are fully 30 m. tall, from 6 to 7 m. in girth of trunk and the blackish gray bark is fissured into thick oblong and rhomboidal plates.

When growing thickly together in forests, as on Tanega-shima, and protected from the wind this Black Pine can behave like an ordinary Pine tree and form a nearly straight trunk, spreading branches and a more or less oval or flattened crown. On Tanega-shima these trees are from 20 to 30 m. tall and in girth of trunk from 2 to 4 m. On the islets at Matsushima it grows from 3 to 20 m. tall and from 1 to 3 m. in girth of trunk. The blackish gray bark is fissured into elongated plates of irregular size and shape. The branches are variable in size, length and disposition and the shoot is yellowish brown. The terminal buds are characteristic and readily distinguish the species, being white or grayish white, ovoid to ovoid-cylindrical and pointed, with fimbriate scales matted together, with their subulate ends free. The leaves are dark green, in pairs, stout, twisted, densely crowded on the branches and spreading, from 6 to 18 cm. long, finely serrulate and pungent, with stomata on both surfaces and medial resin-ducts. The cones are subterminal, clustered and spreading on short stalks, and are firmly attached to the branches, symmetrical ovoid to ovoid-conic in shape, from 4 to 6 cm. long and nut-brown in color; the apophysis is flat or convex with a transverse ridge and the umbo is usually armed with a minute prickle. The wood is similar in appearance to that of *P. densiflora* S. & Z., but is coarser grained, more brittle, more resinous and of considerably less value for all purposes except as fuel.

Under long cultivation in Japanese gardens several distinct forms have developed, some dwarf, some pendulous in habit, others with variegated or otherwise abnormal foliage. Another name for this Pine in Japan is O-Matsu (Male Pine).

Mayr speaks of hybrids between *P. Thunbergii* and *P. densiflora* S. & Z. and I inquired about them in Japan, but all I could learn was that in nurseries of seedlings, raised from one or other of these Pines, plants intermediate in appearance were occasionally found. I saw none, however. In Japan *P. Thunbergii* is used as the stock in grafting all the other native Pines and their varieties. Mayr mentions ten different forms of *P. Thunbergii* as cultivated in Japan; of these the f. *pendula* Mayr, which makes an ugly tree, f. *variegata* Mayr and f. *monophylla*

Mayr are the most distinct. The last two were discovered by Siebold and by Siebold & Zuccarini were referred to their *P. Massoniana* as varieties.

Like the Red Pine (*P. densiflora* S. & Z.) the Black Pine was discovered by Thunberg and introduced into Holland by von Siebold in 1855 and into England by John Gould Veitch in 1861. The largest plants growing in this Arboretum are from seeds received from the Agricultural College, Sapporo, Hokkaido, in June 1880; there are other good specimens raised from seeds collected in Japan in 1892 by Professor Sargent. In eastern North America this species is hardy and grows rapidly as far north at least as Boston, Massachusetts. It would appear to be of value for planting on the seashore and on sand dunes and in such exposed situations deserves a thorough trial.

LARIX Mill.

Ten species of this genus, with possibly two well-marked geographical varieties, are now recognized and two Larches of hybrid origin are also in cultivation. All the species are confined to the Northern Hemisphere, where they are widely distributed from the Arctic Circle southward and reach their southern limits on the mountains of Yunnan province, China, and on the Himalayas. Three species are North American and of these *L. laricina* K. Koch is dispersed over an immense region from Newfoundland and Labrador westward to the valley of the Mackenzie River and beyond to the Yukon, Alaska.[1] The other two species (*L. Lyallii* Parl. and *L. occidentalis* Nutt.) are confined to western North America and have a rather restricted geographical range. The European Larch (*L. decidua* Mill.) is wild on the Alps from Dauphiné to the Tyrol, on the Carpathians and on the mountains of Bohemia and Moravia. In some places it forms extensive and pure forests. Its Siberian relative (*L. sibirica* Ledeb.) covers large areas in northern Russia as far north as latitude 67° and spreads eastward through Siberia to the Yenesei River and possibly beyond; from the Altai Mountains to Lake Baikal it finds the southern limits of its range.

On the Himalayas there is one species (*L. Griffithii* Hook. f. & Thoms.) and this is distributed eastward from eastern Nepal to the mountains bordering Yunnan in southwestern China. In China two species (*L. Potaninii* Batal. and *L. Mastersiana* Rehd. & Wils.) are endemic and grow on the mountains from Shensi province westward to those of the Chino-Thibetan borderland. *Larix Mastersiana*, however, may prove when better known only a condition of *L. Potaninii* with abnormal bracts. In northeast Asia from near Lake Baikal east and north grows *L. dahurica* Turcz., but the geographical limits and range of variation of this species are not yet properly known. In Saghalien, Kamtchatka and the Kuriles, and possibly also in the coastal region of the Amur province, it is represented by the variety *japonica* Maxim.; in parts of Korea, Mandshuria and in extreme northeastern China it is represented by the large-coned variety *Principis Rupprechtii* Rehd. & Wils. From Olga Bay, northeast of Vladivostock, Henry has recently (in *Gard. Chron.* ser. 3, LVII. 109, fig. 31, 32 [1915]) described a new species (*L. olgensis*), but it is doubtful if this is anything more than a state of the variety *japonica*, itself very questionably distinct from typical *L. dahurica*. In Japan one species is endemic in the central parts of the main island of Hondo.

[1] From Alaska a new species (*L. alaskensis* Wight in *Smithsonian Misc. Coll.* L. 174, t. 17 [1908]) has recently been described and Henry (in *Gard. Chron.* ser. 3, LVIII. 178 [1915]) states that it may be *L. dahurica* Turcz. I have seen the type specimen of this supposed new species and can find no character by which it can be distinguished from typical *L. laricina* K. Koch.

KEY TO THE JAPANESE SPECIES

Cone-scales reflexed at the apex, numerous, with lepidote glands on the back; leaves on short shoots gray-green, markedly stomatiferous on both surfaces . L. KAEMPFERI.
Cone-scales not reflexed at the apex, few in number, glabrous or glandularly puberulous; leaves on short shoots grass-green, with or without obscure and broken stomatiferous lines on the upper surface . . . . L. DAHURICA, var. JAPONICA.

LARIX KAEMPFERI Sarg.

PLATES XV AND XVI

LARIX KAEMPFERI Sargent, *Silva N. Am.* XII. 2, note 2 (not Carrière[1]) (1898). — Silva Tarouca, *Uns. Freiland-Nadelh.* 60, fig. 53 (1913).

Pinus Larix Thunberg, *Fl. Jap.* 275 (not Linnaeus) (1784).
Pinus Kaempferi Lambert, *Pinus,* ed. 2, preface, vi (1828).
Abies Kaempferi Lindley in *Penny Cycl.* I. 34 (1833).
Abies leptolepis Siebold & Zuccarini, *Fl. Jap.* II. 12, t. 105 (1842).
Pinus leptolepis Endlicher, *Syn. Conif.* 130 (1847).
Larix japonica Hort. ex Endlicher, *Syn. Conif.* 130 (as a synonym) (1847). — Carrière, *Traité Conif.* 272 (1855). — Murray, *Pines & Firs Jap.* 94, fig. 178–188 (1863). — Regel in *Gartenfl.* XX. 104, t. 685, fig. 7 (1871).
Larix leptolepis Gordon, *Pinet.* 128 (1858). — Murray in *Proc. Hort. Soc. Lond.* II. 633, fig. 154, 156–171 (1862); *Pines & Firs Jap.* 89, fig. 172–177 (1863). — Miquel in *Ann. Mus. Lugd.-Bat.* III. 166 (1867); *Prol. Fl. Jap.* 330 (1867). — Regel in *Gartenfl.* XX. 102, t. 685, fig. 5 (1871). — Franchet & Savatier, *Enum. Pl. Jap.* I. 466 (1875). — Masters in *Jour. Linn. Soc.* XVIII. 523 (1881). — Mayr, *Monog. Abiet. Jap.* 63, t. 5, fig. 14 (1890). — Sargent, *Forest Fl. Jap.* 83 (1894). — Shirasawa, *Icon. Ess. For. Jap.* I. 13, t. 2, 1–16 (1900). — Kent in Veitch, *Man. Conif.* ed. 2, 397, fig. 102 (1900). — Matsumura, *Ind. Pl. Jap.* II. pt. 1, 11 (1905). — Miyoshi, *Atlas Jap. Veget.* pt. II. 6, t. 12 (1905); pt. V. 5, t. 38 (1906). — Elwes & Henry, *Trees Gr. Brit. & Irel.* II. 384, t. 108 (1907). — Clinton-Baker, *Ill. Conif.* II. 58, t. (1909). — Hayata, *Veget. Mt. Fuji,* 93, fig. 5, 16, 31 (1911).
Larix leptolepis, var. *minor* Murray in *Proc. Hort. Soc. Lond.* II. 637, fig. 155 (1862).
Larix leptolepis, β *Murrayana* Maximowicz in *Ind. Sem. Hort. Petrop.* 1866, 3. — Franchet & Savatier, *Enum. Pl. Jap.* I. 366 (1875). — Beissner, *Handb. Nadelh.* ed. 2, 309, fig. 73 (1909).
Larix Japonica macrocarpa Carrière, *Traité Conif.* ed. 2, 354 (1867).
Larix orientalis Jackson in *Ind. Kew.* II. 31 (as a synonym) (1895).
Larix Kaempferi, var. *minor* Sargent, *Silva N. Am.* XII. 2, in a note (1898).

As a wild tree this Larch, the Kara-matsu, is confined to volcanic soils of recent formation in central Hondo from Hak-san, in Kaga province in the south and west through Shinano province to that of Shimotsuke, where it reaches its northern limit in the Nikko region. Within these limits it is common on nearly every mountain, but especially on Yatsuga-dake and on Fuji-san. Its altitudinal range is from 500 to 2300 m., but on the south side of Fuji-san above this altitude it forms scrub up to 2900 m. On Fuji-san *Pinus pumila* Regel does not grow and its place is in a measure taken by scrub Larch. That this low scrubby growth is the direct result of local ecological conditions and not of fixed character is proved by plants

---

[1] *Larix Kaempferi* Carrière is *Pseudolarix Kaempferi* Gordon (*Pinet.* 292 [1858]), the Chinese Golden Larch, a tree unknown in Japan and to Kaempfer.

growing in this Arboretum. Seeds were collected by Philip Codman in 1892 at the upper limit of this scrubby Larch, and the trees raised from them are now 12 m. tall and have grown just as rapidly as trees raised from seeds collected from the ordinary tree form.

This Japanese Larch is inclined to form pure stands and these are often of very considerable extent, but it grows also in mixed woods with *Pinus densiflora* S. & Z., *Picea jezoënsis* Carr., *Tsuga diversifolia* Mast. and such broad-leaved trees as Oak, Birch, Hornbeam and Beech, and with *Abies homolepis* S. & Z. at its lowest and *A. Veitchii* Lindl. at its upper altitudinal limit. The maximum size of *Larix Kaempferi* is about 33 m. by 4 m., but such trees are rare and the average size is from 25 to 26 m. tall and from 2 to 3 m. in girth of trunk. The bark is gray and scales off in narrow strips, leaving behind red scars; on old trees near the base of the trunk the bark is deeply furrowed into more or less oblong plates. The branches are numerous, slender and short, horizontally spreading, sometimes slightly ascending, sometimes slightly decurved, and form a narrow, somewhat pyramidal crown. The shoot is glabrous or pubescent, yellowish to reddish brown and often more or less pruinose. The leaves are glaucous green, strongly keeled on the lower side and stomatiferous on both surfaces. The cone is broadly ovoid, from 1.6 to 3 cm. long, and the upper margin of the lepidote cone-scale is reflexed. The wood is very durable in and near the ground and on this account is valued for mine-props, railway-ties, telegraph-poles and the like; it is also used in ship-building. In Japan this tree is esteemed as the source of very useful timber and on this account it has been extensively planted in many parts of Hondo, and in Hokkaido as far north as Sapporo, where it thrives. In eastern North America *Larix Kaempferi* is perfectly hardy as far north as Boston, and in this Arboretum its rate of growth is more rapid than that of the European Larch (*L. decidua* Mill.). The common Japanese name for this Larch is Kara-matsu, and it is also known as Fuji-matsu and Rakuyōshō.

This Larch was first mentioned by Kaempfer (*Amoen.* fasc. V. 883 [1712]) under its vernacular name of Kara-maatz and as *Larix conifera, nucleis pyramidatis, foliis deciduis*. Thunberg took it to be the same as the European species and cites Linnaeus' description, but Lambert, suspecting the Japanese species was distinct, named it for Kaempfer. It was first introduced into Europe by John Gould Veitch, who sent seeds to England in 1861, and one of the trees raised from these seeds was planted in the Hunnewell Pinetum.

LARIX DAHURICA Turcz.

LARIX DAHURICA Turczaninow apud Trautvetter, *Imag. Pl. Fl. Russ.* 48, t. 32 (1844). — Carrière, *Traité Conif.* 271 (1855). — Trautvetter & Meyer in Middendorff, *Reis. Sibir.* I. pt. 2, Bot. abt. 2, 88 (*Fl. Ochot.*) (1856). — Ruprecht & Maximowicz in *Bull. Phys.-Math. Acad. Sci. St. Pétersbourg*, XV. 140 (1857). — Ruprecht & Maack in *Bull. Phys.-Math. Acad. Sci. St. Pétersbourg*, XV. 382 (1857). — Regel & Tiling, *Fl. Ajan.* 119 (1858). — Maximowicz in *Mém. Sav. Étr. Acad. Sci. St. Pétersbourg*, IX. 262 (*Prim. Fl. Amur.*) (1859). — Fr. Schmidt in *Mém. Acad. Sci. St. Pétersbourg*, sér. 7, XII. no. 2, 177 (*Reis. Amur. Sachal.*) (1868). — Glehn in *Act. Hort. Petrop.* IV. 86 (1874). — Herder in *Act. Hort. Petrop.* XII. 98 (1892). — Korshinsky in *Act. Hort. Petrop.* XII. 424 (1892). — Komarov in *Act. Hort. Petrop.* XX. 190 (*Fl. Mandsh.* I.) (1901). — Beissner, *Handb. Nadelh.* ed. 2, 319, fig. 77

(1909). — Nakai in *Jour. Coll. Sci. Tokyo*, XXXI. 382 (*Fl. Kor.* pt. 2) (1911). — Henry in *Gard. Chron.* ser. 3, LVIII. 178, fig. 58, 59 (1), 60 (3) (1915).

Larix dahurica Lawson, *Agric. Man.* 389 (name only) (1836).
Pinus dahurica Fischer apud Turczaninow in *Bull. Soc. Nat. Mosc.* XI. 101 (name only) (*Cat. Pl. Baical.*) (1838).
Larix europaea, var. *dahurica* Loudon, *Arb. Brit.* IV. 2352 (1838).
Abies Gmelinii Ruprecht in *Beitr. Pflanz. Russ. Reich.* II. 56 (1845).
Larix dahurica, a typica Regel in *Gartenfl.* XX. 105, t. 684, fig. 9, 10 (1871); in *Act. Hort. Petrop.* I. 160 (*Revis. Spec. Crataeg. Dracaen. Laric.* 59) (1871–72).
Larix Cajanderi Mayr, *Fremdl. Wald- u. Parkb.* 297, fig. 88 (1906).

This Larch is distributed over an immense tract of country from near the eastern shores of Lake Baikal northward and eastward; in the south it extends into Mandshuria and Korea, where, however, as well as in extreme northeast China, it is chiefly represented by its large-coned variety *Principis Rupprechtii* Rehd. & Wils. Although many references to *L. dahurica* can be cited and Lawson states that it was introduced into England in 1827, very little has been recorded concerning the habit and general appearance of this Larch.[1] It is doubtful if there are any good specimens of this tree in cultivation in Europe,[2] except perhaps in Russia, and there are certainly none in this country. In this Arboretum we have small plants growing under this name and received from various sources. Some of these are *L. sibirica* Ledeb., some *L. pendula* Salisb., others *L. dahurica*, var. *japonica* Maxim. and one plant only is referable to typical *L. dahurica*. In the Botanic Gardens at Petrograd[3] and Moscow I have seen trees labelled *L. dahurica*, but unfortunately I made no notes on the habit and appearance of these trees. I have a poor photograph of the trees in the Botanic Gardens, Moscow, but these are crowded together, have crooked trunks and have evidently suffered from the influence of strong winds and nothing of value is shown by it. One of these trees has flat, stiff, wide-spreading horizontal branches. I have before me specimens collected near Khabarovsk and others near Sryetinsk by Professor Sargent in August 1902 and by him named *L. dahurica*. They have the typical small cone as figured by Trautvetter, and most of the shoots are pale-colored and glabrous or nearly so, but some shoots are densely clothed with a short, crisped, red-brown pubescence and are reddish in appearance, as in typical *L. dahurica*, var. *japonica* Maxim. In this herbarium there are a number of specimens of *L. dahurica* collected in various parts of continental northeastern Asia, and in these the cones, cone-scales and bracts vary in size and shape and in some the cone-scales are glandularly puberulous on the dorsal surface; the leaves on the short shoots vary in size and may be without stomata on the upper side or these may be present in broken and obscure lines; the shoots are glabrous or nearly

---

[1] A note on this subject to Mr. W. J. Bean, Assistant Curator, Royal Gardens, Kew, elicited the following reply. "I am afraid I cannot help you about *L. dahurica* and *L. sibirica*. They both do so very badly here and have no cones, so that one has no basis to go on. I must say, however, that there seems to be nothing to distinguish them as they grow here. *Larix kurilensis*, as we grow it, is absolutely distinct in every way — most of all by its very pubescent shoots."

[2] The *L. dahurica* of Elwes & Henry (*Trees Gr. Brit. & Irel.* II. 379 [1907]) is mainly *L. pendula* Salisb., a hybrid between *L. decidua* Mill. and *L. laricina* K. Koch (see Henry in *Gard. Chron.* ser. 3, LVIII. 178, fig. 58 a, b, fig. 59, 2 (1915).

[3] Specimens with cones in this herbarium received from the Botanic Garden, Petrograd, as *L. dahurica* do not belong to that species, but to *L. pendula* Salisb. From cultivated trees of the true *L. dahurica* I have seen no cone-bearing material.

so and pallid, or more or less densely clothed with a reddish pubescence. These variations are present on one and the same branch. A similar range of variation occurs on material which I gathered in Japanese Saghalien in August 1914, and also on the numerous specimens in this herbarium that came from the Kurile Islands or from plants raised from seeds collected on these islands. Whether these Larches are absolutely identical or not can well be left to the future to decide, and in order not to complicate the question I retain for the insular Larch, characterized in its typical form by its reddish shoots, the varietal name of

LARIX DAHURICA, var. JAPONICA Maximowicz apud Regel in *Gartenfl.* XX. 105, t. 685, fig. 6 (not *L. japonica* Carrière) (1871). — Regel in *Act. Hort. Petrop.* I. 160 (*Revis. Spec. Crataeg. Dracaen. Laric.* 59) (1871-72); in *Belge Hort.* XXII. 105, t. 10, fig. 1 (1872). — Miyabe in *Mem. Boston Soc. Nat. Hist.* IV. 261 (*Fl. Kurile Isl.*) (1890). — Beissner, *Handb. Nadelh.* 329, fig. 91 (1891). — Sargent, *Forest Fl. Jap.* 84, t. 26 (1894). — Patschke in *Bot. Jahrb.* XLVIII. 651 (1913).

Abies kamtschatica Ruprecht in *Beitr. Pflanz. Russ. Reich.* II. 57 (1845).
Pinus kamtschatika Endlicher, *Syn. Conif.* 135 (1847).
Larix Kamtschatica Carrière, *Traité Conif.* 279 (1855).
Larix Kurilensis Mayr, *Monog. Abiet. Jap.* 66, t. 5, fig. 15 (1890). — Elwes & Henry, *Trees Gr. Brit. & Irel.* II. 383, t. 107 (1907). — Shirasawa, *Icon. Ess. For. Jap.* II. t. 1, fig. 1-16 (1908). — Beissner, *Handb. Nadelh.* ed. 2, 321, fig. 78 (1909). — Clinton-Baker, *Ill. Conif.* II. 57, t. (1909). — Takeda in *Jour. Linn. Soc.* XLII. 486 (1914).
Larix Dahurica, var. *Kurilensis* Sargent, *Silva N. Am.* XII. 4, in a note (1898).
Larix sibirica Masters in *Bull. Herb. Boiss.* VI. 272 (not Ledebour) (1898). — Matsumura, *Ind. Pl. Jap.* II. pt. 1, 12 (1905).
Larix dahurica Miyoshi, *Atlas Jap. Veget.* pt. IX, 4, t. 67 (possibly of Turczaninow) (1908). — Miyabe & Miyake, *Fl. Saghal.* 620, t. 11, fig. 4-8 (1915).
Larix dahurica, var. *pubescens* Patschke in *Bot. Jahrb.* XLVIII. 651 (1913).

This tree (Plates XVII and XVIII) is abundant in swampy places throughout Japanese Saghalien, where it forms immense pure forests or is mixed with *Abies sachalinensis* Mast., *Picea jezoënsis* Carr., *Alnus hirsuta* Turcz., *Betula japonica* Sieb., *B. Ermanii* Cham. and various species of Willow. It grows also on the Kurile Islands, where its southern limit is on the island of Shikotan, but it is not known in a wild state in Hokkaido or in any other part of Japan proper. As I saw it in Saghalien it is a somewhat sparsely branched tree growing from 20 to 30 m. tall, with a trunk from 2 to 3 m. in girth; the bark is dark gray, scaly on young trees, but becoming fissured into shallow plates and finally on old trees very deeply furrowed. The branches are rather long, slender, and straight, and spread horizontally, but are usually somewhat upturned at the ends and give the tree a characteristic appearance. The shoots are usually densely or sparsely clothed with crisped brownish pubescence, but occasionally this is wanting. In color the young shoot varies from pale to reddish and it often is slightly covered with a pale bloom; the second year shoot is red or yellowish brown and sometimes gray. The leaves on the shoots are curved, pointed, about 2.5 to 3 cm. long, and have the stomatic lines prominent on both surfaces, and in consequence the color is rather glaucous green. On the spurs the leaves are grass-green, from 1 to 2.8 cm. long, broadest at the apex, which is blunt, and the stomatic lines are absent or nearly so from the upper side, which is perfectly flat. The cone is cylindric-ovoid, from 1.5 to 2.5 cm. high and composed usually of from 20 to 25 scales, but the number varies from 18 to 30. In the typical form the cone is reddish brown, but from small trees growing near Toyohara I gathered on August 5, 1916, specimens (No. 7333), in which the cone-scales were green in the centre, red-brown round the margins and perfectly intermediate between the type and its green-coned form (f. *ochrocarpa* Wils.). The scales of the ripe cone are ascending-spreading, either perfectly smooth or glandularly puberulous on the outside, with the margin thin, often slightly crenulate, truncate and normally emarginate at the summit. The wood is of about the same value as that of the Japanese Larch (*L. Kaempferi* Sarg.) and is used in Saghalien for telegraph-poles, railway-ties and for planking and posts in general building work.

Some years ago Maximowicz informed Dr. K. Miyabe that the tree from which came the specimens on which he based his *L. dahurica*, var. *japonica* grew in the town of Hakodate in Hokkaido. Acting on this information I succeeded in locating in Hakodate the only large tree of this Larch known to grow there and in all probability Maximowicz's type. Through the courtesy of the military authorities I was able to photograph this interesting tree, which is about 15 m. tall, with a trunk 2 m. in girth and a flat, wide-spreading crown some 13 m. through. It grows in what is now a private garden at 101, Yachigashira. On comparing specimens from this tree with a cotype from Dr. Mayr of his *L. kurilensis* I can detect no difference except that the shoots on the Hakodate specimens are rather more pubescent and redder brown. They agree exactly with Mayr's figure. No one has really questioned the identity of Maximowicz's variety and Mayr's species, but admitting this it remains exceedingly doubtful if the variety is distinct from typical *L. dahurica* Turcz. In a letter recently received Professor A. Henry points out certain differences which he has detected and which he considers distinguish the Kuriles Larch from that of Saghalien and of the mainland. I have carefully examined the many specimens in this herbarium and find the characters pointed out by Henry to be extremely variable and common to material from the Kuriles, from Saghalien and from continental eastern Asia. At my request my several colleagues have kindly undertaken an independent examination of the material and their conclusions are identical with my own. From my study of cultivated trees of the Kuriles Larch in Hokkaido and in this Arboretum, of the forests of Larch in Saghalien and of the mass of dried material in this herbarium I am strongly of the opinion that Messrs. Miyabe and Miyake are correct in reducing Maximowicz's variety (the *L. kurilensis* Mayr) to typical *L. dahurica* Turcz. Nevertheless, in the present imperfect state of our knowledge and in order to avoid any possible confusion it is best to keep them separate.

Larix dahurica, var. *japonica* is a very hardy tree, but it is not probable that it will have value for forestry purposes in lands where the Japanese Larch (*L. Kaempferi* Sarg.) can be grown. The forestry officers at Kushiro informed me that an experimental planting had been recently made on part of the Nemuro peninsula in northeastern Hokkaido, but it was too early to form any opinion of its value. In the Botanic Garden at Sapporo this Larch grows well, but is not the equal in this respect of *L. Kaempferi* Sarg. In this Arboretum trees raised from seeds received in February 1894 are now only 6 m. tall, with trunks 0.4 m. in girth, and their clear grass-green leaves and characteristic habit make them very distinct. It was introduced into Europe by Dr. Mayr in 1888. A form of this Larch is

LARIX DAHURICA, var. JAPONICA, f. OCHROCARPA Wilson n. forma.

Larix dahurica, forma *chlorocarpa* Miyabe & Miyake, *Fl. Saghal.* 621 (possibly of Schröder) (1915).

This tree is abundant in swamps in Saghalien, where it grows with the typical var. *japonica* and from which it does not differ except in the color of the cone, which is pale yellowish green. This form is based on my No. 7331, collected on August 4, 1914, at Konuma near Toyohara. It is possible that Messrs. Miyabe and Miyake are correct in referring this form to Schröder's *chlorocarpa*, which is founded on a tree cultivated at Moscow. Its origin is not stated, but it is much more probable that it came from Dahuria than from Saghalien. To avoid any possibility of confusion it appears best to keep the Saghalien tree separate under a distinct name.

PICEA A. Dietr.[1]

The genus Picea is widely distributed in the colder and temperate regions of the Northern Hemisphere from the Arctic Circle southward, reaching the Tropic of Cancer on the mountains of Formosa in the Old World. Thirty-eight species are now recognized and of these no fewer than 18 are endemic in central and western China. One other species is recorded from Formosa, but this is probably identical with the Chinese *P. Watsoniana* Mast. The central Asian *P. Schrenkiana* Fisch. & Mey. also grows in the province of Kansu, so that more than half the known species are Chinese. It is of course probable that when better known the Chinese species may be somewhat reduced in number. Nearly all of them are now in cultivation and it must be admitted that even in a juvenile condition they are mostly dissimilar. A majority of them promise to thrive in this Arboretum and in a few years it will be possible to judge their value and distinctness.

In North America seven species are found, ranging from the Arctic Circle to the slopes of the southern Appalachian Mountains and to the mountains of northern New Mexico and Arizona. In Europe three species are indigenous, one of which (*P. obovata* Ledeb.) extends far into Siberia. In the Taurus and the Caucasus is found *P. orientalis* Carr. and two species are indigenous on the Himalayas. The central Asian and southern Siberian *P. Schrenkiana* Fisch. & Mey. has been mentioned as growing in northwest China, but the eastern limit of the range of this species is not properly known. Six species occur in Japan and of these four (possibly five) are endemic; the other is widely spread in Korea, Mandshuria and the Amur region of northeastern Asia.

KEY TO THE JAPANESE SPECIES

Leaves quadrangular in section.
  Branchlets quite glabrous.
    Shoots shining yellow-brown; winter-buds ovoid, acute or obtuse, chestnut-brown, very slightly or not at all resinous; cone ovoid-cylindrical, from 8 to 10 cm. long . . . . P. POLITA.
    Shoots rusty to yellowish brown; winter-buds conical, acute, reddish brown and resinous; cone cylindrical, from 2.5 to 6.5 cm. long . . . . P. MAXIMOWICZII.
  Branchlets glandular-pubescent; reddish brown, slightly pruinose; winter-buds conical, swollen at the base, shining brown and resinous; cone cylindrical, from 4 to 10 cm. long . . . . P. KOYAMAI.
Leaves slightly compressed, rhombic in section.
  Branchlets with dense rust-red pubescence; winter-buds conical to ovoid, swollen at the base, shining chestnut-brown and resinous; cone cylindrical, from 5 to 8 cm. long . . . . P. GLEHNII.

---

[1] Link (in *Abh. Akad. Berl.* 1827, 179) is usually cited as the author of the genus Picea, but it was founded by A. Dietrich (*Fl. Berl.*, I. abh. 2, 794 [1824]).

Branchlets glabrous or with more or less gray pubescence; winter-buds not swollen at the base, dull- to chestnut-brown; cone ovoid-cylindrical, from 6 to 12 cm. long.
. . . . P. BICOLOR.

Leaves flattened, narrowly elliptic in section, with white lines on one surface; branchlets glabrous and shining; winter-buds swollen at the base, broad-conical, resinous and shining . . . . P. JEZOËNSIS.

PICEA POLITA Carr.

PLATES XIX AND XX

PICEA POLITA Carrière, *Traité Conif.* 256 (1855). — Masters in *Gard. Chron.* n. ser. XIII. 233, fig. 44 (1880); in *Jour. Linn. Soc.* XVIII. 507, t. 19 (1881). — Mayr, *Monog. Abiet. Jap.* 46, t. 3, fig. 7. — Sargent, *Forest Fl. Jap.* 80 (1894). — Kent in Veitch, *Man. Conif.* ed. 2, 446, fig. 110 (1900). — Matsumura, *Ind. Pl. Jap.* II. pt. 1, 13 (1905). — Shirasawa, *Icon. Ess. For. Jap.* II. t. 2, fig. 18–29 (1908). — Beissner, *Handb. Nadelh.* ed. 2, 250, fig. 51, 52 (1909). — Clinton-Baker, *Ill. Conif.* II. 45, t. (1909). — Hayata, *Veget. Mt. Fuji*, 93, fig. 12, 28 (1911). — Elwes & Henry, *Trees Gr. Brit. & Irel.* VI. 1370 (1912).

Abies torano Siebold in *Verh. Batav. Genoot.* XII. pt. 1, 12 (*Syn. Pl. Oecon. Jap.*) (name only) (1830). — K. Koch. *Dendr.* II. pt. 2, 233 (1873).

Abies polita Siebold & Zuccarini, *Fl. Jap.* II. 20, t. 3 (1842). — Lindley & Gordon in *Jour. Hort. Soc. Lond.* V. 212 (1850). — Franchet & Savatier, *Enum. Pl. Jap.* I. 466 (1875).

Pinus polita Antoine, *Conif.* 95, t. 36, fig. 1 (1846). — Endlicher, *Syn. Conif.* 121 (1847).

Abies Smithiana Gordon, *Pinet.* 12 (as to the Japanese plant, not Loudon) (1858); *Pinet.* suppl. 12 (as to the synonym *Abies Thunbergii*) (1862).

Abies Khutrow Henkel & Hochstetter, *Syn. Nadelh.* 199 (as to the Japanese plant, not Loudon) (1865).

Picea Khutrow Willkomm, *Forstl. Fl.* 95 (as to the Japanese plant, not Carrière) (1887).

Picea Torano Koehne, *Deutsch. Dendr.* 22 (1893). — Sargent, *Silva N. Am.* XII. 21 (1898).

Pinus torano Voss in *Mitt. Deutsch. Dendr. Ges.* XVI. 93 (1907).

Around the northerly end of Lake Yamanaka, situated at the base of the northern slope of Fuji-san, there is a pure forest of this Spruce. This most interesting forest is growing on an old lava flow. The lava is broken into a maze of irregular, rugged blocks and is very porous in structure and water is present below. Not far away on the slope above Kagozaka pass there is a park-like area with many trees of this Spruce growing in cinders and ashes and among coarse grasses and shrubs. At Subashiri on the eastern slope of Fuji-san there are a few trees of *P. polita* growing isolated, or in company with *Abies homolepis* S. & Z., *Larix Kaempferi* Sarg., *Pinus densiflora* S. & Z. and broad-leaved trees such as *Zelkova serrata* Mak., *Quercus mongolica*, var. *grosserrata* Rehd. & Wils., and *Prunus Maximowiczii* Rupr. Higher up on the slopes of Fuji-san this Spruce grows in mixed forests in the same zone as *P. bicolor* Mayr, but is not very common. In the ascent from Nikko to Lake Chuzenji I saw a few young trees growing among Beech, Oak, Maple, and Birch, and Sargent collected cones in the same locality and noted that the trees were small and decrepit in appearance. I have seen material collected by Mayr on Shirane-san in Kai province and it has been reported from Tosa province in Shikoku.

Forestry officials inform me that it grows on the island of Kyushu, in three localities in Higo province, and on Nishi-Kirishima on the borders of Osumi and Satsuma provinces, but I did not see it when collecting on this mountain. The species is therefore distributed from the Nikko region southward and grows apparently always on volcanic soils of recent formation, but it is nowhere plentiful except at Lake Yamanaka. In Tokyo and other places in central Hondo it is occasionally met with in gardens, parks and temple grounds, and the tallest tree I saw was in the grounds of the Suwa Temple at Kamisuwa in Shinano province and about 40 m. tall.

The pure forest of *P. polita* on the flat shores of Lake Yamanaka is unique and the most interesting thing of its kind that I saw in Japan, where I did not meet with any other species of Spruce in pure stands of any extent (see Plate XIX). The forest is dense and from the near distance has a very black appearance. The trees are uniform in size, being from 20 to 26 m. tall and from 2.3 to 3 m. in girth of trunk; they grow thickly together and are pyramidal in outline, although the tops of many are flattened. The bark is pale gray, rough, but not very thick and is shallowly fissured and broken into small thin flakes of irregular shape, which exfoliate and leave behind pale brown scars. The branches are numerous, slender, of moderate length, spread horizontally and are often slightly ascending or sometimes somewhat decurved. The shoots are stout, shining yellow-brown, quite glabrous and change to pale gray in the second or third year. The winter-buds are ovoid, acute or obtuse, chestnut-brown, only slightly or not at all resinous and are composed of closely imbricated scales. The leaves are pungent and spread outward on all sides of the shoot and on lateral branchlets the leaf tips curve upwards; they are stout, dark green, curved, slightly compressed, but 4-angled in section, from 1.5 to 2 cm. long, oblique at the apex, which terminates in a sharp point, and furnished with several lines of stomata on each of the four surfaces. The cone is ovoid-cylindrical to ovoid, from 8 to 10 cm. long, yellowish green when growing, yellow-brown to cinnamon when ripe and with age becomes somewhat shining brown. The cone-scales are broad, rounded and have a few irregular denticulations. The wood is white, resinous, fairly close-grained and of ordinary quality, but the tree is not sufficiently common to be of much economic importance. The logs are cut into boards and planking and are used for general construction purposes and also for making cheap furniture. Immediately below the bark the resin is most abundant.

In Japan this tree is known as the Bara-momi, Hari-momi and Toranoo-momi, the first name in each instance having reference to the sharp, stout leaves. It is one of the most distinct of all the species of Picea and at its best is a strikingly handsome tree. In eastern North America it is quite hardy as far north as Boston, and on the Hall estate there is a specimen 19 m. tall with a trunk 1.5 m. in girth.

Picea polita appears to have been first discovered by von Siebold [1] and was introduced into England by John Gould Veitch in 1861. It was introduced into this country by Dr. George R. Hall in 1862.

---

[1] Siebold & Zuccarini cite *Pinus Abies* Thunberg (*Fl. Jap.* 275, not Linnaeus [1784]; syn. *Pinus Thunbergii* Lambert, *Descr. Pinus*, II. preface, vi [1828]; *Abies Thunbergii* Lindley in *Penny Cycl.* I. 34 [1833]) as a synonym of their *Picea polita* and this has been copied by many authors. Since this, if correct, would make Lambert's specific name the oldest, we wrote to Professor O. Juel and he kindly informs us "that in Thunberg's herbarium there is no specimen from Japan of *Pinus Abies*. Thunberg in his *Flora Japonica* only repeated the diagnosis given by Linnaeus in *Species plantarum*, but made a slight alteration: instead of 'foliis . . . bifariam versis' he wrote 'foliis . . . bifariis.' This most certainly is of no significance." What plant Thunberg intended to describe must forever remain uncertain; in and around Tokyo he must have seen *Abies firma* S. & Z. and *Tsuga Sieboldii* Carr., whereas it is very doubtful if he saw *Picea polita*. His "foliis . . . bifariis" would fit either this Abies or Tsuga, but certainly not *P. polita*.

PICEA MAXIMOWICZII Regel

PLATES XXI AND XXII

PICEA MAXIMOWICZII Regel in *Ind. Sem. Hort. Petrop.* 1865, 33 (name only). — Carrière, *Traité Conif.* ed. 2, 347 (1867). — Masters in *Gard. Chron.* n. ser. XIII. 363, fig. (1880); in *Jour. Linn. Soc.* XVIII. 507, fig. 6 (1881). — Mayr, *Monog. Abiet. Jap.* 98 (1890). — Elwes & Henry, *Trees Gr. Brit. & Irel.* VI. 1374 (1912). — Shirasawa & Koyama in *Tokyo Bot. Mag.* XXVII. 130, t. 11, fig. 18-27 (1913). — Clinton-Baker, *Ill. Conif.* III. 68, t. (1913). — Silva Tarouca, *Uns. Freiland-Nadelh.* 215, t. 225 (1913). — Shirasawa in *Mitt. Deutsch. Dendr. Ges.* XXIII. 255, fig. 18-27 (1914); in *Gard. Chron.* ser. 3, LVIII. 99, t. 36, fig. 18-27 (1915).

Abies obovata, var. *japonica* Maximowicz in *Ind. Sem. Hort. Petrop.* 1866, 1, 3. — Franchet & Savatier, *Enum. Pl. Jap.* I. 466 (1875).
Abies Maximowiczii Neumann, *Cat.* 1865 ex Carrière, *Traité Conif.* 347 (as a synonym) (1867). — Veitch, *Man. Conif.* 80 (1881).
Picea obovata japonica Beissner, *Handb. Nadelh.* 370 (1891).
Picea Tschonoskii Mayr, *Fremdl. Wald- u. Parkb.* 339 (1906).
Picea excelsa, var. *obovata japonica* Beissner, *Handb. Nadelh.* ed. 2, 220 (1909).

This little-known Spruce is usually a tree from 10 to 25 m. tall, with a trunk from 1 to 2.5 m. in girth, but exceptionally fine specimens from 40 to 50 m. tall and from 4 to 5 m. in girth of trunk are known in temple grounds. The bark is grayish brown to light gray, thick, fissured and rough, but firmly coherent. The branches are very numerous, slender, moderately long, on young trees ascending-spreading, but on larger trees horizontally disposed and upturned at the ends. The shoots are glabrous, rusty to yellowish brown, becoming pale whitish gray in the second and third years. The winter-buds are conical, pointed, reddish brown and resinous. The leaves spread on all sides of the shoot and point slightly forward; they are deep green, 4-angled in section, short and stout, with a blunt tip, but on young trees and on the inner branches of adult trees the leaves are longer and more slender and are very pungent. The cone is cylindrical or nearly so, varies in length from 2.5 to 6.5 cm., is pale green in color and when ripe rather shining brown; the cone-scales are rounded, entire and slightly oblique at the apex. The wood is white and of the average value of Spruce timber.

Until its rediscovery in October 1911 by Mr. Mitsua Koyama, this Spruce had not been met with growing wild since Tschonoski discovered it and sent seeds and herbarium material to Maximowicz in 1865. Indeed there has been much speculation as to its origin and Mayr and others have doubted if it was a Japanese species. This can be explained by the fact that it is not met with in Japanese gardens and temple grounds in the parts of Japan readily accessible to travellers. It is in fact a very rare and local tree and grows only in remote mountainous parts of central Hondo, where the population is very sparse and access exceedingly difficult. Dr. H. Shirasawa told me of the discovery of this tree on the Yatsugadake, a high mountain on the borders of Kai and Shinano provinces, and acting on this information I visited the place in company with Mr. Koyama. The mountain or mountain ridge has three peaks, the highest being about 3000 m. above sea-level, and is probably the richest mountain for conifers in the empire. The lower slopes, doubtless once well forested, are now moor-like and covered with coarse grasses and shrubs, with small scattered woods of mixed trees. Above 1600 m. the moorland gives place to forest, mainly coniferous. On the open, wind-swept moorland, between 1200 and 1600 m. altitude and growing with low bushes of *Juniperus rigida* S. & Z., and a scrubby growth of *Pinus densiflora* S. & Z. I found *Picea Maximowiczii* to be fairly common as a low bushy tree, pyramidal in outline and very densely branched. It also grows scattered through mixed woods, where trees 20 m. tall are met with. However, the only really large trees known are in temple grounds. One tree at Nakashinden I measured was 25 m. tall with a trunk 2 m. in girth. This was the largest specimen I saw, but I was told of trees 40 m. tall with trunks 4 m. in girth, and Shirasawa writes of a specimen in the grounds of the village temple at Kawakami which is 50 m. tall and has a trunk 5 m. in girth. From what I saw and gathered in conversation this Spruce is on the verge of extinction and the large trees that are known are but few in number. Tschonoski's original discovery was made on Fuji-san, but the species has not since been met with on that mountain.

Adult trees strikingly resemble those of *Picea polita* Carr., although less massive in appearance and there is no doubt that these species are closely related. This affinity is well expressed by the vernacular name for *P. Maximowiczii*, which is Hime-bara-momi, i. e. Daughter, or small Bara-momi, which is the vernacular name for *P. polita*.

Picea Maximowiczii was discovered by Maximowicz's Japanese collector Tschonoski, who sent seeds to Petrograd in 1865, and these were distributed by Regel to various botanic gardens in Europe. It is quite hardy in this Arboretum, but grows slowly. A specimen in the Hunnewell Pinetum is 5 m. tall.

PICEA KOYAMAI Shiras.

PLATES XXIII AND XXIV

PICEA KOYAMAI Shirasawa in *Tokyo Bot. Mag.* XXVII. 127, t. 11, fig. 28–35 (1913); in *Mitt. Deutsch. Dendr. Ges.* XXIII. 254, fig. 28–35 (1914); in *Gard. Chron.* ser. 3, LVIII. 98, t. 36, fig. 28–35 (1915).

This recent and most interesting addition to the Japanese flora is known to grow only on the slopes of Yatsuga-dake, on the borders of Kai and Shinano provinces. On my visit to this mountain I was fortunate to have as a companion Mr. Mitsua Koyama, who discovered this new Spruce in October 1911. The mountain, though not very far from Kaminosuwa on the Kofu-Shiojiri Junction railway, is rather difficult of access as it is situated in the very heart of central Hondo. Only one small grove, which I estimated contained not more than 100 trees, is known of this Spruce. It is growing on a rather steep, rocky slope, facing nearly north between 1700 and 1800 m. altitude. The trees are small and the largest I measured was 20 m. tall with a trunk 1.5 m. in girth. Dead stumps of larger trees occur, but apparently it is never a tree of large size. It grows mixed with *Larix Kaempferi* Sarg. and an undergrowth of miscellaneous broad-leaved shrubs. The bark is gray-brown, scaly, shallowly fissured, and easily peels off in thin, small, papery, more or less oblong flakes, which leave behind brown scars. The branches are dense, horizontally spreading, upturned at the ends, rather slender, only moderately long and form a narrow pyramidal crown. The shoots are of medium stoutness, reddish brown and slightly pruinose, becoming paler and more shining with age and finally pale gray; the main shoots are glabrous or have a few scattered glandular hairs, but the weaker shoots are very distinctly glandular-pubescent, more especially so between the pulvini. The winter-buds are conical, shining brown, resinous, and swollen at the base, which appears as if imbedded in the apex of the shoot. The leaves are crowded on the shoots and point upward and forward; they are dark green or often somewhat glaucous, stout, slightly curved or straight, 0.7 to 1.3 cm. long, oblique and acute or obtuse at the apex, 4-angled in section, with lines of stomata on all four faces. The cone is cylindrical, from 4 to 10 cm. long and averages much longer than stated (3 to 6 cm.) by Shirasawa; when growing it is pale green and changes to shining pale brown when ripe; the cone-scales are very firm, broad, rounded and finely denticulate. The wood is white, slightly resinous and of the ordinary quality of that of other Spruces. The tree is too rare to be of economic value and, indeed, it would be vandalism to cut it down for any purpose. It is to be hoped that the Government Forestry service will have the grove set aside as a preserve and cut a wide fire barrier round it. At present it is in danger of extermination. The Japanese name for this Spruce is Yatsuga-dake-tōhi. It is a shapely and a decidedly ornamental tree, and with its dense branching habit and dark green leaves it presents a black appearance from the near distance. I secured seeds in 1914, and a nice stock of young seedlings is growing in this Arboretum, but it is too early to say anything about their hardiness. Whether *P. Koyamai* is confined to Japan or grows also on the mainland cannot yet be decided. Material collected by W. Purdom in the Weichang, and near Jehol in southwestern Mandshuria, which Rehder & Wilson (in Sargent, *Pl. Wilson.* II. 29 [1914]) refer to *P. Schrenkiana* Fisch. & Mey., is very similar in every way to *P. Koyamai* collected by me. The specific and geographic limits of *P. Schrenkiana* and *P. obovata* Ledeb. require fuller investigation in the field. It is by no means certain that the trees growing in extreme eastern continental Asia, Korea and Mandshuria, and referred by different authors to one or other of the above species really belong to either, but until more is known about the conifers of Korea it is idle to speculate on this subject. From other Japanese species *P. Koyamai* is abundantly distinct and in all probability the name will stand even if it is found to grow on the mainland and to have been confused with other species.

PICEA GLEHNII Mast.

Plates XXV and XXVI

Picea Glehnii Masters in *Gard. Chron.* n. ser. XIII. 300, fig. 54 (1880); in *Jour. Linn. Soc.* XVIII. 512, fig. 13 (1881). — Mayr, *Monog. Abiet. Jap.* 56, t. 4, fig. 11 (1890). — Sargent, *Forest Fl. Jap.* 80 (1894); *Silva N. Am.* XII. 21 (1898). — Kent in Veitch, *Man. Conif.* ed. 2, 437 (1900). — Matsumura, *Ind. Pl. Jap.* II. pt. 1, 12 (1905). — Shirasawa, *Icon. Ess. For. Jap.* II. t. 3, fig. 19–42 (1908). — Elwes & Henry, *Trees Gr. Brit. & Irel.* VI. 1369 (1912). — Miyabe & Miyake, *Fl. Saghal.* 597 (1915).

Abies Glehni Fr. Schmidt in *Mém. Acad. Sci. St. Pétersbourg*, sér. 7, XII. no. 2, 176, t. 4, fig. 8–12 (*Reis. Amur. Sachal.*) (1868).
Pinus glehnii Voss in *Mitt. Deutsch. Dendr. Ges.* XVI. 93 (1907).

Near Rubeshibe in Kitami province, Hokkaido, I saw a few trees of this Spruce and in forests about 10 miles from Oketo in the same province I found it to be fairly common. The forestry officers told me that in more remote parts of Kitami and of northern Kushiro there exist pure forests of this Spruce. I have specimens collected for me in the extreme southeast corner of Hidaka province and have seen others from Iburi and Tokachi provinces. It has not yet been reported from southwestern Hokkaido and is rare around Sapporo, according to Miyabe, and appears to be so everywhere except in the more remote parts of northeastern Hokkaido. I did not meet with this species in Japanese Saghalien and the forestry officers there informed me that it is very uncommon. Masters has identified as belonging to this species a specimen collected along the Ussuri River in Amurland by R. Maack, but this determination is very doubtfully correct and there is no other evidence to show that Glehn's Spruce grows on the mainland. It is not known to grow on the Kurile Islands and from the evidence available appears to be confined to southern Saghalien and to northern and eastern Hokkaido.

The trees I saw were all growing on moist rocky slopes and appeared to favor northerly and westerly exposures and were easily recognized by the characteristic bark. The species grows with *Picea jezoënsis* Carr., *Abies sachalinensis* Mast. and occasional trees of *Ulmus japonica* Sarg., *Tilia Maximowicziana* Shiras., *Acer pictum* Thunb., *Acanthopanax ricinifolius* Seem. and *Taxus cuspidata* S. & Z. In the rich forests of Kitami it is a lofty tree from 26 to 40 m. tall, with a trunk from 3 to 5 m. in girth and clean of branches for fully half its height. The bark is red-brown or chocolate-brown and is fissured into thin, loose flakes of irregular size and shape which become gray as they exfoliate. The branches are slender, relatively short, horizontally spreading and usually slightly upturned at the ends and form a narrowly oblong crown. The shoots are yellow-brown to rust-red; they change to gray in the second to fourth years and have a persistent, short, rust-red pubescence on both the pulvini and the furrows between them. The winter-buds are conical to ovoid, resinous, shining chestnut-brown, swollen at the base and composed of few closely imbricated scales; on terminal buds the basal scales end in long subulate points as in the winter-buds of *P. mariana* B. P. S. The leaves are crowded and on erect shoots are more or less appressed on all sides of the shoot and point forward, but on the lateral branchlets on the lower side they are twisted into two ranks exposing the twig, and most of them are directed upward and forward. On very young trees the leaves are slender, straight and pungent, but normally they are stout, straight or curved, from 0.6 to 1.2 cm. long, oblique at the apex, which is acute or obtuse, deep green, and rhombic in section, with lines of stomata on all four faces. The cone is cylindrical, from 5 to 8 cm. long, violet when growing, with reddish scale-margins becoming brown and somewhat shining when ripe and finally gray-brown. The scales of ripe cones spread from the axis at right angles; they are rather thin, rounded or with the central part more or less prolonged, and entire or more usually finely denticulate. The wood is white, has a satiny lustre and is considered to be superior in quality to that of *P. jezoënsis* Carr. In Hokkaido *P. Glehnii* is generally known as the Aka-yezo-matsu, i. e. "Red-Yezo-Pine," a name doubtless suggested by the reddish color of its bark, shoots and cones in contrast with those of *P. jezoënsis*, the true Yezo-matsu. *Picea Glehnii* was introduced to this Arboretum by seeds received from the Government Forestry School, Tokyo, in 1894 and the species is well established here. The best plants are 6 m. tall, spire-like in outline, and are growing here more satisfactorily than any other species of Japanese Spruce. It is easily recognized by its habit and more especially by its pubescent shoots, which in autumn and winter are decidedly redder than those of any other species. Of the Japanese Spruces it is most closely related to *P. bicolor* Mayr.

Picea Glehnii was discovered in Saghalien in August 1861 by P. von Glehn, the comrade of Fr. Schmidt on the expedition sent out by the Russian Geographical Society to eastern Asia. It was subsequently found in Hokkaido by Charles Maries in 1877. According to Beissner (*Handb. Nadelh.* 377 [1891]) young seedling plants were growing in Germany in 1891.

PICEA BICOLOR Mayr

PICEA BICOLOR Mayr, *Monog. Abiet. Jap.* 49, t. 3, fig. 8 (1890). — Sargent, *Forest Fl. Jap.* 80 (1894); *Silva N. Am.* XII. 21 (1898). — Shirasawa, *Icon. Ess. For. Jap.* I. 19, t. 4, fig. 1–14 (1900). — Elwes & Henry, *Trees Gr. Brit. & Irel.* VI. 1372 (1912). — Dümmer in *Jour. Hort. Soc. Lond.* XXXIX. 88 (1913). — Silva Tarouca, *Uns. Freiland-Nadelh.* 22, fig. 12 (1913).

> *Abies Alcoquiana* J. G. Veitch apud Lindley in *Gard. Chron.* 1861, 23 (in part); 1862, 308. — Murray in *Proc. Hort. Soc. Lond.* II. 426, fig. 106–110 (in part) (1862); *Pines & Firs Jap.* 66, fig. 116, 125–128 (1863). — Gordon, *Pinet.* suppl. 8 (*A. Alcoqueana* sic, in part). — K. Koch, *Dendr.* II. pt. 2, 245 (in part) (1873).
> *Picea japonica* Regel in *Ind. Sem. Hort. Petrop.* 1865, 33 (name only); 1866, 3 (as a synonym).
> *Abies bicolor* Maximowicz in *Bull. Acad. Sci. St. Pétersbourg*, sér. 3, X. 488 (1866); in *Mél. Biol.* VI. 24 (1866). — Franchet & Savatier, *Enum. Pl. Jap.* I. 467 (1875).
> *Picea Alcockiana* Carrière, *Traité Conif.* ed. 2, 343 (1867). — Masters in *Gard. Chron.* n. ser. XIII. 212, fig. 41, 43 (1880); in *Jour. Linn. Soc.* XVIII. 508, fig. 7–9 (1881). — Hennings in *Gartenfl.* XXXVIII. 216, t. 40, fig. 1, b–f (1889). — Kent in Veitch, *Man. Conif.* ed. 2, 429 (1900). — Matsumura, *Ind. Pl. Jap.* II. pt. 1, 12 (1905). — Clinton-Baker, *Ill. Conif.* II. 35, t. (1909). — Hayata, *Veget. Mt. Fuji*, 93 (1911).
> *Pinus Alcoquiana* Parlatore in De Candolle, *Prodr.* XVI. pt. 2, 417 (1868).
> *Abies acicularis* Maximowicz in *Ind. Sem. Hort. Petrop.* 74 (name only) (1868).
> *Abies excelsa*, var. *acicularis* Hort. ex Masters in *Gard. Chron.* n. ser. XIII. 212 (as a synonym) (1880).
> *Picea acicularis* Beissner, *Handb. Nadelh.* 380 (1891).
> *Picea bicolor*, var. *reflexa* Shirasawa & Koyama in *Tokyo Bot. Mag.* XXVII. 129, t. 11, fig. 9–17 (1913).—Shirasawa in *Mitt. Deutsch. Dendr. Ges.* XXIII. 255, fig. 9–17 (1914); in *Gard. Chron.* ser. 3, LVIII. 99, t. 36, fig. 9–17 (1915).
> *Picea bicolor*, var. *acicularis* Shirasawa & Koyama in *Tokyo Bot. Mag.* XXVII. 129, t. 11, fig. 1–8 (1913). — Shirasawa in *Mitt. Deutsch. Dendr. Ges.* XXIII, 254, fig. 1–8 (1914); in *Gard. Chron.* ser. 3, LVIII. 98, t. 36, fig. 1–8 (1915).

I met with this Spruce only on the slopes of Fuji-san where I saw but few trees and none more than 26 m. tall and 3 m. in girth of trunk, the majority of them being much weather worn. In the ascent from Subashiri on the east side and in that from Yoshida on the north, between 900 and 1600 m., there are scattered trees and here and there small groups of this Spruce, but it is far from common. It grows in the zone represented by the upper limits of *Abies homolepis* S. & Z. and the lower limits of *Abies Veitchii* Lindl. and in company with the much more common *Picea jezoënsis* Carr., *Larix Kaempferi* Sarg., *Tsuga diversifolia* Mast. and such broad-leaved trees as *Quercus mongolica*, var. *grosseserrata* Rehd. and Wils., *Betula grossa* S. & Z., *B. Ermanii* Cham., *Alnus hirsuta*, var. *sibirica* Schneid., *Sorbus commixta* Hedl. and *Prunus Maximowiczii* Rupr. I had specimens collected for me on Yatsuga-dake on the borders of Kai and Shinano provinces, where it is said to grow with *Larix Kaempferi* Sarg., *Pinus koraiensis* S. & Z. and *P. parviflora* S. & Z., although I did not see it on this mountain. It grows on Shirane-san in Kai province and Sargent collected it on the Wada-tōge in Shinano province. I have also a specimen collected for me on Sangai-san near Ena-san in Mino province, and Mayr collected it on the Chichibu Mountains in Musashi province. From this evidence it is clear that this Spruce grows on many of the high mountains in central Hondo, but apparently it is nowhere common. In a list of the conifers which grow on the southern island of Kyushu, compiled for me from the forestry records by Mr. T. Miyoshi of the Government Forestry service and stationed at Kagoshima, *P. bicolor* is reported from four localities in Bungo province, from two in Higo province and from one in Osumi province. I have seen, however, no specimens from any of these localities and suspect that in some cases at least the Spruce reported is *P. jezoënsis* Carr. From Nantai-san in the Nikko region Shirasawa reports *P. bicolor*, but I did not see it on that mountain nor in that region.

As I saw it growing on the volcanic soil and wind-swept slopes of Fuji-san, *P. bicolor* was not a handsome or attractive tree, but in sheltered woods I met with a few young trees of good appearance. The bark is gray, usually pale gray, but sometimes gray-brown, fissured and broken into small, thin, scale-like flakes of irregular size, which on old trees are more or less firmly coherent. The branches are rather slender, spread horizontally, are often slightly ascending and form a rather broad pyramidal crown; the shoots vary in color from shining yellowish brown to reddish brown and change to gray the second, third or fourth year. On young trees the shoots may all be quite glabrous, but on adult trees usually the principal shoots are pubescent and the weak lateral shoots glabrous, but often on fruiting branches all the shoots are more or less hairy. The pubescence is short and gray, and is confined to the furrows between the pulvini or clothes the whole shoot and even occurs on the margin of the basal part of the leaf itself. The winter-buds are dull-brown to chestnut-brown, ovoid to conical, obtuse or somewhat acute and usually slightly resinous; the scales are firmly appressed and often slightly scarious on the margin. The leaves are more or less bluish green, sometimes glaucous, from 1 to 2 cm. long, mostly curved, rhombic in section, with lines of stomata on all four surfaces; on erect and main shoots they are appressed to the twig on all sides and point forward, but on the lateral shoots the arrangement is more or less pectinate and the under side of the twig is exposed. On young trees the leaves are pungent and on fruiting branches and adult trees they are oblique at the apex which ends in a short cartilaginous point. The cone is ovoid-cylindrical to cylindrical, from 6 to 12 cm. (usually from 7 to 10 cm.) long, pale reddish purple when growing, changing to cinnamon-brown when ripe and becoming shining or dull mud-brown when old. The cone-scales vary from obovate to rhombic and are appressed or more or less reflexed at the apex, which is broad and rounded or narrowed, denticulate, often finely so, and occasionally erose. The wood is white, somewhat lustrous and of the same quality as that of *P. jezoënsis* Carr., but the tree is too scarce to be of economic importance.

Shirasawa and Koyama have described two varieties of the Spruce based largely upon the character of the cone-scales. The differences are very slight and have been observed on cultivated trees in this country and in Europe, but I do not think they have taxonomic value. The cone-scales of *P. Abies* Karst. are notoriously variable in shape; other species, too, exhibit similar variation, and it would appear that a tendency toward rhombic cone-scales is inherent in most species of Picea.

In Japan *P. bicolor* is known as Iramomi. It is seldom cultivated in Japanese gardens and is very rare[1] in the gardens of Europe and North America. In eastern North America the few examples known are thriving better than those of any other Japanese Spruce. In the Hunnewell Pinetum there are growing several fine specimens of *P. bicolor*, the largest of which is 13 m. tall, with a trunk 1 m. in girth and a 12 m. spread of branches. Another is 11 m. tall, with a trunk 1.4 m. in girth and has a 13 m. spread of branches.

In regard to the name of this Spruce there has never been any doubt that Veitch, when he discovered it in 1860, intended to name a new Spruce for Sir Rutherford Alcock, but unfortunately the material he sent home came from trees belonging to two distinct species and the description of *Abies Alcoquiana* drawn from it by Lindley covers both. Murray's figures show that the leaves are those of *Picea jezoënsis* and the cone that of a quite different species, and of this species Maximowicz in 1866 gives a good description under the name of *A. bicolor*. Carrière's description of his *P. Alcockiana* in 1867 is correct, but Maximowicz's specific name is a year older and has priority. Masters in 1880 clearly separated the two species confused by Veitch and Lindley; more recently Henry and Dümmer have both examined the type specimen of *A. Alcoquiana* Veitch apud Lindley and state that it consists of "leaves of *P. hondoënsis* and the cones[2] of *P. bicolor*."

Picea bicolor was not only first discovered by John Gould Veitch, but was also first introduced into Europe by him in 1861, but unfortunately the seeds were mixed with those of *P. jezoënsis* Carr. In 1865 Tschonoski, Maximowicz's Japanese collector, sent seeds to Petrograd, and these were distributed by Regel under the name of *P. japonica*. In 1868 Tschonoski sent more seeds to Petrograd, and these were distributed as *Abies acicularis* Maxim.

PICEA JEZOËNSIS Carr.

Plates XXVII and XXVIII

Picea jezoënsis Carrière, *Traité Conif.* 255 (1855). — Beissner, *Handb. Nadelh* 389 (1891). — Sargent, *Silva N. Am.* XII. 21 (1898). — Rehder in Bailey, *Stand Cycl. Hort.* V. 2620 (1916).

Abies jezoënsis Siebold & Zuccarini, *Fl. Jap.* II. 19, t. 110 (1842). — Murray in *Proc. Hort. Soc. Lond.* II. 496, fig. 119–126, 128 (1862); *Pines & Firs Jap.* 72, fig. 137–144, 146 (1863). — Veitch, *Man. Conif.* 72 (1881).

Pinus jezoënsis Antoine, *Conif.* 97, t. 37, fig. 1 (1847).

Abies ajanensis Knight & Perry, *Syn. Conif.* (Errata, name only) (1850?). — Ruprecht & Maximowicz in *Bull. Phys.-Math. Acad. Sci. St. Pétersbourg*, XV. 140 (1857). — Ruprecht & Maack in *Bull. Phys.-Math. Acad. Sci. St. Pétersbourg*, XV. 382 (1857). — F. Schmidt in *Mém. Acad. Sci. St. Pétersbourg*, sér. 7, XII. no. 2, 177 (*Reis. Amur. Sachal.*) (1868).

Abies ajonensis Lindley & Gordon in *Jour. Hort. Soc. Lond.* V. 212 (name only) (1850).

Picea Ajanensis Fischer apud Carrière, *Traité Conif.* 259 (1855). — Trautvetter & Meyer in Middendorff, *Reis. Sibir.* I. pt. 2, Bot. abt. 2, 87 (*Fl. Ochot.*) (1856). — Regel & Tiling, *Fl. Ajan.* 119 (1858). — Maximowicz in *Mém. Sav. Étr. Acad. Sci.*

---

[1] The Spruce cultivated in most gardens in Great Britain as *P. Alcockiana* is *P. jezoënsis* Carr.
[2] Dümmer says "cone-scales."

where the Stanovoi Mountains approach the Sea of Okhotsk, southward through the coast and Amur provinces to Korea and westward through Mandshuria, where it reaches its southern limits of distribution in the Weichang, near Jehol, in about longitude 117° E. and latitude 42°. Over the greater part of this area it is from all accounts a common tree. In Saghalien and Hokkaido it is abundant, and it also grows on the most southern of the Kurile Islands. In Hondo it, like all other Spruces, has a somewhat restricted distribution, but even here its range possibly exceeds that of the other species. On this island the Yezo Spruce is known to me personally from the mountains of the Nikko region southward to the mountains of the Shinano province, and I also have material collected for me near Kanabu village in the Nara prefecture, Yamato province, latitude about 34°. Very probably it grows on the high mountains of Shikoku, although I did not meet with it there, and possibly also in a few localities on the high mountains of Kyushu, since the Japanese foresters report *P. bicolor* Mayr from this island, but these men do not all clearly distinguish between the two species. Shirasawa, in his *Iconographie des Essences Forestières du Japon*, text, p. 20, states that the flat-leaved Spruce grows on Chokai-san in Ugo province, but this is an error, as subsequent investigations by Shirasawa and other forestry officials and by myself have proved. Neither this nor any other Spruce is known in Hondo north of latitude 37° 30', and the mountains of the Nikko region represent very exactly the northern limits of its range in Hondo.

The finest trees of *Picea jezoënsis* I saw were in Hokkaido, especially in the moist rich forests round Rubeshibe and Oketo in Kitami province, where specimens 50 m. tall, with trunks 6 m. in girth, are not rare, although the average is about 30 to 35 m. by 3 to 4 m. It is associated with broad-leaved deciduous trees such as *Ulmus japonica* Sarg., *Acer pictum* Thunb., *Fraxinus mandshurica* Rupr., *Acanthopanax ricinifolius* Seem., *Populus Maximowiczii* Henry, *Cercidiphyllum japonicum* S. & Z. and *Betula Ermanii* Cham.; and with *Abies sachalinensis* Mast. and *Picea Glehnii* Mast. At its best in these rich moist forests the Yezo Spruce is a truly magnificent tree, spire-like in habit, often glaucous in appearance, with rather long and slender branches, which sweep downwards and outwards in a graceful manner and are often slightly upturned at the ends.

In Saghalien it grows with *Abies sachalinensis* Mast. and *Larix dahurica*, var. *japonica* Maxim., but is less fond of the swamps than the Larch and is more common with the Fir on the lower slopes of the mountains. The largest trees I saw measured 26 m. in height and were 3 m. in girth of trunk, but in this more northern land it is never so fine as in Hokkaido.

In the Nikko region this Spruce is rare, though there is considerable of it near Lake Yumoto, growing in company with *Larix Kaempferi* Sarg., *Abies homolepis* S. & Z., *Abies Veitchii* Lindl. and *Tsuga diversifolia* Mast. On the middle slopes of Fuji-san it is common and grows among the same kind of trees as at Nikko. On Mt. Ontake and the neighboring mountains in the Shinano province it is plentiful between 1600 and 2800 m. above the sea, growing with *Tsuga diversifolia* Mast., *Abies Veitchii* Lindl., *Pinus parviflora* S. & Z. and *Pinus koraiensis* S. & Z. On the Tsubakura-dake, one of the granite peaks of the high mountains in Shinano province, at about 2000 m. altitude, I saw many fine specimens of the Yezo Spruce, but I did not see anywhere on the volcanic soils in Hondo trees comparable with those met with in central and northern Hokkaido. In the Hondo forests the tree averages from 25 to 30 m. in height and from 2 to 3 m. in girth of trunk. It is usually much less spire-like in outline and generally very ragged in appearance.

St. Pétersbourg, IX. 261 (*Prim. Fl. Amur.*) (1859). — Masters in *Gard. Chron.* n. ser. XIII. 115, fig. 22 (1880); XIV. 427, fig. 80–84 (1880); in *Jour. Linn. Soc.* XVIII. 508, fig. 10–12 (1881). — Hooker f. in *Bot. Mag.* CX. t. 6743 (1884). — Mayr, *Monog. Abiet. Jap.* 53, t. 4, fig. 10 (1890). — Sargent, *Forest Fl. Jap.* 81 (1894). — Kent in Veitch, ed. 2, *Man. Conif.* 425, t. (1900). — Komarov in *Act. Hort. Petrop.* XX. 197 (*Fl. Mandsh.* I.) (1901). — Matsumura, *Ind. Pl. Jap.* II. pt. 1, 12 (1905). — Elwes & Henry, *Trees Gr. Brit. & Irel.* I. 85 (1907). — Shirasawa, *Icon. Ess. For. Jap.* II. t. 3, fig. 1–18 (1908). — Beissner, *Handb. Nadelh.* ed. 2, 289, fig. 64 (1909). — Clinton-Baker, *Ill. Conif.* II. 33, t. (1909). — Nakai in *Jour. Coll. Sci. Tokyo*, XXXI. 381 (*Fl. Kor.* pt. 2 (1911). — Hayata, *Veget. Mt. Fuji*, 93 (1911). — Takeda in *Jour. Linn. Soc.* XLII. 486 (1914). — Miyabe & Miyake, *Fl. Saghal.* 596 (1915).

Picea ajanensis, β *subintegerrima* Trautvetter & Meyer in Middendorff, *Reis. Sibir.* I. pt. 2, Bot. abt. 2, 87 (*Fl. Ochot.*) (1856).

Abies microsperma Lindley in *Gard. Chron.* 1861, 22. — J. G. Veitch in *Gard. Chron.* 1862, 308. — Murray in *Proc. Hort. Soc. Lond.* II. 429, fig. 111–118 (1862); *Pines & Firs Jap.* 69, fig. 129–136 (1863).

Abies Alcoquiana J. G. Veitch apud Lindley in *Gard. Chron.* 1861, 23 (in part); 1862, 308. — Murray in *Proc. Hort. Soc. Lond.* II. 426, fig. 98–105 (in part) (1862); *Pines & Firs Jap.* 66, fig. 117–124 (1863). — Gordon, *Pinet.* suppl. 8 (*A. Alcoqueana* sic, in part) (1862).

Veitchia japonica Lindley in *Gard. Chron.* 1861, 265.

Picea microsperma Carrière, *Traité Conif.* ed. 2, 339 (1867).

Abies microcarpa Miquel, *Prol. Fl. Jap.* 389 (*Conspec. Fl. Jap.*) (1867).

Pinus Menziesii Parlatore in De Candolle, *Prodr.* XVI. pt. 2, 418 (in so much as relates to the Asiatic plant, not D. Don) (1868).

Abies Sitchensis K. Koch, *Dendr.* II. 247 (in so much as relates to the Asiatic plant, not Lindley & Gordon) (1873).

Abies Menziesii Franchet & Savatier, *Enum. Pl. Jap.* I. 467 (not Lindley) (1875).

Abies Schrenkiana Gordon, *Pinet.* n. ed. 18 (as to synonyms *Picea Ajanensis* and *Abies Ajanensis*, not Lindley & Gordon) (1880).

Picea ajanensis, var. *microsperma* Masters in *Gard. Chron.* n. ser. XIII. 115 (1880); in *Jour. Linn. Soc.* XVIII. 509 (1881). — Beissner, *Handb. Nadelh.* ed. 2, 291 (1909).

Picea ajanensis, var. *japonica* Maximowicz ex Masters l. c. (as a synonym) (1880).

Abies ajanensis microsperma Veitch, *Man. Conif.* 66 (1881).

Tsuga Ajanensis Regel, *Russ. Dendr.* ed. 2, pt. 1, 39 (1883).

Picea Hondoënsis Mayr, *Monog. Abiet. Jap.* 51, t. 4, fig. 9 (1890). — Shirasawa, *Icon. Ess. For. Jap.* I. 20, t. 5, fig. 1–22 (1900). — Miyoshi, *Atlas Jap. Veget.* pt. II. 7, t. 14 (1905); pt. VIII. 5, t. 58 (1907). — Elwes & Henry, *Trees Gr. Brit. & Irel.* I. 89 (1907). — Hayata, *Veget. Mt. Fuji*, 93, fig. 7 (1911). — Dümmer in *Jour. Hort. Soc. Lond.* XXXIX. 88 (1913). — Silva Tarouca, *Uns. Freiland-Nadelh.* 221, 225, fig. 232, 236 (1913). — Bean, *Trees & Shrubs Brit. Isl.* II. 158 (1914).

Picea obovata Miyabe in *Mem. Boston Soc. Nat. Hist.* IV. 261 (*Fl. Kurile Isl.*) (exclude synonyms, not Ledebour) (1890).

Pinus hondoënsis Voss in *Mitt. Deutsch. Dendr. Ges.* XVI. 93 (1907).

Pinus jezoensis, f. *microsperma* Voss in Putlitz & Meyer, *Landlexikon*, IV. 772 (1913)

Picea jezoensis, var. *hondoensis* Rehder in *Mitt. Deutsch. Dendr. Ges.* XXIV. (1915 in Bailey, *Stand. Cycl. Hort.* V. 2620 (1916).

This is the flat-leaved Spruce of northeastern Asia and of Japan and is only species of the section Omorica so far known from those regions. Its geogr ical range is very great, greater in fact than that of any other species of es Asia, for it is found spread over 30 degrees of longitude and 22 degrees of lat On the mainland it extends from near Port Aian (Ayan) about latitude 5

In the early summer the yellow male catkins and bright crimson young cones, borne in remarkable profusion, make the tree very conspicuous, but in Hondo generally it cannot be called a handsome Spruce. It is essentially a northern tree which delights in a moist cold climate and a soil rich in humus.

The bark is gray and broken into circular scales about 5 or 6 cm. broad, which are gradually exfoliated and leave behind gray patches; on old trees the bark is 3 to 4 cm. thick, deeply longitudinally fissured and cracked in irregular narrowly oblong plates. The shoots are quite glabrous and shining, pale orange-yellow to yellowish brown and occasionally a little pinkish the first year, becoming slightly darker until they change to pale gray, which on vigorous and healthy branches takes place in the third, fourth or fifth year. Weak shoots and those much exposed to wind may be yellowish the first year and pale gray in the second. The winter-buds are large, swollen at the base, broadly conical, resinous and shining. The leaves are thin, flattened, dark green on the ventral surface and silvery white on the dorsal surface, from 0.8 to 3 cm. (usually 1.2 to 1.8 cm.) long, straight or curved, sharp-pointed on young trees and on adults oblique at the apex which ends in a short acute or blunt point. The very young cones are crimson and change as they develop to green tinged with pale brown, and when ripe they are leather-brown and slightly shining; they vary in length from 3 to 7.5 cm. and are cylindrical in shape. The cone-scales are rhombic, erose and denticulate. The wood is white, fine-grained, light and of good quality, and since the tree is plentiful this species as a source of timber is by far the most valuable of all the Japanese Spruces. The wood is used for a variety of purposes, such as boat-masts, planking, for making matchboxes, luncheon-boxes so common in Japan, and chip-braid. Japanese foresters in Hokkaido told me that it was difficult to reafforest with this Spruce, and in consequence in its stead they were experimenting with the Norway Spruce (*Picea Abies* Karst.).

In the study of Japanese conifers this flat-leaved Spruce has furnished one of the principal problems, and in consequence I devoted much attention to it. The synonymy is involved and Mayr is emphatic in his statement that the Hondo and Hokkaido trees belong to two distinct species. In the field, after a detailed and critical study, I failed to detect any real or essential difference, and this view is confirmed by a study of a mass of herbarium material collected at many points over the entire range of its distribution. On specimens from the mainland, from Saghalien, Hokkaido and Hondo I find the leaves straight or curved, oblique and obtuse or acute at the apex. Whether the peg-like part of the pulvinus points forward or is recurved, whether it is straight or twisted depends upon the position of the shoot. This peg-like part of the pulvinus may be smooth or swollen and grooved on the same branchlet, and these conditions are present on nearly every specimen before me. The color of the shoot is the most pronounced character put forward by Mayr, but this again I find inconstant, and specimens from Saghalien and from Hondo have shoots indistinguishable in color. Such pale gray shoots as were figured by Mayr under *P. ajanensis* can be found on trees in Hondo or Saghalien or on the mainland, but they are the exception and not the rule and are usually those of weak lateral branches or of unhealthy trees. The relative size of the cones as figured by Mayr cannot be considered of specific importance, and of the material gathered by myself cones from trees growing on Mt. Ontake in Hondo exceed in size those collected in Saghalien. The largest cone I have seen measures nearly 8 cm. in length and is from a tree cultivated on the estate of the late Dr. George R. Hall; this tree is about 22 m. tall with a trunk

1.25 m. in girth with the lower branches resting on the ground; probably this is the finest specimen of this species in the United States.

Mayr says that the young leaves of his *P. hondoënsis* are tinged with red on the upper side when they issue from the bud, and Henry transposing the statement applies it to those of *P. ajanensis*. I did not notice this phenomenon, which is indicated in Siebold & Zuccarini's plate.

In this Arboretum there is growing a very poor tree of *P. jezoënsis*, received under this name from Veitch in 1889, and this differs from other plants of the species growing here in starting into growth a week or ten days earlier. In all probability the plant was raised from seeds collected in Hokkaido by Maries and in beginning to grow early it behaves like many other northern trees. In eastern North America the Yezo Spruce rarely thrives and it is seldom seen in gardens. In Great Britain it is usually known as *P. Alcockiana*. In Hokkaido this tree is known as the Yezo-matsu and in Hondo as the Tōhi.

Picea jezoënsis was first recognized from a plant cultivated in Tokyo by von Siebold and was discovered growing wild by Dr. A. Th. von Middendorff on the Stanovoi Mountains during his journey in northern and eastern Siberia in 1843–44. In 1860 John Gould Veitch discovered it on Fuji-san and sent seeds to England in 1861 mixed with those of *P. bicolor* Mayr. In 1860 Veitch visited Hakodate and sent to England seeds of the Flat-leaved Spruce, and this Hokkaido plant received the name of *Abies microsperma* from Lindley. In 1879 Charles Maries sent to Messrs. Veitch seeds from Hokkaido of *P. jezoënsis*.

TSUGA Carr.

This genus is confined to the temperate regions of North America, Japan, Formosa, central and western China and the Himalayas as far west as northeastern Kumaon. Nine species are now known. Of these two are indigenous in eastern North America and two in western North America. One of the latter species (*T. Mertensiana* Sarg.) differs markedly in its leaves and cones from other species of Tsuga and by some is placed in another genus (Hesperopeuce). Of the Asiatic species *T. chinensis* Pritz. is common on the mountains from western Hupeh to the Chino-Thibetan borderland and also grows on the mountains of Formosa. The second Chinese species, *T. yunnanensis* Mast., is distributed on the mountains of western Szech'uan and western Yunnan and is possibly not specifically distinct from *T. Brunoniana* Eichl. which grows on the Himalayas. Two species are found in Japan, one being endemic and the other reaching the Korean island of Ooryöng.

KEY TO THE JAPANESE SPECIES

Shoots glabrous; winter-buds ovoid, slightly acute at the apex; leaves not crowded, lustrous; cone-scales glabrous and ciliate . . . . T. SIEBOLDII.
Shoots pubescent; winter-buds pyriform to subglobose, obtuse at the apex; leaves crowded, not lustrous; cone-scales puberulous . . . . T. DIVERSIFOLIA.

TSUGA SIEBOLDII Carr.

PLATES XXIX AND XXX

TSUGA SIEBOLDII Carrière, *Traité Conif.* 186 (1855).—Masters in *Jour. Linn. Soc.* XVIII. 512 (1881).—Mayr, *Monog. Abiet. Jap.* 59, t. 4, fig. 12 (1890).—

Kent in Veitch, *Man. Conif.* ed. 2, 472, fig. 118 (1900). — Matsumura, *Ind. Pl. Jap.* II. pt. 1, 20 (1905). — Elwes & Henry, *Trees Gr. Brit. & Irel.* II. 246 (1907). — Shirasawa, *Icon. Ess. For. Jap.* II. t. 4, fig. 16–31 (1908). — Beissner, *Handb. Nadelh.* ed. 2, 80, fig. 11 (1909). — Clinton-Baker, *Ill. Conif.* I. 68, t. (1909). — Hayata, *Veget. Mt. Fuji*, 93, fig. 16, 2 (1911). — Silva Tarouca, *Uns. Freiland-Nadelh.* 107, 288, fig. 104, 302 (1913).

Abies araragi Siebold in *Verh. Batav. Genoot.* XII. pt. 1, 12 (*Syn. Pl. Oecon. Jap.*) (name only) (1830).

Abies Tsuga Siebold & Zuccarini, *Fl. Jap.* II. 14, t. 106 (1842). — Lindley in *Gard. Chron.* 1861, 23. — Murray, *Pines & Firs Jap.* 84, fig. 159–171 (1863). — Maximowicz in *Bull. Acad. Sci. St. Pétersbourg*, sér. 3, XII. 230 (1868); in *Mél. Biol.* VI. 374 (1868). — Franchet & Savatier, *Enum. Pl. Jap.* I. 468 (1875).

Pinus Tsuga Antoine, *Conif.* 83, t. 32, fig. 2 (1846). — Endlicher, *Syn. Conif.* 83 (1847).

Micropeuce Sieboldii Spach apud Gordon, *Pinet.* suppl. 13 (as a synonym) (1862).

Tsuga Tsuja Murray in *Proc. Hort. Soc. Lond.* II. 508, fig. 141–153 (1862). — Sargent, *Forest Fl. Jap.* 81 (1894).

Picea (Tsuga) Sieboldii, Bertrand in *Ann. Sci. Nat.* sér. 5, XX. 89 (1874).

Pinus Sieboldii McNab in *Proc. R. Irish Acad.* ser. 2, II. 213, t. 23, fig. 6 (1875).

Tsuga Araragi Koehne, *Deutsch. Dendr.* 10 (1893). — Sargent in *Garden & Forest*, X. 491, fig. 62 (1897); *Silva N. Am.* XII. 60 (1898).

This is the southern Hemlock of Japan and it has much the same distribution as *Abies firma* S. & Z. and *Thea Sasanqua* Nois., with which it is very generally found growing. It is particularly prominent in the moist rich forests on the steep mountains of Shikoku, southern Hondo and Kyushu, where it reaches its maximum size. Dr. Nakai informed me that it grows on the island of Ooryöng, off the east coast of Korea, in company with *Pinus Thunbergii* Parl. and *P. parviflora* S. & Z., but it does not reach the mainland. In the gardens and parks in and around Tokyo, Siebold's Tsuga is frequently planted, but good specimens are rare. The latitude of Tokyo corresponds very closely with the northern limits of the range of the species. I did not meet with it as a wild tree north of Mitsumine-san in Musashi province, where it is local. It occurs here and there on the lower slopes of Fuji-san and also in Shinano province up to 800 m. altitude in small, scattered groves. On Koya-san in Kii province it is plentiful up to 1000 m. altitude and grows with *Pinus densiflora* S. & Z., *Chamaecyparis obtusa* S. & Z. and *Sciadopitys verticillata* S. & Z. On the mountains in Tosa province, Shikoku, this Tsuga grows in abundance, with *Pinus parviflora* S. & Z., *Abies firma* S. & Z., *Pseudotsuga japonica* Beissn. and the conifers mentioned as growing on Koya-san. On various mountains in Kyushu I saw *Tsuga Sieboldii* and on the island of Yaku-shima it is very plentiful between 600 and 1500 m. altitude, in company with *Cryptomeria japonica* D. Don, *Abies firma* S. & Z. and such broad-leaved trees as *Stewartia monadelpha* S. & Z., *Distylium racemosum* S. & Z., *Trochodendron aralioides* S. & Z., *Daphniphyllum macropodum* Miq., *Thea japonica* Nois., *T. Sasanqua* Nois. and *Clethra barbinarvis* S. & Z.

Yaku-shima, the southern limit of its range, is a gigantic upthrust of granite, but most of the mountains on which I saw this tree growing were of recent volcanic origin and the nature of the soil apparently has little influence on its growth or, indeed, on that of the closely related *T. diversifolia* Mast. Steep mountain slopes where a mild climate and an abundant rainfall prevail are the natural conditions under which the tree grows. On Yaku-shima, where the finest development of

Tsuga Sieboldii is found, the trees rarely exceed 26 m. in height, but many are fully 6 m. in girth of trunk, and are picturesque in appearance. The forests on this island are dense and the Hemlock trees are clean of branches for two-thirds of their height and have flat-topped crowns composed of short, stout branches. Usually the trunk is somewhat inclined, occasionally conspicuously so, and the contrast between the Tsuga and the Cryptomeria, with its towering, mast-like trunk, is very striking. On the mountains of Shikoku and of Hondo the trunks of this Hemlock are upright or nearly so, and more clothed with branches which are rather thin, spread horizontally and form a more or less oval crown. The bark is gray, firm, fissured and shows red beneath. It is used for tanning fish nets. The shoot is shining, yellowish brown and always perfectly glabrous, and this is the best character by which to distinguish this species from *T. diversifolia* Mast. The winter-buds are ovoid to subglobose, reddish and glabrous, and the scales are ciliate. The leaves are entire, of uniform width and relatively broad, from 0.6 to 2 cm. long, emarginate, not crowded, and are shining dark green above, with a green midrib and two broad white stomatic lines on the under side. The ripe cone is narrowly ovoid, from 1.6 to 3 m. long, shining pale brown and is composed of rather broad scales which are truncated or rounded and slightly oblique on the margin. The wood is pale yellowish brown, with a wavy figure and is of good quality; it is valued for building purposes and for shingles. Native names for this tree are Tsuga and Toga-matsu.

Tsuga Sieboldii was discovered by von Siebold and introduced by him into Europe in 1850. In this Arboretum it has not proved very hardy, but in the Hunnewell Pinetum there is a rather poor specimen 6 m. tall.

TSUGA DIVERSIFOLIA Mast.

PLATES XXXI AND XXXII

TSUGA DIVERSIFOLIA Masters in *Jour. Linn. Soc.* XVIII. 514 (1881); in *Jour. Hort. Soc. Lond.* XIV. 255 (1892). — Mayr, *Monog. Abiet. Jap.* 61, t. 4, fig. 13 (1890). — Sargent, *Forest Fl. Jap.* 81, t. 25 (1894); in *Garden & Forest*, X. 491, fig. 63 (1897); *Silva N. Am.* XII. 60 (1898). — Kent in Veitch, *Man. Conif.* ed. 2, 467 (1900). — Matsumura, *Ind. Pl. Jap.* II. pt. 1, 20 (1905). — Miyoshi, *Atlas Jap. Veget.* pt. V. 3, t. 34, 35 (1906). — Elwes & Henry, *Trees Gr. Brit. & Irel.* II. 249 (1907). — Shirasawa, *Icon. Ess. For. Jap.* II. t. 4, fig. 1-15 (1908). — Clinton-Baker, *Ill. Conif.* I. 66, t. (1909). — Hayata, *Veget. Mt. Fuji*, 93 (1911). — Silva Tarouca, *Uns. Freiland-Nadelh.* 289, t. 303 (1913).

Abies diversifolia Maximowicz in *Bull. Acad. Sci. St. Pétersbourg*, sér. 3, XII. 229 (1868); in *Mél. Biol.* VI. 373 (1868). — Franchet & Savatier, *Enum. Pl. Jap.* I. 468 (1875).
Pinus Tsuga, β *nana* Endlicher, *Syn. Conif.* 83 (1847).
Tsuga Sieboldii, β *nana* Carrière, *Traité Conif.* 186 (1855).
Abies Tsuga nana Siebold apud Gordon *Pinet.* suppl. 13 (1862).
Tsuga Araragi, var. *nana* Sargent, *Silva N. Am.* XII. 60, in a note (1898).
Pinus araragi, var. *diversifolia* Voss in *Mitt. Deutsch. Dendr. Ges.* XVI. 93 (1907).
Pinus araragi, var. *nana* Voss in Putlitz & Meyer, *Landlexikon*, IV. 773 (1913).

On the mountains of the Nikko region and northward this is the only representative of the genus and it is common in the forests on nearly all the high mountains of central and northern Hondo. Its most northerly habitat is Hakkoda-yama, near Aomori, where it is fairly common as a small tree at altitudes between 700 and 1000 m. above the sea. On the upper wind-swept slopes of Hayachine-san in Rikuchu province it is reduced to scrub and with *Abies Mariesii* Mast. covers a great area between 1600 and 2000 m. altitude. On the same mountain, but near its base, this Tsuga is a common tree in the forests with *Abies Mariesii* Mast., *Pinus parviflora* S. & Z. and *Thujopsis dolabrata*, var. *Hondai* Mak. In the Nikko region and on the northern slopes of Fuji-san, between 1500 and 2000 m. altitude, this northern Tsuga reaches its maximum development and forms nearly pure forests. At its lowest level on the mountains of these regions it is associated with *Abies homolepis* S. & Z., and at its upper limits with *Abies Veitchii* Lindl., and growing with it throughout its altitudinal range are such conifers as *Larix Kaempferi* Sarg., *Thujopsis dolabrata* S. & Z., *Thuja Standishii* Carr., *Picea jezoënsis* Carr., *Pinus parviflora* S. & Z. and broad-leaved trees like *Betula Ermanii* Cham., *B. corylifolia* Regel, *B. Maximowicziana* Regel, *Sorbus japonica* Hedl., *S. commixta* Hedl., *Alnus hirsuta*, var. *sibirica* Schneid., *Prunus ssiori* Schmidt and *Quercus mongolica*, var. *grosseserrata* Rehd. & Wils. On the upper middle slopes of the volcanic Mt. Ontake *Tsuga diversifolia* forms with *Abies Veitchii* Lindl., *Picea jezoënsis* Carr. and with occasional trees of *Pinus koraiensis* S. & Z. extensive forests. It forms forests also on the granite Tsubakura-dake in the same province of Shinano. I did not meet with this Tsuga south of these alps of Shinano, but I have before me a specimen collected on Sobo-san in Bungo province, Kyushu. In this connection it is interesting to recall that the species was founded by Maximowicz on material collected in an alpine region of this southern island. Very probably this tree occurs on many of the high mountains in Kyushu, Shikoku and southern Hondo, but it is plentiful only on the Shinano mountains and northward.

Like *T. Sieboldii* Carr. this Hemlock selects steep, rocky slopes and is seen at its best in rich moist forests. When the forests are mixed there is usually a dense undergrowth composed of dwarf Bamboo, *Rhododendron Metternichii* S. & Z., *R. brachycarpum* G. Don, *Enkianthus campanulatus* Nichols., *Viburnum furcatum* Bl., *V. urceolatum* S. & Z. and *Menziesia pentandra* Maxim., but where the Tsuga forms pure or nearly pure forests, as on Tsubakura-dake in Shinano, the upper middle slopes of Nantai-san and elsewhere in the Nikko region there is no undergrowth whatever and the large roots of the Hemlock trees are exposed.

At its best, as seen in the Nikko region, on Fuji-san and in the Shinano province, *Tsuga diversifolia* is as large and as handsome as its southern relative *T. Sieboldii* Carr., but generally it is a smaller tree. The largest I saw measured 26 m. tall and had a trunk 4 m. in girth, but the average is from 16 to 22 m. tall and from 2 to 2.5 m. in girth of trunk, and on wind-swept slopes in northern Hondo it becomes reduced to scrub from 1.5 to 2 m. high. The branches are slender, horizontally spreading, very numerous and are retained low down on the trunk, and the outline of the crown is more or less pyramidal. Although abundantly distinct, in general appearance this species closely resembles *T. Sieboldii* Carr., the bark is similar, the branching, more especially in young trees, is more dense and intricate, the leaves are shorter, crowded on the twigs and less lustrous, the cone is smaller and its peduncle is less apparent and the wood is perhaps denser; but all these characters are relative and old trees of these two species are sometimes difficult to distinguish. The winter-buds of *T. diversifolia* are pyriform to subglobose, flattened at the apex and often puberulous; the shoots are pubescent and these characters, particularly the latter, best distinguish the species. The short, gray pubescence may occur over the whole of the shoot or it may be confined to the furrows between the pulvini, but it is always present.

As may be expected from its habitat, *T. diversifolia* is much the hardier of the two Japanese species and in this Arboretum withstands uninjured the severest winters. In Japan it is known as Kome-tsuga or Kuro-tsuga.

Although first distinguished as a distinct species by Maximowicz, this Hemlock was known to Siebold, who regarded it as a dwarf form of the species which now bears his name. It was introduced into England by John Gould Veitch in 1861, and the plants were afterward distributed under the name of *Abies Tsuga*, var. *nana*.

PSEUDOTSUGA Carr.

A genus confined to western North America, Japan, Formosa and southwestern China, of which five species are now recognized. The two western North America species are the only ones properly known. One of these, *P. taxifolia* Britt., the Douglas Fir or Oregon Pine, is one of the most famous and useful of all conifers, and is one of the commonest and most widely distributed from latitude 55° southward to northern Mexico. The second species, *P. macrocarpa* Mayr, has a restricted range in southern California from the Santa Inez Mountains in Santa Barbara County to the Cuyamaca Mountains. Very little is known concerning the Formosan *P. Wilsoniana* Hayata and the species from Yunnan, southwestern China. The latter is presumably the *P. sinensis* Dode (in *Bull. Soc. Dendr. France*, 1912, 59, fig.) which was founded on fragmentary material. It is probable, however, that the Formosan and Chinese species are identical. The Japanese species is endemic.

PSEUDOTSUGA JAPONICA Beissn.

PLATES XXXIII AND XXXIV

PSEUDOTSUGA JAPONICA Beissner in *Mitt. Deutsch. Dendr. Ges.* V. 62 (1896); XI. 53 (1902); XV. 84, 144 (1906); *Handb. Nadelh.* ed. 2, 111 (1909). — Sargent, *Silva N. Am.* XII. 84, note 2 (1898).—Shirasawa, *Icon. Ess. For. Jap.* I. 21, t. 7 (1900). — Mayr, *Fremdl. Wald- u. Parkb.* 406 (1906). — Elwes & Henry, *Trees Gr. Brit. & Irel.* IV. 812 (1909). — Clinton-Baker, *Ill. Conif.* I. 59, t. (1909). — Jackson in *Gard. Chron.* ser. 3, XLV. 307, fig. 132 (1909). — Bean, *Trees & Shrubs Brit. Isl.* II. 260 (1914).

Tsuga (Pseudo-tsuga) japonica Shirasawa in *Tokyo Bot. Mag.* IX. 86, t. 3 (1895). — *Garden & Forest*, VIII. 129 (1895). — *Gard. Chron.* ser. 3, XVII. 462 (1895).

Tsuga japonica Matsumura, *Ind. Pl. Jap.* II. pt. 1, 20 (1905).

To see this conifer I made a special journey in Tosa province, Shikoku, to Nishinokawa, some 40 miles north from the town of Kochi. There, at about 1000 m. altitude in government forests, is set aside a preserve of about 16 acres, where this rare and local tree forms fully 10 per cent of the forests in which *Tsuga Sieboldii* Carr. is the dominant tree. Other associate trees are *Abies firma* S. & Z., *Chamaecyparis obtusa* S. & Z. and *Torreya nucifera* S. & Z., which is here very rare indeed. The sparse undergrowth is of such evergreens as *Thea japonica* Nois., *Pieris japonica* D. Don, *Skimmia japonica* Thunb., *Eurya japonica* Thunb. and *Osmanthus Aquifolium* S. & Z. The forest is dense and has been known to the Japanese for over 200 years, but only quite recently has the preserve been made. It is on a very steep slope facing east, but sheltered by a parallel spur. The rocks are of old volcanic origin and are overlaid with humus. As seen in this forest the Japanese Pseudotsuga is a tree from 23 to 30 m. tall, with a trunk from 2 to 5 m. in girth. The branches are comparatively few and near the top of the tree, and are wide-spreading, not very thick, horizontally disposed and form a loose, broad, flattened crown. Shirasawa describes the habit as conical, but I saw no trees that could be so described. However, in mixed forests where Shirasawa discovered this tree its habit may be different. The trunk is straight and clean of branches for two-thirds the height of the tree. The bark is dull reddish brown, becoming grayish brown on very old trees and on exposed trunks and is fissured into thin narrow plates in which long corky lenticels are prominent; the plates split transversely and flake off from below upward. On very old trees and near the base of the trunk the plates may be half an inch thick. The shoot is perfectly glabrous and pale yellowish gray, becoming whitish gray the second season. The winter-buds are elongated and acute, as in other species of the genus; they are without resin and are composed of shining chestnut-brown chaffy scales. The leaves are pale green above, white beneath, straight or slightly curved, pectinately arranged and point forward; they are from 1.5 to 2.5 cm. long, soft to the touch and on fruiting branches at least of almost equal width throughout and rounded and always notched at the apex. On seedlings and very young plants the leaves are acute. The cones are ovoid to cylindrical-ovoid and vary in length from 4 to 6 cm.; they are chocolate-brown, somewhat resinous and more or less pruinose when ripe, becoming nearly black with age. The cone-scales are broad, rounded and oblique on the margin; the bract is strongly recurved in its exserted part, is easily broken and the central awn-like lobe is much narrower and longer than the lateral lobes, which are erose or laciniate. The wood is pale brown (dun color), easily worked, of good quality and withstands damp very well. It is used for making coffins, boards for ceilings and other interior work, but the tree is too rare to be of commercial importance. It is evidently of slow growth, for on a piece 5.5 cm. in diameter I have counted with the aid of a lens over 50 annual rings and a strip of board 6.3 cm. wide shows 30 such rings. As I saw this tree in the forest it had nothing of special ornamental character to recommend it. Seedlings of this Pseudotsuga were raised in this Arboretum in the spring of 1899, but the plants did not prove hardy. The Arboretum is experimenting again with seeds I secured from Nishinokawa in 1914. According to Beissner (in *Mitt. Deutsch. Dendr. Ges.* XI. 53 [1902]) young plants were in cultivation in Ansorge's nursery, at Klein-Flottbeck in Holstein, and in the Botanic Garden at Hamburg in 1902.

This Pseudotsuga, Japanese names for which are Toga-suwara and Goyō-toga, grows in small numbers in other parts of Tosa province, round Tanabe and between Owashii and Yoshino on the Kishu peninsula, Hondo, and in Kyushu, where it is very rare indeed. It has not been reported[1] from anywhere else and is apparently limited to a few localities in southeastern Japan and as far as is known is everywhere a rare tree. This tree was discovered in July 1893 by Dr. Homi Shirasawa.

[1] In the herbarium of the Imperial Botanic Garden, Tokyo, Dr. Hayata showed me material of the Formosan plant which he had referred (in *Tokyo Bot. Mag.* XIX. 45 [1905]) to *Pseudotsuga japonica*, and it certainly belongs to another species. Among other differences the Formosan plant has orange-brown puberulous shoots, smaller bracts and a larger, differently shaped wing to the seeds. It has been named *P. Wilsoniana* Hayata (*Icon. Pl. Formos.* V. 204, t. 15 [1915]).

ABIES Juss.

Abies is widely distributed in the temperate regions of the Northern Hemisphere, especially at high altitudes. In North America Fir trees are found from Labrador and the valley of the Athabasca River to the mountains of North Carolina in the eastern part of the continent, and in the west from Alaska through the Pacific and Rocky Mountain regions to the highlands of Guatemala. In the Old World they range from Siberia, Saghalien and the mountains of central Europe to Formosa, southwestern China, the Himalayas and the highlands of northern Africa. Some 35 species are now recognized, 10 in North America and 25 in the Old World. Five species are native of Japan; one of these is common to Hokkaido, Saghalien and the Kurile Islands, the other four are found only in Hondo and the southern islands.

KEY TO THE JAPANESE SPECIES

Bark on adult trees rough and dark gray; winter-buds large.
  Shoots pubescent on young trees, glabrous or nearly so on adults, shallowly furrowed; winter-buds ovoid or conical, acute, shining gray-brown with little or no resin; leaves bifid and pungent on young trees, lower sterile branches and adventitious shoots, with two resin-ducts; on fertile and adult branches obtuse, often emarginate, with four resin-ducts; cone green, bracts exserted . . . A. FIRMA.
  Shoots glabrous, deeply furrowed and wrinkled; winter-buds conical, obtuse and resinous; leaves rounded and emarginate, those at the ends of shoots often acutish; resin-ducts 2, median, in young plants and adventitious shoots marginal; cone often umbilicate, violet-purple (green in var. *umbellata*), bracts included . A. HOMOLEPIS.
Bark on adult trees smooth, grayish white; winter-buds small.
  Shoots clothed with rufous-brown pubescence, terete; winter-buds brownish purple, globose; leaves rounded and emarginate; resin-ducts 2, lateral; cone ovoid or somewhat barrel-shaped, violet-purple, bracts included . . . . . A. MARIESII.
  Shoots more or less clothed with gray or occasionally brownish gray pubescence; winter-buds reddish brown, subglobose to ovoid; leaves truncate and emarginate; resin-ducts 2, lateral; cone slender, cylindrical, violet-purple (green in var. *olivacea*), bracts as long as the cone-scale or slightly longer and reflexed.
A. VEITCHII.
  Shoots more or less clothed with short rufous-gray or gray pubescence; winter-buds bluish, subglobose; leaves rounded and emarginate at the apex; resin-ducts 2, median; cone cylindrical, slightly tapering, greenish purple, bracts longer than the cone-scales (shorter in var. *nemorensis*), recurved . . . . A. SACHALINENSIS.

ABIES FIRMA S. & Z.

PLATES XXXV AND XXXVI

ABIES FIRMA Siebold & Zuccarini, *Fl. Jap.* II. 15, t. 107 (1842). — Murray, *Pines & Firs Jap.* 53, fig. 96–108, 110–112, 115 (1863). — Miquel in *Ann. Mus. Lugd.-Bat.* III. 166 (1867); *Prol. Fl. Jap.* 330 (1867). — Bertrand in *Ann. Sci. Nat.* sér. 5, XX. 93 (1874). — Franchet & Savatier, *Enum. Pl. Jap.* I. 467 (1875). — Masters in *Gard. Chron.* n. ser. XII. 198 (1879); in *Jour. Linn. Soc.* XVIII. 514 (exclude synonyms *Abies holophylla* and *Pinus holophylla*) (1881). — Mayr, *Monog. Abiet. Jap.* 31, t. 1, fig. 1 (1890). — Sargent, *Forest Fl. Jap.* 82 (1894). — Kent in Veitch, *Man. Conif.* ed. 2, 506, fig. 130–132 (1900). — Shirasawa, *Icon. Ess. For.*

Jap. I. 17, t. 6, fig. 1-21 (1900). — Matsumura, *Ind. Pl. Jap.* II. pt. 1, 5 (1905). — Elwes & Henry, *Trees Gr. Brit. & Irel.* IV. 762, t. 216 (1909). — Clinton-Baker, *Ill. Conif.* II. 12, t. (1909). — Hayata, *Veget. Mt. Fuji*, 46, 89 (1911). — Silva Tarouca, *Uns. Freiland-Nadelh.* 147, t. 146 (1913). — Pardé, *Icon. Conif.* t. 26 (1914).

?Pinus Abies Thunberg, *Fl. Jap.* 275 (not Linnaeus) (1784).
?Pinus Thunbergii Lambert, *Descr. Pinus*, II. preface, vi (1828).
Abies momi Siebold in *Verh. Batav. Genoot.* XII. pt. 1, 12 (*Syn. Pl. Oecon. Jap.*) (name only) (1830).
?Abies Thunbergii Lindley in *Penny Cycl.* I. 34 (1833).
Abies bifida Siebold & Zuccarini, *Fl. Jap.* II. 18, t. 109 (1842). — Bertrand in *Ann. Sci. Nat.* sér. 5, XX. 93 (1874).
Pinus firma Antoine, *Conif.* 70, t. 27 (1846).
Pinus bifida Antoine, l. c. 79, t. 31, fig. 2 (1846). — McNab in *Proc. Roy. Irish Acad.* ser. 2, II. 688, t. 47, fig. 15 (1877).
Picea firma Gordon, *Pinet.* 147 (1858). — Murray in *Proc. Hort. Soc. Lond.* II. 351, fig. 63-75, 77-79 (1862).
Picea firma, var. B Murray in *Proc. Hort. Soc. Lond.* II. 409 (1862).
Picea firma, var. *bifida* Masters in *Gard. Chron.* n. ser. XII. 199 (1879).
Abies firma, var. *bifida* Masters in *Jour. Linn. Soc.* XVIII. 514 (1881).
Pinus momi Voss in *Mitt. Deutsch. Dendr. Ges.* XVI. 94 (1907).

This is the Momi of the Japanese and the only Fir known from southern Japan. It is the common low-level species of central Japan from Nagoya northward to Mito and is abundant throughout Kyushu, Shikoku and southern Hondo including the Kishu peninsula, where its altitudinal limit is from 1300 to 1600 m. On the slopes of Fuji-san it ascends to about 1000 m. altitude. On the Chichibu Mountains to the west-northwest of Tokyo it also reaches 1000 m. altitude. Mayr gives latitude 40° as the northern limit of this species, but I saw no wild trees north of latitude 37°. It is also commonly planted in temple grounds and parks throughout the region where it grows naturally. In and around Tokyo and at Nikko it is common as a planted tree and good specimens are plentiful.

On the island of Yaku-shima off the extreme south of Japan and 90 miles south of the city of Kagoshima this Fir is common in the forest mixed with *Cryptomeria japonica* D. Don, *Tsuga Sieboldii* Carr. and various dicotyledonous trees, and I saw there individuals more than 30 m. tall, with trunks 6 m. in girth. Around the base of Mt. Kirishima in southern Kyushu in mixed forest it is common, and there too I saw many magnificent specimens. In Shikoku I again met with it in mixed forest with *Pinus parviflora* S. & Z. and *Pseudotsuga japonica* Beissn. On Koya-san it grows with *Chamaecyparis obtusa* S. & Z., *Sciadopitys verticillata* S. & Z. and various deciduous leaved trees. On the slopes of Takao-san, a low mountain about 24 miles west and slightly south of Tokyo, this Fir grows with *Torreya nucifera* S. & Z. I did not see it forming pure forest, but always associated with other coniferous and dicotyledonous trees. It attains its maximum size in the moist warm valleys of southern Japan. The trees I saw on Yaku-shima impressed me most. On the steep slopes of this island *Abies firma* is first seen at about 500 m. altitude and ascends nearly to the peak (alt. 1928 m.). None of the trees here exceed 40 m. in height, but the average girth of the trunks is from 5 to 6 m. In Tosa province, Shikoku, I saw trees perhaps taller, but the average girth of trunk was rather less.

As it grows in southern Japan *A. firma* is a noble tree with massive branches spreading horizontally and forming an oval or flattened and rounded crown. The bark is dark gray, rough and scaly and in the forests the trunk is clean of branches for from 10 to 18 m. from the ground. On young trees the shoots are clothed with a short, erect, dark gray pubescence or this pubescence is confined to the shallow furrows between the pulvini; the short shoots and the fruiting branchlets are glabrous or nearly so. The winter-buds are large, ovoid to conical, shining gray-brown, with little or no resin. The leaves are dark shining green, and on young trees and adventitious branches are spreading, bifid and pungent, and on older branches rounded and emarginate. On the fruiting branches the leaves are upturned, short, obtuse and often quite entire. With the difference in age of the branchlets and character of the leaf there are correlated differences in the position and number of the resin-ducts. In its juvenile condition with bifid leaves the resin-ducts are two in number, sub-epidermal and lateral; in its adolescent stage, where the leaves are merely spreading and emarginate, the resin-ducts are two in number and are median; on adult, fruiting branches the leaves have each four resin-ducts, two larger median and two smaller sub-epidermal and lateral. In all the stages stereom tissue is present scattered through the mesophyll and its presence distinguishes *A. firma* from all the other Japanese Firs. In its adolescent stage the position of the resin-ducts is the same as in *A. homolepis* S. & Z., but this species is without stereom tissue scattered through the mesophyll. The variations in the character of the leaf in young and old trees caused Siebold & Zuccarini to distinguish their *A. firma* and *A. bifida*, and the differences in the position of the resin-ducts led to the misunderstanding of *A. firma* by Bertrand and by McNab and to their confusing it in part with the totally distinct *A. homolepis* S. & Z. Masters was the first to doubt that the position of resin-ducts was an all-important taxonomic character in the genus Abies. The conclusions I have reached have been verified from material taken from a living tree growing in this Arboretum, supplemented by similar microscopic sections made from material of all ages collected in Japan by myself and others. The cone is green and cylindrical, changes to gray or grayish brown when ripe and is from 12 to 15 cm. long; the apical part of the bract is lance-shaped and is always exserted, erect and pungent. The wood is white, coarse-grained, soft and of little value except for pulp and for making packing cases. Most of the boxes in which Japanese Lily bulbs are packed for export are made of this wood.

As stated under *Pinus Thunbergii* Parl. and under *Picea polita* Carr., this Fir is probably the tree seen by Thunberg near Tokyo and by him referred to Linnaeus' *Pinus Abies*, but as no specimens of Thunberg's plant exist this must ever remain a matter of doubt. It must have been common in Tokyo gardens and temple grounds in Thunberg's time as it is now, and it is a reasonable assumption that he saw it even if he did not recognize its botanical character. Von Siebold was the first to make us properly acquainted with this Fir; it was introduced into England in 1861 by John Gould Veitch, and into America by Dr. George R. Hall in 1862. On the Hall estate there is a fine specimen about 26 m. tall with a trunk 2.25 m. in girth, but in eastern Massachusetts the climate is too severe, and though it just manages to exist and to cone annually in this Arboretum, the species is not really hardy and has no ornamental value here.

ABIES HOMOLEPIS S. & Z.

PLATES XXXVII AND XXXVIII

ABIES HOMOLEPIS Siebold & Zuccarini, *Fl. Jap.* II. 17, t. 108 (1842). — Miquel in *Ann. Mus. Lugd.-Bat.* III. 166 (1867); *Prol. Fl. Jap.* 331 (1867). — Bertrand in *Ann. Sci. Nat.* sér. 5, XX. 93 (1874). Masters in *Gard. Chron.* n. ser. XII. 823, fig. 136 (1879); in *Jour. Linn. Soc.* XVIII. 518 (1881). — Mayr. *Monog. Abiet. Jap.* 35, t. 2, fig. 3 (1890). — Sargent, *Forest Fl. Jap.* 82 (1894). — Shirasawa, *Icon. Ess. For. Jap.* I. 14, t. 3 (1900). — Kent in Veitch, *Man. Conif.* ed. 2, 513, fig. (1900). — Elwes & Henry, *Trees Gr. Brit. & Irel.* IV. 764 (1909). — Hayata, *Veget. Mt. Fuji*, 92 (1911). — Silva Tarouca, *Uns. Freiland-Nadelh.* 86, fig. 81 (1913).

> *Pinus homolepis* Antoine, *Conif.* 78, t. 31, fig. 1 (1846).
> *Picea firma*, var. *A*. Murray in *Proc. Hort. Soc. Lond.* II. 409, fig. 76, 80–81 (1862).
> *Abies firma* Murray, *Pines & Firs Jap.* 53 (in part, not Siebold & Zuccarini), fig. 109, 113, 114 (1863).
> *Abies Tschonoskiana* Regel in *Ind. Sem. Hort. Petrop.* 32 (name only) (1865).
> *Abies brachyphylla* Maximowicz in *Bull. Acad. Sci. St. Pétersbourg*, sér. 3, X. 488 (1866); in *Mél. Biol.* VI. 23 (1866). — Masters in *Gard. Chron.* n. ser. XII. 556, fig. 91, 92 (1879); in *Jour. Linn. Soc.* XVIII. 515, fig. 14 (1881). — Hooker f. in *Bot. Mag.* CXVI. t. 7114 (1890). — Matsumura, *Ind. Pl. Jap.* II. pt. 1, 4 (1905). — Elwes & Henry, *Trees Gr. Brit. & Irel.* IV. 765 (1909). — Clinton-Baker, *Ill. Conif.* II. 8, t. (1909). — Silva Tarouca, *Uns. Freiland-Nadelh.* 85, fig. 80 (1913).
> *Pinus brachyphylla* Parlatore in De Candolle, *Prodr.* XVI. pt. 2, 428 (1868).
> *Abies Finhonnoskiana* Neumann, *Cat.* 1865 ex Parlatore in De Candolle, *Prodr.* XVI. pt. 2, 431 (1868).
> *Pinus Finhonnoskiana* Parlatore in De Candolle, *Prodr.* XVI. pt. 2, 431 (1868).
> *Picea brachyphylla* Gordon, *Pinet.* ed. 2, 201 (1875).
> *Pinus (Abies) firma* McNab in *Proc. Roy. Irish Acad.* ser. 2, II. 686, t. 47, fig. 14 (not *P. firma* Antoine) (1877).
> *Pinus (Abies) Harryana* McNab in *Proc. Roy. Irish Acad.* ser. 2, II. 689, t. 47, fig. 16 (1877).
> *Abies Veitchii* Hort. ex McNab l. c. (as a synonym, not Lindley) (1877).

This is the common Fir of the mountains of central Japan at altitudes between 800 and 2000 m. above the sea, from the alps in Shinano and Hida provinces to the mountains around Nikko. It always grows associated with Larch and broad-leaved deciduous trees. At its lowest altitudinal limit it is associated with *A. firma* S. & Z. and at its highest with *A. Veitchii* Lindl. It is common on Mt. Ontake, on Tsubakura-dake in Shinano province, and on the Yatsuga-dake on the borders of Shinano and Kai provinces. On the lower middle slopes of Fuji-san and on the Chichibu Mountains west-northwest of Tokyo it is fairly plentiful. Around Nikko it is abundant and here grow the finest trees of this Fir I saw in Japan. At Chuzenji on the shores of the lake are trees from 30 to 35 m. tall and from 5 to 6 m. in girth of trunk, with thick horizontally spreading branches and often round-topped heads. The bark is gray and rough and the shoots are stout, glabrous, pale-colored, deeply fissured, with prominent pulvini. The winter-buds are conical, obtuse and resinous. The leaves are variable in length, rounded and emarginate at the apex and often acutish at the ends of the shoots; the upper side is shining green, the lower normally very white. There is no stereom tissue scattered through the mesophyll and the resin-ducts are normally median, but on young trees and adventitious shoots they are marginal. The cone is resinous, violet-purple, cylindrical, from 7.5 to 9 cm. long and from 2.5 to 3.75 cm. wide, occasionally umbilicate, and changes to brownish purple when ripe.

The figure of Siebold & Zuccarini is poor, but it does show, though somewhat diagrammatically, the characteristically deeply grooved shoot which distinguishes this species from other Japanese Firs. Differences that have been pointed out between supposed plants of *Abies homolepis* and *A. brachyphylla* Maxim. are merely variations, dependent on the different ages of the specimens compared.

The name Dake-momi, very generally applied to this tree by the Japanese, signifies Mountain Fir. The wood is used for the same purposes as that of *A. firma* S. & Z. and is of equal value.

Abies homolepis was discovered by von Siebold, who saw it cultivated in gardens in Osaka and Nagasaki and who states on the authority of Keiske Ito and other Japanese that it grows wild in the provinces of Owari and Shinano. We know today that this is perfectly true. Apparently it was first introduced to Europe by John Gould Veitch, who sent seeds from Japan in 1861, under the impression that they were those of *A. Veitchii* Lindl., and under this name the plants were distributed until the error was discovered in 1880 through the introduction of Lindley's species by Maries in 1879. Seeds were sent to Petrograd by Maximowicz's collector, Tschonoski in 1865 and distributed by Regel under the name of *A. Tschonoskiana;* the same collector again sent seeds in 1866 and this was distributed as *A. brachyphylla* Maxim. In eastern North America this Fir is a very satisfactory tree, grows freely and is extremely ornamental. In this Arboretum it is perfectly hardy and for landscape purposes is the best of the Japanese species and one of the most valuable of all exotic Firs. Our largest tree was received from Messrs. Veitch in 1882 and is now about 12 m. tall and well furnished with wide-spreading branches from the ground up. In the Hunnewell Pinetum there is an older and finer specimen 17 m. tall. A variety of this species is

ABIES HOMOLEPIS, var. UMBELLATA Wils. n. var.

> *Abies umbellata* Mayr, *Monog. Abiet. Jap.* 34, t. 1, fig. 2 (1890). — Shirasawa, *Icon. Ess. For. Jap.* II. t. 2, fig. 1-17 (1908). — Elwes & Henry, *Trees Gr. Brit. & Irel.* IV. 768 (1909). — Matsumura, *Ind. Pl. Jap.* II. pt. 1, 5 (1905). — Hayata, *Veget. Mt. Fuji*, 92 (1911).
> *Abies umbilicata* Mayr in *Mitt. Deutsch. Dendr. Ges.* III. 31 (1894).
> *Pinus umbilicata* Voss in *Mitt. Deutsch. Dendr. Ges.* XVI. 94 (1907).

Except in the color of the cones I can find no difference whatever between this Fir (Plate XXXIX) and the typical *A. homolepis* S. & Z. The habit of the tree, the bark, the shoot, the winter-buds, the leaves, the character of their mesophyll and the position of the resin-ducts are the same. In both the cone is occasionally umbilicate, but this is the exception rather than the rule. All the specimens of Mayr's Fir so far recorded have been found growing mixed with typical *A. homolepis*. On Mitsumine-san, where Mayr discovered it, there are growing in the temple grounds two trees of this variety *umbellata* and the priests declare they are the only ones on the mountain. To these trees the name Urajiro-momi has been applied and they are well known to Japanese botanists. Unfortunately no young cones could be found and I had to be contented with male flowers. Both *Abies homolepis* and *A. firma* S. & Z. grow in the same temple grounds and are wild on the mountain.

On the shores of Lake Chuzenji, on June 3, I discovered a tree of the variety *umbellata* growing with the type and laden with flowers. The young cone is green and retains this color until it is ripe, when it changes to pale gray-brown.

If Mayr's figures of his *A. umbellata* and of *A. homolepis* be compared, it will appear that the bracts are of different shape and the cone-scale and seed are smaller in *A. homolepis*. These differences, however, are not constant, as a careful comparison between actual cones of the variety and type proves.

That individual trees of a species of Abies, which normally has purple or violet-colored cones, produce green-colored cones is known in *A. concolor* Lindl. & Gord., *A. Veitchii* Lindl. and other species. This phenomenon of viridescence is analogous to albinism in ordinary flowering plants.

This Fir was discovered by Dr. H. Mayr presumably in 1889, and this Arboretum received seeds from him on June 11, 1891. Trees raised from these seeds have grown more rapidly than those of any other Fir and our largest are about 11 m. tall. They produced cones in 1914 and a tree of the same origin has also borne cones in the Hunnewell Pinetum. As they grow in this Arboretum the trees of var. *umbellata* are somewhat less densely branched, the branches are slightly ascending and the leaves a more yellowish green than those of the type species.

In 1892, in Yokohama, Professor Sargent purchased some seeds under the name of *Abies firma*. Many trees raised from these seeds are growing in this Arboretum and in habit and appearance are identical with those of the variety *umbellata*, raised from Mayr's seeds. In this connection it may be of interest to record that in Japan I showed cones of variety *umbellata* to a man who lives on the lower slopes of the Yatsuga-dake and who makes a business of collecting seeds of *Larix Kaempferi* Sarg. and of other conifers. He at once declared them to be the cones of the Momi (*A. firma* S. & Z.) and added that a few trees grew near his home. Questioned as to his reason for considering them to have come from the Momi, he pointed to the color of the cones.

ABIES MARIESII Mast.

Plates XL and XLI

Abies Mariesii Masters in *Gard. Chron.* n. ser. XII. 788, fig. 129 (1879); in *Jour. Linn. Soc.* XVIII. 519, fig. 17, 18 (1881). — Mayr, *Monog. Abiet. Jap.* 40, t. 2, fig. 5 (1890). — Sargent, *Forest Fl. Jap.* 82 (1894). — Shirasawa, *Icon. Ess. For. Jap.* II. t. 4, fig. 15-28 (1900). — Matsumura, *Ind. Pl. Jap.* II. pt. 1, 5 (1905). — Elwes & Henry, *Trees Gr. Brit. & Irel.* IV. 771 (1909). — Clinton-Baker, *Ill. Conif.* II. 18, t. (1909).

Pinus mariesii Voss in *Mitt. Deutsch. Dendr. Ges.* XVI. 94 (1907).

This is the alpine Fir of central Japan and the only species known in a wild state in Hondo north of the Nikko region. The most southern station where I saw this Fir was on Mt. Ontake, in Shinano province, where above 2600 m. it is common as a small tree or bush and grows with *Tsuga diversifolia* Mast., *Pinus pumila* Regel and *Juniperus communis*, var. *nipponica* Wils. From here northward it probably occurs on all the high mountains. It is common on and near the summit of Yatsuga-dake on the borders of Kai and Shinano provinces. On Nantai-san in the Nikko region, in the form of small trees or scrub, it covers large areas above 2400 m., and on the Onsenga-dake beyond Yumoto it forms with *Abies Veitchii* Lindl. pure woods, the trees being from 16 to 20 m. tall. Immediately over the

Konseitōge Pass, travelling from Yumoto village, there is a fine forest of this and Veitch's Fir and the trees are from 20 to 25 m. tall and have trunks from 1.5 to 2.3 m. in girth. On a spur of Adzuma-san which I ascended from Tōge on the borders of Iwashiro and Uzen provinces there is a pure forest of *Abies Mariesii* in which the lumbermen were unfortunately very busy. Here I saw in quantity the finest trees of this Fir I met with. Specimens from 25 to 30 m. tall and from 2 to 3 m. in girth of trunk were common. On the crest of this spur this Fir is reduced to a small tree or bush.

On the northern slopes of Hayachine-san in Rikuchu province Maries' Fir is abundant. On the upper slopes it forms, with *Tsuga diversifolia* Mast., *Pinus pumila* Regel and broad-leaved deciduous trees, a dense scrub. Lower down on the mountain it forms woods. On Hakkoda-yama in Mutsu province, where Maries first discovered it, most of the trees have been cut down or have been destroyed by fire, but a number still grow there and the trees, though less tall, equal in girth of trunk any I saw elsewhere. It does not grow in Hokkaido; neither has it been reported from Hondo south of the central provinces. The specimens from Formosa and from China which have been referred to this species are now known to belong to other species.

As it grows in the forests of Japan this is a more handsome Fir than *A. Veitchii* Lindl., with stouter, more wide-spreading branches forming normally an oval or even flattened round crown. The bark is very pale gray (almost white) as in Veitch's Fir, but on old trees it becomes somewhat rough near the base of the trunk — a condition I never observed in *A. Veitchii* Lindl. The shoots are clothed with a rufous-brown pubescence, and the winter-buds are brownish purple, globose and resinous. The leaves are unequal in length and on fruiting branches more or less appressed. The cone is violet-purple, from 4 to 9 cm. long and from 3 to 4.5 cm. wide, and ovoid or somewhat barrel-shaped. The wood is white, becoming very pale brown on exposure, and is of good quality for that of a Fir.

In Japan this tree is known as the Aomori-todomatsu in northern Hondo, and around Nikko as the Oh-shirabiso. It was discovered on Hakkoda-yama by Charles Maries in 1878 and by him introduced into the nurseries of Messrs. Veitch in 1879. In eastern North America Maries' Fir does not thrive and in this Arboretum can be kept alive only in a sheltered place. The fact that it is an alpine species is probably the reason why it does so badly here at sea-level. In the Hunnewell Pinetum there is a healthy plant about 4 m. tall, and this has produced cones.

A. VEITCHII Lindl.

Plates XLII and XLIII

Abies Veitchii Lindley in *Gard. Chron.* 1861, 23.—Murray, *Pines & Firs Jap.* 39, fig. 69–79 (1863).—Miquel, *Prol. Fl. Jap.* 389 (1867).—Bertrand in *Ann. Sci. Nat.* sér. 5, XX. 93 (1874).—Masters in *Gard. Chron.* n. ser. XIII. 275, fig. 50, 51 (1880).—Veitch, *Man. Conif.* 107, fig. 11, 27, 28 (1881).—Mayr, *Monog. Abiet. Jap.* 38, t. 2, fig. 4 (1890).—Sargent, *Forest Fl. Jap.* 83 (1894).—Shirasawa, *Icon. Ess. For. Jap.* I. 16, t. 5, fig. 23–42 (1900).—Matsumura, *Ind. Pl. Jap.* II. pt. 1, 6 (1905).—Beissner, *Handb. Nadelh.* ed. 2, 190, fig. 42 (1909).—Elwes & Henry, *Trees Gr. Brit. & Irel.* IV. 768 (1909).—Clinton-Baker, *Ill. Conif.* II. 28, t. (1909).—Hayata, *Veget. Mt. Fuji*, 48, 92, fig. 16 (1) (1911).—Silva Tarouca, *Uns. Freiland-Nadelh.* 102, fig. 99 (1913).

Picea Veitchii Murray in *Proc. Hort. Soc. Lond.* II. 347, fig. 52–62 (1862).
Abies spec. nova (Pichtae aff.) No. 9668 Regel in *Ind. Sem. Hort. Petrop.* 1865, 32.
Pinus selenolepis Parlatore in De Candolle, *Prodr.* XVI. pt. 2, 427 (1868).
Pinus (Abies) Veitchii McNab in *Proc. Roy. Irish Acad.* ser. 2, II. 686, t. 47, fig. 13 (1877).
Abies Eichleri Lauche in *Gartenzeit.* I. 63, t. (1882). — Hennings in *Gartenfl.* XXXIX. 377, fig. 66 (1890).
Abies Veitchii, var. *Nikkoënsis* Mayr, *Monog. Abiet. Jap.* 39, 86 (1890).
Abies japonica Hort. ex Sargent in *Garden & Forest,* VI. 525 (as a synonym) (1893).
Pinus nephrolepis, var. *veitchii* Voss in *Mitt. Deutsch. Dendr. Ges.* XVI. 94 (1907).
Abies Veitchii, var. *reflexa* Koidzumi in *Tokyo Bot. Mag.* XXX. 327 (1916).

I met with this Fir only on the high mountains of central Japan from those of Shinano and Hida provinces in the south to those round Nikko in the north. According to Mayr it occurs very sparingly on the summit of Ishitzuchi-yama in Shikoku, but I have seen no specimens from that island. In central Japan its altitudinal range is usually from 1300 to 2300 m., but on the slopes of Fuji-san on the Gotemba side it descends to 1050 m. At its lower altitude it is associated with *Abies homolepis* S. & Z. and at its highest with *A. Mariesii* Mast. On Mt. Ontake in Shinano province it forms extensive forests mixed with *Picea jezoënsis* Carr., *Tsuga diversifolia* Mast., Birch and a few other broad-leaved deciduous trees. On Tsubakura-dake, a granite peak in the same province, this Fir is exceedingly rare and I saw only a few small trees. On the Yatsuga-dake, on the borders of Kai and Shinano provinces, I saw, at about 2300 m. altitude, almost pure forests of this Fir. Above Yumoto in the Nikko region it is abundant in woods of Birch, Maple and other broad-leaved deciduous trees. On the Onsenga-dake and over the Konseitoge Pass, both near Yumoto, it forms with *Abies Mariesii* Lindl. nearly pure forests. North of the Nikko mountains I did not meet with *A. Veitchii.*

Veitch's Fir is the smallest of the Japanese Abies. The largest tree I saw was 24 m. tall and had a girth of 2.3 m. In the forests it is a narrow, tapering, pyramidal tree with very numerous short, slender branches. In more open country, as on the slopes of Fuji-san, it is not so tall and the branches are longer. The shoot is slender, more or less clothed with short, erect gray or occasionally reddish gray pubescence and the winter-buds are reddish brown, small, subglobose to ovoid and resinous. The bark is perfectly smooth and very pale gray (almost white) and resin-pustules are prominent. The leaves are soft to the touch, shining dark green above, white beneath and truncate and emarginate at the apex. The violet-purple cone is slender, cylindrical, from 4.5 to 6.5 cm. long and from 2 to 2.5 cm. broad. The bracts are very slightly or are distinctly exserted and reflexed. The wood is white and of no particular value. Mayr has separated a variety (*nikkoënsis*), but the characters on which he relies are trivial and, moreover, inconstant and I do not consider that it can be kept distinct from the type.

Abies Veitchii was discovered on Fuji-san in 1860 by John Gould Veitch, for whom it is named. Veitch failed to obtain seeds, but in 1865 Maximowicz's Japanese collector, Tschonoski, sent seeds to Petrograd, and these were distributed by Regel under the name of *Abies spec. nova (Pichtae aff.).* Whether any plants are in cultivation from this seed I do not know. In 1876 it was sent from Japan to the Parsons nurseries at Flushing, New York, by Thomas Hogg, and for many years was known in American gardens as *Abies japonica* Hort. In 1879 Maries sent seeds in quantity to Messrs. Veitch and the plants raised from them have been widely distributed. This Fir grows satisfactorily in this country. It is perfectly hardy in this Arboretum and as an ornamental tree ranks among the Asiatic species next to *A. homolepis* S. & Z. In the Hunnewell Pinetum there is a very fine specimen 16 m. tall. Japanese names for this Fir are Shirabiso, Shirabe-momi and Shira-tsuga. A variety of this species is

ABIES VEITCHII, var. OLIVACEA Shirasawa in *Tokyo Bot. Mag.* XXVII. 132 (1913); in *Mitt. Deutsch. Dendr. Ges.* XXIII. 256 (1914); in *Gard. Chron.* ser. 3, LVIII. 99 (1915).

This variety is distinguished from the type by the color of the cones, which are green and change to gray-brown when ripe. On all the specimens I collected the pubescence on the shoot is ferruginous. I met with this variety first on the Onsenga-dake beyond Yumoto in the Nikko region and afterwards collected ripe seeds and cones at 2000 m. altitude on the Yatsuga-dake, on the borders of Shinano and Kai provinces. In both places it was growing mixed with the typical species. Apparently Maries was the first to discover this variety, as Masters in the *Gardeners' Chronicle*, n. ser. XIII. 275 (1880), says Maries speaks of a "green-coned variety." Many young plants are now growing in this Arboretum from seeds I collected in Japan in 1914.

ABIES SACHALINENSIS Mast.

PLATES XLIV AND XLV

ABIES SACHALINENSIS Masters in *Gard. Chron.* n. ser. XII. 588, fig. 97 (1879); in *Jour. Linn. Soc.* XVIII. 517, fig. 16 (1881). — Veitch, *Man. Conif.* 106, fig. 26 (1881). — Mayr, *Monog. Abiet. Jap.* 42, t. 3, fig. 6 (1890). — Sargent, *Forest Fl. Jap.* 83 (1894). — Shirasawa, *Icon. Ess. For. Jap.* I. 18, t. 6, fig. 22–43 (1900). — Matsumura, *Ind. Pl. Jap.* II. pt. 1, 5 (1905). — Miyoshi, *Atlas Jap. Veget.* pt. IX. 5, t. 68 (1908); pt. X. 1, t. 69, 70 (1908). — Elwes & Henry, *Trees Gr. Brit. & Irel.* IV. 760 (1909). — Clinton-Baker, *Ill. Conif.* II. 26, t. (1909). — Takeda in *Jour. Linn. Soc.* XLII. 486 (1914). — Miyabe & Miyake, *Fl. Saghal.* 598 (1915).

Abies homolepis, var. β *Toknaiae* Carrière, *Traité Conif.* 216 (1855).
Abies Veitchii, var. *sachalinensis* Fr. Schmidt in *Mém. Acad. Sci. St. Pétersbourg*, sér. 7, XII. no. 2, 175, t. 4, fig. 13–17 (*Reis. Amur. Sachal.*) (1868).
Pinus sachalinensis Voss in Putlitz & Meyer, *Landlexikon*, IV. 777 (1913).

This Fir is abundant in Hokkaido and is the only species known from that island. Occasionally it forms pure forests, but usually it is associated with *Picea jezoënsis* Carr. and broad-leaved deciduous trees and in the more northern part of the island with *Picea Glehnii* Mast. At Nopporo, a few miles from Sapporo, there is a government forest reservation where this tree is abundant, forming extensive and pure stands; it also occurs there mixed with broad-leaved deciduous trees, but is the dominant tree. In Kitami province in the north it is abundant and forms extensive forests mixed with *Picea jezoënsis* Carr. and *P. Glehnii* Mast. In Japanese Saghalien I saw it in great abundance and with *Picea jezoënsis* Carr. and *Larix dahurica*, var. *japonica* Maxim. it covers enormous areas. It is more partial to the low mountain slopes than to the swamps, where the Larch is most at home.

On the slopes of Shiribeshi-san near the town of Kutchan up to 1000 m. altitude there are trees of this Fir from 25 to 30 m. tall and from 2 to 2.5 m. in girth, and these are the largest I saw. In Saghalien the maximum size is from 16 to 25 m. by about 1.6 m. in girth of trunk. In habit and general appearance this Fir strongly resembles *A. Veitchii* Lindl. The bark is perfectly smooth, almost white and full of resin-pustules. The branches are short and slender and the leaves are rather long, soft to the touch, rounded and emarginate. The shoots are more or less densely clothed with short, gray or rufous-gray pubescence; the winter-buds are small, bluish, subglobose and are covered with resin. The cone is greenish purple with exserted pale green recurved bracts which when dry are pale and shining brownish gray; it is cylindrical, tapering at the summit, from 5 to 7.5 cm. long and from 2.5 to 3 cm. wide. Colloquially known as Todo-matsu, this Fir is the only species appreciated by the Japanese for the value of its wood, which is white and is extensively used in house and ship building, and in making furniture and paper. For these purposes it is used locally and is exported from Hokkaido in quantity to other parts of Japan.

This species does not occur on the main island (Hondo) of Japan and is, as far as our present knowledge goes, confined to Hokkaido, the Kurile Islands and to Saghalien. It has not been reported from continental eastern Asia. In the forest it reproduces itself readily from self-sown seeds, but the forestry officials informed me that their efforts at reafforesting with this Fir had not been successful. *Abies sachalinensis* was discovered in 1866 by Fr. Schmidt on the island of Saghalien; in July 1878 seeds were received in this Arboretum from W. A. Clark of the Agricultural College, Sapporo, and plants of this origin were growing here until quite recently. In 1879 Maries sent seeds from Hokkaido to Messrs. Veitch and in 1892 Professor Sargent secured seeds, and many plants from this source are now growing here, the largest being about 6 m. tall. It is perfectly hardy in this Arboretum and it grows fairly well, but with its short sparse branches and spire-like habit it cannot be called ornamental. One or two of our plants, however, are bushy and have fairly long branches. The small bluish winter-buds are very characteristic and in winter afford a ready means for identifying this species.

Of the form with red bark, dark red wood and red cone-bracts discovered by Dr. K. Miyabe (Sargent, *Forest Fl. Jap.* 83 [1894]) I saw nothing. Plants of this form raised from seed received from Miyabe in December 1892 are growing in this Arboretum, but are indistinguishable from those of the type. A variety of this species is

ABIES SACHALINENSIS, var. NEMORENSIS Mayr, *Monog. Abiet. Jap.* 43, 86, t. 3, fig. 6 (1890).

Pinus sachalinensis, f. *nemorensis* Voss in Putlitz & Meyer, *Landlexikon*, IV. 777 (1913).
Abies nemorensis Miyabe & Miyake, *Fl. Saghal.* 598 (1915).

I saw this variety in Saghalien only, growing in the forests at Konuma, a few miles from Toyohara, mixed with the type. In my specimens the bracts are quite included and this and their more violet hue give the cone an entirely different aspect. There are no apparent differences in the habit and general appearance of this variety and I do not think it is entitled to higher rank. The cone of *Abies Veitchii* Lindl., which is somewhat like that of this variety, may be distinguished by its much smaller cone-scales. The shape of the cones is also rather different.

Mayr gives northeastern Hokkaido and the Kurile Islands as the region of distribution of this variety. Japanese forestry officers informed me that their efforts to find this variety in northeastern Hokkaido had failed. I secured seeds in 1914 through the forestry officials at Toyohara and many young plants are now growing in this Arboretum.

Subfam. TAXODIEAE Parl.

SCIADOPITYS S. & Z.

PLATES XLVI AND XLVII

SCIADOPITYS VERTICILLATA Siebold & Zuccarini, *Fl. Jap.* II. 3, t. 101, 102 (1842). — Lindley in *Gard. Chron.* 1861, 22, 360, fig. — Murray in *Proc. Hort. Soc. Lond.* II. 719, fig. 184–196 (1862); *Pines & Firs Jap.* 109, fig. 202–213, 215 (1863). — Carrière in *Rev. Hort.* 1868, 150, fig. 16. — Franchet & Savatier, *Enum. Pl. Jap.* I. 468 (1875). — Masters in *Jour. Linn. Soc.* XVIII. 502 (1881); XXVII. 276, 320, fig. 26, 27 (1890); XXX. 21 (1893); in *Jour. Bot.* XXII. 97, fig. 1, 4 (1884). — Sargent, *Forest Fl. Jap.* 77 (1894). — Shirasawa, *Icon. Ess. For. Jap.* I. 22, t. 8, fig. 15–35 (1900). — Matsumura, *Ind. Pl. Jap.* II. pt. 1, 17 (1905). — Thiselton-Dyer in *Bot. Mag.* CXXXI. t. 8050 (1905). — Mayr, *Fremdl. Wald- u. Parkb.* 407, fig. 136–138 (1906). — Elwes & Henry, *Trees Gr. Brit. & Irel.* III. 568, t. 159 (1908). — Beissner, *Handb. Nadelh.* ed. 2, 448, fig. 106–108 (1909). — Silva Tarouca, *Uns. Freiland-Nadelh.* 267, fig. 279 (1913). — Bean, *Trees & Shrubs Brit. Isl.* II. 506, fig. (1914).

Taxus verticillata Thunberg, *Fl. Jap.* 276 (1784).
Pinus verticillata Siebold in *Verh. Batav. Genoot.* XII. pt. 1, 12 (*Syn. Pl. Oecon. Jap.*) (1830).

In a wild state this interesting tree is confined principally to the valley of the Kiso-gawa in central, and to Koya-san and its immediate neighborhood in east-central, Hondo. It has also been reported from one or two mountains in Shikoku, but is very rare there and I did not meet with it. Through the Kiso-gawa Valley in the provinces of Mino and Shinano, between 600 and 1000 m., the Sciadopitys is common. Occasionally it forms pure stands of some size, but usually it occurs in small groves and as solitary trees scattered through dense mixed forests of *Chamaecyparis pisifera* S. & Z., *C. obtusa* S. & Z., *Pinus parviflora* S. & Z., *Abies firma* S. & Z., *Tsuga Sieboldii* Carr. and such broad-leaved trees as *Aesculus turbinata* Bl., *Magnolia obovata* Thunb., *Acanthopanax innovans* Fr. & Sav., *A. sciadophylloides* Fr. & Sav., *Cercidiphyllum japonicum* S. & Z. and *Acer rufinerve* S. & Z. In these forests the Sciadopitys is easily recognized from a distance by its narrow plume-like crown, which towers well above those of its neighbors. On Koya-san, situated on the borders of Kii and Yamato provinces and famed for its monasteries, the Umbrella Pine is common and it is from this mountain that the tree gets its Japanese name Koya-maki (the Podocarpus of Mt. Koya). There, between 800 and 1000 m. altitude, it forms pure stands of considerable size, but more usually it is scattered in small groves or as individual trees among *Chamaecyparis obtusa* S. & Z., *Tsuga Sieboldii* Carr., *Pinus densiflora* S. & Z. and *Torreya nucifera* S. & Z., the Chamaecyparis being the dominant tree. Usually the slopes where the Sciadopitys grows are so densely wooded that there is no undergrowth except Ferns, Mosses and Liverworts, although sometimes *Skimmia japonica* Thunb., *Ilex Sugeroki* Maxim. and other shade-loving shrubs occur. Seedlings of the Umbrella Pine abound in the forest floor, and it is by this means that the stands and groves of this tree are perpetuated.

The Sciadopitys delights in steep, rocky situations, sheltered from strong winds and where it is cool and moist. On Koya-san the trees average from 20 to 30 m. in height and from 1.6 to 2.6 m. in girth of trunk, and the largest I saw was about 35 m. tall and 4 m. in girth of trunk. In Shinano I saw trees from 40 to 45 m. tall, but none more than 3.5 m. in girth and the majority much less. The branches are short and slender and in the forest shade spread horizontally and are slightly upturned toward the end, but in the open and on the upper part of the tree the branches are ascending-spreading and even quite ascending. New leaders are readily formed and trees with three or four are common. Those familiar with this conifer only as a lawn tree, where it forms usually a dense pyramid branched from the ground, would be surprised at its appearance in the forest, where it is gaunt and thin, so that, standing close to its bole and looking upward, the sky is clearly visible through the narrow crown. The bark is thin and nearly smooth, gray to gray-brown without and red-brown within, and splits into long thin sheets which easily strip off. This bark is made into a rough tow and is employed in calking boats, in packing the joints of steampipes, etc. The wood is soft, white, fragrant and withstands water and damp well. It is used for making small boats, bathtubs, etc. The wood of the trees on Koya-san is said to be superior to that of the trees which grow in the valley of the Kiso-gawa.

The cones mature the second season and are produced in great numbers, and as mentioned before seedlings from self-sown seeds abound on the forest floor. Proliferous cones are not uncommon and as mementoes of their visit are much sought after by the pilgrims who annually journey to Koya-san in great crowds. In old gardens, parks and temple grounds in Nara, Kyōto, Kobe, Nagoya, Yokohama, Tokyo and other wealthy cities small plants of the Umbrella Pine are occasionally met with, but it does not appear to be one of the popular trees in Japan. The only large planted tree I saw is the one growing in the courtyard of one of the temples in Shiba Park, Tokyo, which is mentioned by Sargent and shown in a figure on p. 102 of *A Traveller's Notes* by James H. Veitch. This specimen is about 26 m. tall with a trunk 3 m. in girth and the habit is remarkable. It has the short slender branches of the species, but they are decurved and their terminal branchlets are all upturned and ascending and the outline of the tree is therefore narrowly columnar. Bean (*Trees & Shrubs Brit. Isl.* II. 507 [1914]) gives the name of var. *pendula* to this tree and says that one of similar habit is growing in the garden of Mr. L. Rothschild at Gunnesbury Park, near London.

In cultivation the Sciadopitys is one of the most distinct and one of the handsomest of all conifers and is deservedly a favorite in many lands. In eastern North America it is perfectly hardy as far north as Boston but grows very slowly.

Sciadopitys verticillata was discovered by Thunberg in 1775–76 and was early introduced by the Dutch to Java. From Buitenzorg a plant was sent to England by Thomas Lobb when collecting for Messrs. Veitch; it arrived in 1853, but died soon afterward. In 1861 John Gould Veitch sent seeds to England and from these many plants were raised. About the same time Robert Fortune also sent seeds home. To this country it was introduced by Dr. George R. Hall, who gave a quantity of seeds to the Parsons Nursery, Flushing, New York, in 1862.

CRYPTOMERIA D. Don

PLATES XLVIII AND XLIX

CRYPTOMERIA JAPONICA D. Don in *Trans. Linn. Soc.* XVIII. 167, t. 13, fig. 1 (1841). — Hooker, *Icon.* VII. t. 668 (1844). — Siebold & Zuccarini in *Abh. Akad. Münch.* IV. pt. 3, 234 (*Fl. Jap. Fam. Nat.* II. 110) (1846). — Miquel in *Ann. Mus. Lugd.-Bat.* III. 168 (1867); in Siebold & Zuccarini, *Fl. Jap.* II. 43, t. 124, 124 b (1870). — Franchet & Savatier, *Enum. Pl. Jap.* I. 469 (1875). — Masters in *Jour. Linn. Soc.* XVIII. 497 (1881); XXVI. 544 (1902); XXXVII. 413 (1906). — Sargent, *Forest Fl. Jap.* 74, t. 24 (1894). — Shirasawa, *Icon. Ess. For. Jap.* I. 24, t. 9, fig. 25–42 (1900). — Matsumura, *Ind. Pl. Jap.* II. pt. 1, 9 (1905). — J. H. Veitch, *A Traveller's Notes*, 133, t. 9 (1906). — Mayr, *Fremdl. Wald- u. Parkb.* 278 (1906). — Elwes & Henry, *Trees Gr. Brit. & Irel.* I. 128, t. 38–41 (1906). — Beissner, *Handb. Nadelh.* ed. 2, 475, fig. 115–117 (1909). — Pardé, *Icon. Conif.* t. 114 (1912). — Silva Tarouca, *Uns. Freiland-Nadelh.* 67, 134, fig. 60, 133 (1913). — Rehder & Wilson in Sargent, *Pl. Wilson.* II. 52 (1914).

Cupressus japonica Linnaeus f., *Suppl.* 421 (1781). — Thunberg, *Fl. Jap.* 265 (1784).
Taxodium japonicum Brongniart in *Ann. Sci. Nat.* sér. I. XXX. 183 (exclude var. *heterophylla*) (1833).
Cryptomeria japonica, var. *Lobbii* Carrière, *Traité Conif.* 154 (1855).
Cryptomeria japonica, var. *japonica* Henry in Elwes & Henry, *Trees Gr. Brit. & Irel.* I. 129 (1906).

My first journey after my arrival in Japan in early February 1914 was to the forests on the island of Yaku-shima, situated some 90 miles south of Kagoshima in Kyushu. In books Yaku-shima is usually mentioned as belonging to the Liukiu group, but this statement is not correct. It is only a small island, yet it is of peculiar interest since it is not only the extreme southern limit of the Japanese archipelago proper, but also marks the southern limit of the Japanese flora. My trip was made easy through the kindness of Dr. H. Shirasawa, who wrote on my behalf to Dr. Naito, head of the Kagoshima forestry bureau, within whose jurisdiction Yaku-shima lies. Dr. Naito, in the most obliging manner, detailed his assistant, Mr. Miyoshi, to accompany me anywhere I wished to go in his district. Mr. Miyoshi, who had recently graduated from the Tokyo School of Forestry under Professor Honda, proved a most charming and enthusiastic travelling companion. At Yaku-shima the local forestry officials did everything they could. But for this assistance it would have been impossible to have made any study of these forests, for there are no roads, only trails laid on logs for the use of the forest guards, and no accommodation other than rough huts for the occasional use of these men.

Yaku-shima is really a mountain of granite blocks upthrust from the bed of the ocean, with numerous spurs, and culminating in a peak, called Miyanoura, 1928 m. above sea-level. From sea-level to about 100 m. altitude is coastal savannah with scattered hamlets, patches of cultivation, isolated trees, chiefly *Pinus Thunbergii* Parl., and along the watercourses shrubs, Bananas, Tree Ferns and miscellaneous trees. Above this, up to about 250 m. altitude, is a narrow belt of mixed and chiefly evergreen forest in which *Castanopsis cuspidata* Schottk. is a prominent tree and Cryptomeria is planted. This belt belongs to the villagers and above it the whole island is a government forest reserve. The summit of Miyanoura is said to be covered with dwarf Bamboo, *Rhododendron Metternichii* S. & Z., Juniper and miscellaneous scrub, but at the time of my visit everything was hidden in snow. Fully 99 per cent. of this forest preserve is of evergreen trees, of which 60 per cent. are conifers. Cryptomeria forms fully 50 per cent. of the entire forest. Of other conifers *Tsuga Sieboldii* Carr., *Abies firma* S. & Z. and scattered trees of *Chamaecyparis obtusa* S. & Z. and *Torreya nucifera* S. & Z. make the other 10 per cent. Of broad-leaved evergreen trees *Trochodendron aralioides* S. & Z., *Distylium racemosum* S. & Z., *Thea japonica* Nois. and *T. Sasanqua* Nois. represent 30 per cent., while *Daphniphyllum macropodum* Miq., *D. glaucescens* Bl., *Michelia compressa* Maxim., *Myrica rubra* S. & Z., various Oaks, Hollies and Lauraceae form the other 9 per cent. *Stewartia monadelpha* S. & Z. forms half of the 1 per cent. of the deciduous trees and the remainder is made up of *Acanthopanax ricinifolius* Seem., *Evodia glauca* Miq., *Aleurites cordata* R. Br., *Clethra barbinervis* S. & Z., Maples and trees which I did not recognize. The principal undershrubs are *Skimmia japonica* Thunb., *Eurya japonica* Thunb., *Damnacanthus indicus* Gaertn., *Pieris japonica* D. Don, *Rhododendron Tashiroi* Maxim., *R. indicum* Sweet (sides of torrents), *Chloranthus brachystachys* Bl., *Ardisia crispa* D.C., *A. Sieboldii* Miq., *Illicium anisatum* L., *Daphniphyllum macropodum* Miq. and *Gilibertia trifida* Mak. The last three are plentiful as shrubs, but they also grow into small trees. Climbing plants are comparatively few, but *Hydrangea petiolaris* S. & Z. is plentiful and climbs to the tops of the tallest trees. *Schizophragma hydrangeoides* S. & Z. is common on old stumps and trunks of low trees, *Stauntonia hexaphylla* Decaisn. is rare and *Rhus orientalis* Schneid., with thick rope-like stems, is fairly common. Ivy (*Hedera japonica* Tobl.) I did not see in the forest depths, but it was frequent on the ascent soon after leaving the savannah. The forest floor and tree trunks support an extraordinary rich Cryptogamic flora; nowhere else, not even on famed Mt. Omei, in western China, have I seen such a wealth of this vegetation. Ferns, especially of the genus Hymenophyllum, in wonderful variety grow on the granite rocks, tree-trunks, dead stumps, and rotting logs and with them Mosses, Liverworts, Lichens and Fungi in endless form and shape. Phanerogamic herbs are scarce, but on boulders in and along the sides of torrents *Astilbe japonica* Miq. abounds. The mountain slopes are very steep and the granite blocks are heaped one upon another in vast confusion. Here and there a yellow, greasy clay is in evidence, but the soil of the forest floor is mainly composed of rotting vegetation. There are no open spaces, but everywhere dense primeval forest. The flora is a wonderful Cryptogamic kingdom with a few low shrubs under a vast evergreen canopy. To me the most interesting and remarkable forest in all Japan is this on Yaku-shima, where the Cryptomeria has its southern home.

In that part of the forest I visited no felling is being done now, and until some special arrangements are made it is next to impossible to get the lumber down to the coast. The wood of fallen trees is made into shingles and carried out on men's backs, but that is all that is being done at present. In old times these forests were known and logs for the pillars and columns of temples were exported to Korea, China and other eastern countries. The Yaku-sugi, as this Cryptomeria is called, is famed throughout Japan and its wood commands a much higher price in the market than that of the same tree from anywhere else in the empire.

From the foregoing description of these forests it will be seen that the Cryptomeria enjoys a rich soil, good drainage and an abundant rainfall. On Yaku-shima it is most abundant on the west and north slopes, where its maximum height is about 40 m. and the average trees are from 30 to 35 m. tall. Most of the oldest trees have the tops broken off and I noticed that occasionally a new leader was formed. The height of the trees, though comparatively low, is remarkably even, and I conclude that strong winds account for it. The average girth of trunk of living trees in these forests is from 6 to 8 m.; the largest I measured were 10 m. in girth. Of dead and rotting stumps I measured several from 16 to 18 m. in girth. The trunk is perfectly straight, buttressed at the base and clean of branches for at least half the height of the tree. The bark is reddish brown, becoming gray where fully exposed, never more than 2.5 cm. thick and seldom as much, shallowly fissured and firm, but eventually peeling in thin narrow flakes. The branches are relatively thin, spread horizontally, seldom exceed 6 m. in length and form a more or less dense, oval crown. The weak, inner branchlets are shed in the same manner as are those of *Sequoia gigantea* Decaisn. Indeed these two trees in appearance and general characteristics strongly resemble one another. The wood of the Cryptomeria on Yaku-shima is fragrant, pale brown, becoming darker and even reddish in the centre of the tree. Often it is beautifully spotted and figured and such wood is especially prized for house decoration and furniture making. That the wood is durable in wet climates is proved by the condition of fallen trees which strew the forest floor. On such trees, which the foresters said had been felled 80 years before, the wood was still perfectly sound a couple of inches below the moss-clad exterior. On fallen stems and decaying butts a younger generation of Cryptomeria is growing from small seedlings to trees 26 m. tall and 6 m. in girth of trunk. The Cryptomeria does not sucker nor sprout from stools, but perpetuates itself only by seeds. In the soil of the forest floor the seedling Cryptomeria does not appear able to survive the struggle with its vigorous competitors, and I saw only on fallen trees and old stumps the Cryptomeria successfully renewing itself unaided by man. On every fallen log and tree stump seedlings of *Trochodendron aralioides* S. & Z. may be seen associated with those of Cryptomeria. The two trees in these forests, it would seem, have a curious predilection for one another. They grow upon the same old dead stump or trunk in close embrace to ripe old age with the Cryptomeria towering above its neighbor and shielding it from wind and storm. On Yaku-shima the Cryptomeria does not form pure forests, being always found growing with other coniferous and dicotyledonous trees, but it is the dominant tree in the forest. Its altitudinal range is from 150 to 1900 m. and it seems to be at its best between 600 and 1200 m.

The Cryptomeria is the most generally useful and popular tree in Japan and has been planted there from time immemorial. Apart from the forests on Yaku-shima, where the evidence is indisputable, it is difficult to say where it is growing in an unquestionably wild state. The Japanese themselves consider it indigenous on certain mountains in Tosa province, Shikoku, and in the northeast corner of Ugo province in extreme northern Hondo, and there is no real reason for questioning this opinion. When in Tosa I did not have time to visit the Cryptomeria forests, but I did visit those in Ugo, and as far as I could judge they are spontaneous. Mr. Elwes, who visited these forests in 1904 and has published an account of them, is also of this opinion. These Ugo forests are situated some 1500 miles north of those on Yaku-shima and about 900 miles north of those in Tosa, so the distribution of the wild forests of this tree is very remarkable. The Ugo forests have been known for over 300 years and formerly were much more extensive than at the present time. In their southern and middle parts they are of pure Cryptomeria, but at the north this tree is mixed with *Thujopsis dolabrata*, var. *Hondai* Mak., and finally it gives way to pure forests of the latter. The total area covered with Cryptomeria is said to be about 25 square miles. In Odate district alone there are some 15,000 acres, and I was told in 1914 that during the past eight years these had yielded lumber to the value of a million dollars annually. The mountain slopes are steep and about 300 m. high and the soil is volcanic ash, grit, pumice, etc. The trees densely crowd the slopes and valleys, average from 30 to 40 m. in height and in girth of trunk from 2 to 3.5 m.; the largest are said to be 60 m. tall and from 5 to 6 m. in girth. The heart-wood is very red and the timber is of exceptionally good quality. At Nagaki-sawa a portion of this forest occupying a valley is preserved by the government as a national monument. A point worthy of note is that the Cryptomeria trees in this northern forest grow taller, but are less in girth than those on Yaku-shima.

The Cryptomeria, or Sugi as it as called in Japan, is the noblest of the Japanese conifers and many famous places in Japan owe much of their charm to stately avenues and groves of this impressive tree. There is a solemnity and a dignity about it, with its perfectly straight trunk towering heavenward and topped with a conical dark green crown, as befits a tree used for enshrouding temples, shrines and sacred places generally. The famous and well-known avenues at Nikko, said to be the humble gift of a Daimyō poor in worldly goods, is the most magnificent of all the monuments raised to the memory of the first Shogun. Although much less well known, there are in different parts of Japan many avenues and groves of Cryptomeria with larger trees than those at Nikko. At the shrines of Ise there are said to be some wonderful old trees, but I did not visit this famous place. The finest tree I saw, and probably the largest in all Japan, is in the grounds of a temple at Sugi, a village in Tosa province, Shikoku, which measures 50 m. in height and 25 m. in girth. It is in perfect health, though the top has been broken off by storms and formerly its height was fully 15 m. more than it is now. At the shrine of Jimmu-Tenno, the first Emperor, at Sano in Osumi province, Kyushu, there is a fine avenue of Cryptomeria planted some 500 years ago, the trees being from 50 to 60 m. tall and from 3 to 6 m. in girth. On the Kasuga-yama at Nara there are trees from 40 to 50 m. tall and from 10 to 12 m. in girth of trunk. In the park and temple grounds, too, at Nara are many magnificent old Cryptomerias. The most impressive avenue I saw is that on Koya-san on the borders of Yamato and Kii provinces, which I was told was planted by one Ogo Shonin, a priest, about 650 years ago. This avenue is more than a mile long and the trees range from 40 to 60 m. in height and from 4 to 8 m. in girth of trunk, and I believe with Elwes that they "surpass in grandeur any other trees planted by man in the world." I have mentioned the curious association of Trochodendron and Cryptomeria, and in these avenues and groves it is a not uncommon thing to see other conifers or even broad-leaved trees growing on living and apparently perfectly sound trees of Cryptomeria. At the entrance to the Futaara Temple at Nikko a tree of *Quercus glandulifera* Bl. a metre in girth may be seen growing from the side of a perfectly healthy Cryptomeria, at about 4 m. from the ground, as if it were a natural branch of the tree. Whatever cavity there was when the acorn was deposited is entirely filled, and above and below the Oak nothing, not even a swelling, is visible. The heart of these trees is often decayed, and I suppose the roots of the Oak have found their way there and then to the ground. That the Cryptomeria can play the part of guest as well as that of host is exemplified at Nara, where at Kasuga shrine a tree of Cryptomeria 25 m. tall and more than 1 m. in girth is growing from the side of a *Juniperus chinensis* L., which is 18 m. tall and 5 m. in girth. In the groves and avenues the Cryptomeria trees were planted very close together, with the result that in time at their base numerous trunks have become fused into one butt of irregular shape, giving the impression of numerous trunks rising from a common stool. The impression is entirely false as the Cryptomeria does not sucker nor stool, nor are adventitious growths developed by it. The Nikko avenue shows this phenomenon remarkably well. Another point of interest is that the planted trees of the Sugi exceed in average height the wild trees in the forests.

The wood of the Sugi, though less valuable than that of the Hinoki (*Chamaecyparis obtusa* S. & Z.), is more generally used, being more plentiful and in consequence cheaper. It is used in house-building generally and is especially valued for making sake-tubs. Wood with particularly fine grain or any odd and curious marking or color is valued for making ceilings, screens, doors and ornamental housefittings. Buried logs of this tree are found in many provinces of Japan, especially Ise, Suruga, Sagami and Rikuzen, and in these the wood is a beautiful dark color and is prized for making valuable furniture and ornaments.

The Cryptomeria is very amenable to cultivation over the greater part of Japan, where it is the most widely planted of all trees for reafforestation. In the government, imperial and private forest-lands it is, and has been from earliest times, planted by the million everywhere from southern Kyushu to the most northern parts of Hondo. Even in Hokkaido attempts to grow this tree have been made in and about Hakodate, but the climate there is evidently too severe. The Sugi takes root readily from cuttings and formerly this mode of propagation was generally employed in forestry work. Branches as thick as the third finger and from 0.3 to 0.5 m. long were put in the ground fairly close together in valley and on hillside during late autumn, winter and early spring, according to climate, and in time these grew and formed new forests. In the government forests to-day this method has been abandoned in favor of seeds, which produce better and more quick-growing trees, but the initial cost is greater than by using cuttings. Apart from its value as a timber-tree or as a tree for avenues and groves, the Cryptomeria is planted in Japanese gardens, where several curious forms have originated. It is very commonly used with great success in making dense thick hedges.

In a general way it may be said that the Cryptomeria does not flourish in Western lands, where few really fine specimens are known, although it was introduced into England in 1842. In eastern North America it is even less happy and is not really hardy as far north as Boston, though it is possible to keep it alive in sheltered spots in this Arboretum. I secured seeds of the Sugi from the Ugo forests and it will be interesting to see if they produce a stock hardier than the trees we now try to cultivate. In the parts of China with which I am familiar the Cryptomeria occurs as an occasional tree planted near temples and over shrines, but neither Henry nor I ever saw it spontaneous in China. Fortune (*Residence among the Chinese*, 189, 277 [1857]) states that it grows wild on the mountains southwest of Ningpo, and Franchet (in *Nouv. Arch. Mus. Paris*, sér. 2, VII. 101 [*Pl. David.* I. 291] [1884]) quotes David to the effect that this tree is wild, but is becoming very rare on the mountains of the Fokien province. Nevertheless, further evidence is desirable before it is accepted as an unquestionable fact that *Cryptomeria japonica* is indigenous in China or anywhere outside of Japan.

The Cryptomeria was first discovered in Japan between 1690 and 1692 by Kaempfer, and in his *Amoenitates Exoticae* (fasc. V. 883 [1712]) he gives a short description of it under its native name of Sugi. In 1701 James Cunningham found it growing on the Chusan Islands, near Shanghai, China, and one of his specimens is figured by Plukenet (*Opera*, IV. t. 386, fig. 3 (*Amalt.* 69) [1705]) under the name of *Cupressus cheusanensis, juniperinus arcuatis foliis*, etc. It was introduced by the Dutch into Java early in the nineteenth century and is said to have been first introduced into Europe by the overland route through Siberia to Petrograd. In 1842 seeds were sent from the Chusan Islands to Kew by Sir Everard Home and plants were raised from them. In 1844 Robert Fortune introduced the tree in quantity to England through seeds sent from Shanghai to the Royal Horticultural Society. This form from China is known in gardens as var. *Fortunei* Hort. (syn. *C. Fortunei* Hooibrenk in *Wien. Jour. Pflanzenk.* 1853, 22) or var. *sinensis* Sieb. (apud Miquel in Siebold & Zuccarini, *Fl. Jap.* II. 52 [1870]) and is less satisfactory in cultivation than the Japanese type. The latter, commonly known in gardens as var. *Lobbii* Carr., was sent to the Buitenzorg Botanic Garden, Java, by von Siebold during his residence in Japan and from Buitenzorg Thomas Lobb sent it to Messrs. Veitch about 1845–46, and the finest Cryptomeria trees in cultivation are of this form.

As already mentioned a number of varieties and forms of Cryptomeria have originated in Japan; the most distinct of these is the var. *elegans* Mast. (in *Jour. Linn. Soc.* XVIII. 497 [1881]), which was introduced into England by John Gould Veitch in 1861 and into this country by Dr. George R. Hall in 1862. This variety has linear, acuminate, spreading or falcately curved leaves and short, thin horizontal branches and branchlets decurved at the tip. When young the foliage is bright green, but in the autumn and winter it changes to bronzy red and the trees are then singularly handsome. I saw many of these plants in Japan and in parts of Kyushu it is used as a hedge plant, but I could learn nothing of its origin. Siebold says it came from China, but this I consider very doubtful. It was sent from Japan to Buitenzorg by von Siebold sometime between 1826 and 1830. There is in cultivation a dwarf form known as *elegans nana* Hort. There are also in gardens dwarf, pendulous, white and yellow variegated and otherwise abnormal forms of the typical *C. japonica*, including one (var. *araucarioides* Hort. apud Carrière, *Traité Conif.* ed. 2, 193 [1867]) with long, pendulous, very remote branchlets and deflexed branches.

Subfam. CUPRESSEAE Lindl.

THUJOPSIS S. & Z.

THUJOPSIS DOLABRATA Siebold & Zuccarini, *Fl. Jap.* II. 34, t. 119, 120 (1842). — Lindley in *Gard. Chron.* 1855, 241, fig. — J. G. Veitch in *Gard. Chron.* 1862, 309. — Franchet & Savatier, *Enum. Pl. Jap.* I. 469 (1875). — Veitch, *Man. Conif.* 265, t. (1881). — Sargent, *Forest Fl. Jap.* 72 (1894). — Shirasawa, *Icon. Ess. For. Jap.* I. 27. t. 11, fig. 1–17 (1900). — Matsumura, *Ind. Pl. Jap.* II. pt. 2, 19 (1905). — Miyoshi, *Atlas Jap. Veget.* pt. V. 4, t. 37 (1906). — Elwes & Henry, *Trees Gr. Brit. & Irel.* II. 202 (1907). — Beissner, *Handb. Nadelh.* ed. 2, 486, fig. 119, 120 (1909).

Thuja dolabrata Linnaeus f., *Suppl.* 420 (1781). — Thunberg, *Fl. Jap.* 266 (1784). — D. Don in Lambert, *Descr. Pinus*, II. append. 2, t. 1 (1824). — Masters in *Jour. Linn. Soc.* XVIII. 486 (1881); in *Gard. Chron.* n. ser. XVIII. 556, fig. 95 (1882). — Kent in Veitch, *Man. Conif.* ed. 2, 236, t. (1900).
Dolophyllum sp. Salisbury in *Jour. Sci. & Arts*, II. 313 (1817).
Platycladus dolabrata, Spach, *Hist. Vég.* XI. 337 (1842).
Libocedrus Dolobrata Nelson, *Pinac.* 65 (1866).
Thujopsis dolabrata, var. *australis* Henry in Elwes & Henry, *Trees Gr. Brit. & Irel.* II. 202 (1907).

I saw this tree growing wild near Tōge station at about 800 m. altitude on the borders of Uzen and Iwashiro provinces, around Yumoto in the Nikko region and in the valley of the Kiso-gawa. Near Tōge there were only a few scrubby trees and this appears to be the northern limit of its range. Around Lake Yumoto, between 1600 and 1800 m. altitude, it grows in dense forests of *Tsuga diversifolia* Mast., *Abies homolepis* S. & Z. and *Thuja Standishii* Carr., among and on humus-clad boulders and on the edges of Sphagnum swamps. In the region drained by the Kiso-gawa it grows on Ena-san and other mountains in Mino province and also on those in southern Shinano, between 1100 and 1800 m. altitude, in dense forests mixed with *Sciadopitys verticillata* S. & Z., *Thuja Standishii* Carr., *Pinus parviflora* S. & Z. and the two species of Chamaecyparis; occasionally it forms pure stands. In Kyushu it is reported by forestry officials from one isolated locality on the mountains south from Oita in Bungo province. It is much grown in parks and gardens in the milder parts of Japan, and round Gotemba and elsewhere on the lower slopes of Fuji-san it is a common hedge plant.

I saw no trees of the typical species comparable in size and beauty with those of its northern variety *Hondai* Mak. Of the type the trees were all small, averaging from 10 to 16 m. in height and from 1 to 1.5 m. in girth of trunk, which is usually curved at the base. In habit, in general appearance and in the character of the wood the type is similar to its variety, but the cones are broadly ovoid, from 1.2 to 1.5 cm. long, and the cone-scales have a prominent, triangular umbo which is pointed and often hooked.

Thujopsis dolabrata is a favorite plant in gardens in Japan, where several dwarf, variegated and otherwise abnormal forms have originated. In eastern North America it has not proved very successful in cultivation and in the neighborhood of Boston it is not hardy, but on the estate of William Minot at Mattapoiset, Cape Cod, there are fine specimens 8 m. tall. Those who wish to cultivate this conifer should bear in mind that it is an inhabitant of moist, dense forests, where even as an adult tree it is shaded by its more lofty neighbors, Hemlock or Fir. In Japan this Thujopsis is generally called Hiba, but it is also known as Asunaro, and in Kiso, where it is counted among the five famous trees, it is called Asuhi.

This tree was first made known to us by Kaemper, who mentions it as "a kind of Finoki" in his *Amoenitates Exoticae* (fasc. V. 884 [1712]), and his specimen was figured by Lambert. Like the Sciadopitys it was introduced by the Dutch to Java at an early date, and was sent to the Botanic Garden, Leyden, in 1853. From Buitenzorg Thomas Lobb sent a plant to Messrs. Veitch in 1853. This plant died soon after its arrival, but in 1859 Captain Fortescue, R.N., successfully introduced a plant from Japan, and descendants of this plant are said to be still growing at Castlehill, Devonshire. It was introduced into this country in 1861 by Dr. George R. Hall, who sent plants by Mr. F. Gordon Dexter to Francis Parkman, the historian, who lived at Jamaica Plain, Massachusetts. In the same year John Gould Veitch and Robert Fortune sent seeds from Japan to England, and from these many plants were raised and distributed.

Of the garden forms the var. *nana* Carrière (*Traité Conif.* 111 [1855], syn. *T. laetevirens* Lindley in *Gard. Chron.* 1862, 428) is perhaps the most useful. It was introduced into England by John Gould Veitch in 1861. A variety of *T. dolabrata* is

THUJOPSIS DOLABRATA, var. HONDAI Makino in *Tokyo Bot. Mag.* XV. 104 (1901). — Elwes & Henry, *Trees Gr. Brit. & Irel.* II. 202 (1907).

Thujopsis dolabrata Elwes & Henry, *Trees Gr. Brit. & Irel.* I. t. 60 (not Siebold & Zuccarini) (1906).

Thujopsis Hondai Henry in Elwes & Henry, *Trees Gr. Brit. & Irel.* II. 202 (1907).

This variety (Plates L and LI), which is well distinguished by its larger and globose cones, is the northern form of the species. I met with it first in the ascent of Adzuma-san, on the borders of Iwashiro and Uzen provinces, between 1100 and 1600 m. altitude. In the same neighborhood, at 800 m. altitude and near Tōge station, I collected the type. This region would appear to be the dividing line, for north of it I saw the variety only and south of it only the typical species. On Adzuma the var. *Hondai* grows on steep, rocky slopes mixed with *Thuja Standishii* Carr., *Tsuga diversifolia* Mast., *Pinus parviflora* S. & Z. and such broad-leaved trees as *Fagus Sieboldii* Endl., *Betula Ermanii* Cham., *B. corylifolia* Regel and *Quercus mongolica*, var. *grosseserrata* Rehd. & Wils., but none of the Thujopsis trees here are large. On Chokai-san, in Ugo province, this tree does not appear to be very common, but on the lower, sheltered northern and northwesterly slopes of Hayachine-san, in Rikuchu province, it is plentiful. Here in rich moist forests at 800 to 1000 m. altitude I saw trees 33 m. tall with trunks 4 m. in girth, growing with *Tsuga diversifolia* Mast., *Abies Mariesii* Mast., *Pinus parviflora* S. & Z., *Aesculus turbinata* Bl., *Pterocarya rhoifolia* S. & Z., *Cercidiphyllum japonicum* S. & Z. and *Betula Ermanii* Cham. In Mutsu, the most northern province of Hondo, this Thujopsis is common in several districts from sea-level to 600 m. altitude and forms a magnificent and almost pure forest. This like that of Akita belongs to the state and with the crown forest of Kiso constitutes the three famous forests of Japan. I paid a visit to Yake-yama (Fire Mountain), a series of sandstone ridges not more than 500 m. above sea-level and some nine miles north from Aomori. Here the forest, which is pure Thujopsis, is very extensive and has been known for more than two hundred years. The trees grow thickly together and from the near distance singularly resemble those of moderately young Cryptomeria, although the crown is more oval and less tapering. The trees average from 18 to 23 m. in height and in girth of trunk from 1.3 m. to 2.5 m. None I saw in this forest exceeded these dimensions, but a forestry officer informed me that the maximum height was about 30 m. and 4.5 m. in girth of trunk. The trunk is often slightly recumbent at the base and occasionally forked quite low down. The bark is thin, reddish brown becoming pale gray when old and on exposed trees; it splits transversely and flakes upward into long, thin, narrow strips. The branches are very numerous and crowded, rather short and slender, and spread horizontally or they may be curved downward. The crown is oval and the branches extend well down the trunk; the inner, weak branchlets are shed in the same manner as those of Cryptomeria. The cone is globose, from 1.5 to 1.8 cm. high, and the umbo is reduced to a thin narrow ridge, or to a short mucro. The wood is soft, fragrant, not resinous, yellowish in color and the heart is frequently decayed; it is easily worked and very durable, and is valued for railway-ties, in bridge and conduit building and for such purposes it lasts from 12 to 15 years. It is useless for boards and thin planks as it very readily cracks.

The young trees when growing freely resemble those of *Chamaecyparis obtusa* S. & Z., of the same age, but more usually the young Thujopsis plants have no particular shape but sprawl over the forest floor and form a dense undergrowth about 1 m. high. With them on Yake-yama as undergrowth *Ilex rugosa* Schmidt, *Daphniphyllum humile* Maxim. and *Aucuba japonica* Thunb. are also found in some quantity. At Shimokita, some 35 miles north of Aomori, there is said to be an area of some 25,000 acres where this Thujopsis grows mixed with *Fagus Sieboldii* Endl. and *Quercus mongolica*, var. *grosseserrata* Rehd. & Wils. On the borders of southern Mutsu and northeast Ugo provinces this Thujopsis grows with *Cryptomeria japonica* D. Don.

The forestry officials at Aomori told me that this Thujopsis grows best from cuttings, not from seeds. Shoots taken from free-growing trees and about as thick as the little finger if inserted in soil in May will form roots in a month and are ready for planting in permanent positions on the mountain-sides at the end of a year. The trees grow slowly and the growth is often strongly excentric. On a piece of this wood 15 cm. across I counted 103 annual rings. It is worthy of mention that many trees have a nearly smooth red-brown bark which makes the trunk look distinct. The forestry officers at Aomori are doubtful if there are not two forms of the var. *Hondai*. Both grow together; the cones are identical, and I could discover no difference between them except in the appearance of the bark.

I collected seeds of the var. *Hondai* and young plants raised from them are growing freely in this Arboretum. It is too early as yet to form any opinion, but I am hopeful that this northern variety will prove hardy here. The Japanese name for this tree is Hinoki-asunaro.

THUJA L.

Five species of this genus are known, two in North America and three in eastern Asia. Of the American species *T. occidentalis* L. is widely distributed from Nova Scotia and New Brunswick northwestward to the mouth of the Saskatchewan River and southward over a large area to southern Virginia and northeastern Tennessee. The other (*T. plicata* D. Don) is found from Yas Bay in Alaska southward along the coast ranges to Mendocino County, California, and eastward to the western slopes of the mountains of Idaho and of northern Montana. Of the Asiatic species *T. orientalis* L., which differs markedly in its wingless seed, is much planted in China generally and its range as a wild plant is not properly understood. It is known to be indigenous in Korea, Mandshuria and northeastern China and may have a wider range in that country. The second Chinese species, *T. sutchuenensis* Franch, is very imperfectly known and only from northeastern Szech'uan. The Japanese species also grows in Korea.

THUJA STANDISHII Carr.

PLATES LII AND LIII

THUJA STANDISHII Carrière, *Traité Conif.* ed. 2, 108 (1867). — Gordon, *Pinet.* ed. 2, 408 (1875). — Masters in *Gard. Chron.* n. ser. X. 397 (1878); XIII. 589, fig. 102 (1880). — Veitch, *Man. Conif.* 263 (1881). — Sargent, *Silva N. Am.* X. 124 in a note (1896). — Beissner, *Handb. Nadelh.* ed. 2, 515 (1909). — Nakai in *Jour. Coll. Sci. Tokyo*, XXXI. 382 (*Fl. Kor.* pt. 2) (1911).

Thuiopsis? Standishi Gordon, *Pinet.* suppl. 100 (1862). — Bailly in *Rev. Hort.* 1896, 160, t.

Thuja japonica Maximowicz in *Bull. Acad. Sci. St. Pétersbourg*, sér. 3, X. 490 (1866); in *Mél. Biol.* VI. 26 (1866). — Masters in *Jour. Linn. Soc.* XVIII. 486 (1881); in *Gard. Chron.* ser. 3, XXI. 258, fig. 87 (1897). — Sargent, *Forest Fl. Jap.* 72 (1894). —

Kent in Veitch, *Man. Conif.* ed. 2, 244 (1900). — Shirasawa, *Icon. Ess. For. Jap.*
I. 28, t. 11, fig. 18–34 (1900). — Komarov in *Act. Hort. Petrop.* XX. 206 (*Fl. Mandsh.* I.) (1901). — Matsumura, *Ind. Pl. Jap.* II. pt. 1, 18 (1905). — Elwes & Henry, *Trees Gr. Brit. & Irel.* I. 195 (1906).

Thuya gigantea Parlatore in De Candolle, *Prodr.* XVI. pt. 2, 457 (as to the Japanese plant, not Nuttall) (1868).

Thuya gigantea, var. *Japonica* Franchet & Savatier, *Enum. Pl. Jap.* I. 469 (1875).

The only place where I saw this tree wild in quantity was in the ascent of Adzuma-san from Tōge on the borders of Uzen and Iwashiro provinces. There on steep slopes beyond the hot springs between 1000 and 1300 m. altitude it is common growing with *Thujopsis dolabrata*, var. *Hondai* Mak., *Tsuga diversifolia* Mast., *Pinus parviflora* S. & Z. and such broad-leaved trees as *Betula Ermanii* Cham., *B. corylifolia* Regel, *Fagus Sieboldii* Endl. and *Quercus mongolica*, var. *grosseserrata* Rehd. & Wils., but all the Thuja trees are small. Around Yumoto, in the Nikko region, between 1800 and 2300 m. altitude it grows scattered through mixed forests with *Tsuga diversifolia* Mast., *Abies homolepis* S. & Z., *Larix Kaempferi* Sarg., *Picea jezoënsis* Carr., *Thujopsis dolabrata* S. & Z. and various broad-leaved trees principally Birches. I saw it wild nowhere else, but it is known from the slopes of the high mountains in Kaga, Hida and Shinano provinces in central Hondo. Komarov and Nakai say that it is wild in northern Korea. In the valley of the Kiso-gawa it is called the Nezu and in former days, when all the forests of Kiso were owned by the Daimyō of Owari, stringent forestry laws were enforced; and although ordinary trees might be cut by any one the Nezu, Hinoki (*Chamaecyparis obtusa* S. & Z.), Sawara (*C. pisifera* S. & Z.), Asuhi (*Thujopsis dolabrata* S. & Z.) and the Keaki (*Zelkova serrata* Mak.) might not have so much as a twig broken off, armed foresters being placed to shoot all wood-poachers. Any peasant found in possession of a utensil made of one of these five forbidden kinds of wood was arrested. This paternal despotism had at least the effect of producing splendid forests. Immense havoc was done during the turmoil which ushered in the new régime and only since about 1890 has serious attention again been turned to forest preservation.

The largest tree of the Japanese Thuja I saw was in the forests beyond Yumoto village and was about 15 m. tall with a short trunk 3.5 m. in girth. The average trees are from 12 to 16 m. tall and from 1.5 to 2.6 m. in girth of trunk. The trunk is short and buttressed and usually divides a few feet from the ground into two or several thick stems. The lateral branches are slender and very numerous, spread horizontally and are upturned at the ends and form a dense, pyramidal crown. The bark is thin, smooth and papery, reddish brown with scattered pale gray blotches of irregular size. The foliage is pale green and the tree is attractive and ornamental. The fruit is narrow-ovoid, 1 cm. long and ascending. The wood is pale brown, light and of good quality and is cut into thin boards and used for ceilings and other interior work; it also makes durable shingles. The tree, however, is now too rare to be of any great economic value.

Like the Chamaecyparis and Thujopsis the Japanese Thuja delights in moist rocky slopes and a northerly exposure. It is rare in cultivation in eastern North America, where it is quite hardy as far north at least as Boston. Other Japanese names for this tree are Kurobi, Nezuko and Gorō-hiba.

Thuja Standishii was discovered in 1860 in the gardens of Tokyo by Robert Fortune, who sent seeds to the nursery of Mr. Standish at Ascot, England. A year or so later it was found in the same gardens by C. Maximowicz. In the Hunnewell Pinetum there is a handsome specimen of this Thuja planted in 1874 and now 13 m. tall.

CHAMAECYPARIS Spach

This genus is confined to the Atlantic and Pacific coast regions of North America and to Formosa and Japan. Six species are now recognized; one (*C. thyoides* Britt.) is confined to eastern North America and two (*C. nootkatensis* Lamb. and *C. Lawsoniana* A. Murr.) to western North America. In Formosa one species (*C. formosensis* Matsum.) is endemic and a form of the Japanese *C. obtusa* S. & Z. also grows wild there. The two Japanese species have in Japan given rise to many abnormal forms and these are now familiar garden plants. These forms, many of them dwarfs, are apt to give a wrong impression of the size to which the parent trees and other species of this genus grow; it is well to remember that *C. Lawsoniana* A. Murr. exceeds 60 m. in height, that the two Japanese species are often over 50 m. high and that *C. formosensis* Matsum. grows 65 m. tall with a trunk 20 m. in girth and exceeds in size all other conifers indigenous in the Old World north of the Equator, its only rival being *Cryptomeria japonica* D. Don.

KEY TO THE JAPANESE SPECIES

Leaves obtuse, not glandular; cone about 1 cm. in diameter; seeds from 1 to 5 on each scale . . . . C. OBTUSA.

Leaves acuminate, obscurely glandular; cone about 0.7 cm. in diameter; seeds from 1 to 2 on each scale . . . . C. PISIFERA.

CHAMAECYPARIS OBTUSA S. & Z.

PLATES LIV AND LV

CHAMAECYPARIS OBTUSA Siebold & Zuccarini apud Endlicher, *Syn. Conif.* 63 (1847). — Carrière, *Traité Conif.* 136 (1855). — Franchet & Savatier, *Enum. Pl. Jap.* I. 471 (1875). — Sargent, *Forest Fl. Jap.* 73 (1894). — Shirasawa, *Icon. Ess. For. Jap.* I. 25, t. 10, fig. 17–32 (1900). — Matsumura, *Ind. Pl. Jap.* II. pt. 1, 7 (1905). — Mayr, *Fremdl. Wald- u. Parkb.* 277, t. 5, fig. 4 (1906). — Beissner, *Handb. Nadelh.* ed. 2, 554, fig. 141 (1909). — Pardé, *Ill. Conif.* t. 134, fig. 1 a–15 (1913).

> *Retinispora obtusa* Siebold & Zuccarini *Fl. Jap.* II. 38, t. 121 (1844). — Lindley in *Gard. Chron.* 1861, 265.
>
> *Chamaepeuce obtusa* Zuccarini ex Gordon, *Pinet.* suppl. 93 (as a synonym) (1862).
>
> *Retinispora Fusinoki* Zuccarini ex Gordon, *Pinet.* suppl. 93 (as a synonym) (1862).
>
> *Cupressus obtusa* K. Koch, *Dendr.* II. pt. 2, 168 (1873). — Sargent, *Silva N. Am.* X. 98 in a note (1896). — Masters in *Jour. Linn. Soc.* XXXI. 355 (1896). — Kent in Veitch, *Man. Conif.* ed. 2, 220, fig. 64 (1900). — Elwes & Henry, *Trees Gr. Brit. & Irel.* V. 1185, t. 303, 304 (1910). — Clinton-Baker, *Ill. Conif.* III. 52, fig. (1913).
>
> *Retinospora obtusa* Gordon, *Pinet.* ed. 2, 367 (1875). — Masters in *Gard. Chron.* n. ser. V. 235, fig. 41 (1876). — Veitch. *Man. Conif.* 245, fig. 56 (1881).
>
> *Thuya obtusa* Masters in *Jour. Linn. Soc.* XVIII. 491, fig. 4 (1881).

I did not see this tree in a wild state north of the Kiso-gawa in Mino and Shinano provinces, where it grows in mixed forests between 600 and 1300 m. above the sea with *Pinus densiflora* S. & Z., *P. parviflora* S. & Z., *Tsuga Sieboldii* Carr., *Sciadopitys verticillata* S. & Z., *Abies firma* S. & Z., *Chamaecyparis pisifera* S. & Z. and such broad-leaved trees as *Aesculus turbinata* Bl., *Acanthopanax sciadophylloides* Fr. & Sav., *Acer rufinerve* S. & Z., *Magnolia obovata* Thunb. and occasional trees of *Quercus mongolica*, var. *grosse-serrata* Rehd. & Wils. On the upper slopes of Koya-san it is the dominant tree in the forests. In Tosa province, Shikoku, I met with it at Nishinokawa in mixed forests with *Pseudotsuga japonica* Beissn., where *Tsuga Sieboldii* Carr. is the principal tree; also on Shiraga-yama between 1000 and 1500 m. altitude with *Tsuga Sieboldii* Carr., *Pinus parviflora* S. & Z., *Abies firma* S. & Z. and broad-leaved trees such as *Stewartia monadelpha* S. & Z., *Magnolia obovata* Thunb. and *Acer palmatum* Thunb. I also collected it on Yaku-shima in the Cryptomeria forests at about 1300 m. altitude, where, however, it is rare. Very probably it is more or less common on the slopes of all the older mountains from the region of the Kiso-gawa in central Hondo southward, but I never met with it on those of active, quiescent or recently extinct volcanoes. It would appear also to grow in Formosa. Dr. Hayata showed me copious material from that island and I could detect no real difference between it and specimens collected in Japan. Nevertheless, until more is known concerning the Formosan tree it is best to consider it distinct as Hayata has done.[1]

As I saw it in Japan *Chamaecyparis obtusa* delights in cool rocky slopes and prefers a northerly aspect and at its best grows 50 m. tall with a trunk from 5 to 6 m. in girth. But the average size of the tree in the forests is from 27 to 35 m. in height, and from 2.5 to 4 m. in girth of trunk. The trunk is straight, more or less buttressed at the base, and clean of branches for from a third to a half of the height of the tree. The branches are slender, horizontally and rather widely spreading, and form a more or less oval crown which is rounded at the summit; the branchlets are more or less pendulous. The bark is smooth, red-brown (grayish when much exposed) and peels off in long thin sheets. This bark is highly valued for roofing purposes, since it withstands the extremes of heat and damp and is very durable. In the old days the palaces of the Emperor and of many feudal princes and the Shinto temples were mainly built of the wood of this tree and always roofed with its bark. The wood is white to straw-color and often slightly pinkish, and when green has a strong rancid smell which persists for a long time; it is straight-grained, light, strong and tough, remarkably free from knots and resin and has a lustrous surface which takes lacquer remarkably well. It is used for the frames of temples, for panels, ceilings and interior finishing of the best houses and for many other purposes. The Japanese consider this wood superior to that of any other of their conifers. On this account the tree is being much used in Japan in reafforestation work and for this purpose it is raised from seeds. Being more exacting in the matter of soil and situation than the only slightly less valuable Cryptomeria, this Chamaecyparis is given the best sites and is planted in annually increasing numbers in all favorable places from southern Kyushu and Shikoku to northern Hondo, where I saw it thriving near Aomori.

The Hinoki, as this tree is called in Japan, is sacred among the disciples of the Shinto faith, and it is planted in the courtyards and in the neighborhood of Shinto and Buddhist temples, where often, as at Mitsumine in Musashi province, fine specimens may be seen. The tree has long been a great favorite in Japanese gardens where dwarf, yellow-leaved variegated and other abnormal forms have originated. In eastern North America it is hardy as far north as Halifax in Nova Scotia. On the estate of the late Dr. George R. Hall, there are trees from 16 to 18 m. tall, with trunks a metre in girth. Unless planted close together the tendency is for

---

[1] *C. obtusa*, f. *formosana* Hayata in *Jour. Coll. Sci. Tokyo*, XXV. 208 (1908).

the lower branches to become stout and wide-spreading and to retard the tree's growth in height. It is a very ornamental tree, but grows rather slowly and resents the summer droughts of New England.

Chamaecyparis obtusa was introduced into England by John Gould Veitch in 1861, and into this country by Dr. George R. Hall in 1862. Of the garden forms the var. *nana* Carrière (*Traité Conif.* ed. 2, 131 [1867]) is perhaps the best and one of the handsomest of all dwarf conifers. There is also a yellow-leaved form known as *nana aurea* Hort. Of the tall-growing yellow-leaved forms one of the best is known in gardens as *gracilis aurea* Hort.

CHAMAECYPARIS PISIFERA S. & Z.

PLATES LVI AND LVII

CHAMAECYPARIS PISIFERA Siebold & Zuccarini apud Endlicher, *Syn. Conif.* 64 (1847). — Carrière, *Traité Conif.* 138 (1855). — Franchet & Savatier, *Enum. Pl. Jap.* I. 470 (1875). — Sargent, *Forest Fl. Jap.* 73 (1894). — Shirasawa, *Icon. Ess. For. Jap.* I. 26, t. 10, fig. 1-16 (1900). — Matsumura, *Ind. Pl. Jap.* II. pt. 1, 8 (1905). — Mayr, *Fremdl. Wald- u. Parkb.* 276, t. 6, fig. 1 (1906). — Beissner, *Handb. Nadelh.* ed. 2, 564, fig. 143 (1909). — Pardé, *Ill. Conif.* t. 134, fig. 16-25 (1913).

Retinispora pisifera Siebold & Zuccarini, *Fl. Jap.* II. 39, t. 122 (1844). — Lindley in *Gard. Chron.* 1865, 265.
Cupressus pisifera K. Koch, *Dendr.* II. pt. 2, 170 (1873). — Sargent, *Silva N. Am.* 99 in a note (1896). — Masters in *Jour. Linn. Soc.* XXXI. 355 (1896). — Kent in Veitch, *Man. Conif.* ed. 2, 224, fig. 67 (1900). — Elwes & Henry, *Trees Gr. Brit. & Irel.* V. 1190, t. 305 (1910). — Clinton-Baker, *Ill. Conif.* III. 51, fig. (1913).
Retinospora pisifera Gordon, *Pinet.* ed. 2, 369 (1875). — Masters in *Gard. Chron.* n. ser. V. 235, fig. 44 (1876).
Thuya pisifera Masters in *Jour. Linn. Soc.* XVIII. 489, fig. 1 (1881).

In the temple grounds of Japan this species is as much and as widely planted as its relative *C. obtusa* S. & Z., but as a wild tree its distribution appears to be more limited. I met with it only in the valley of the Kiso-gawa in Mino and Shinano provinces, and around the hot springs at the foot of the ascent of Tsubakura-dake in the more northern part of Shinano. It is very common on the moist, rocky slopes of the low mountains which surround Mt. Ontake on the Otake-Kurasawa side and it was here that I saw the finest specimens of this tree. In these regions it is much more plentiful than *C. obtusa* S. & Z. with which it grows. The finest trees I saw of *C. pisifera* were nearly 50 m. tall with trunks 5 m. in girth and strongly buttressed at the base. The trunk is mast-like and free of branches for from a third to a half the height of the tree. The branches are shorter than those of *C. obtusa* S. & Z., spread horizontally, are somewhat inclined upward near their extremities and form a narrow pyramidal or spire-like crown. The bark is indistinguishable from that of *C. obtusa* and the wood has the same peculiar rancid smell, but it is brownish in color and though of good quality and employed for the same purposes is considered inferior to that of *C. obtusa* S. & Z.

In Japan *C. pisifera* is known as the Sawara and has long been cultivated in gardens and it is a common tree in temple grounds, but I did not see it anywhere in Japan used in reafforestation work. In eastern North America this Chamaecyparis is as hardy as *C. obtusa* S. & Z., but, although it grows more rapidly than the latter, it is decidedly less ornamental and is inclined to become scrawny at an early age. It was introduced into England in 1861 by John Gould Veitch and into this country by Dr. George R. Hall, in 1862. Of the numerous varieties and forms of garden origin var. *plumosa* Beissner (*Handb. Nadelh.* 87 (1891), which is a small tree, conical in outline, with plumose branchlets, is very distinct. In the Hunnewell Pinetum there are specimens of this variety 13 m. tall. Another well-marked form is var. *squarrosa* Beissner and Hochstetter (in *Gartenfl.* XXIX. 364 (1880). This forms a large bush or bushy tree of irregular outline with very numerous spreading branchlets and bluish white acicular leaves in opposite pairs. In the Hunnewell Pinetum there is a good specimen of this plant fully 13 m. tall. A third form widely known in gardens is var. *filifera* Hort. (apud Beissner, *Handb. Nadelh.* 90, fig. 23, 24 [1891]), which forms a large bush and has long, slender, pendent whiplike branches and branchlets. There are also yellow-leaved and variegated forms of these varieties and many other more or less abnormal forms in cultivation; indeed, *C. pisifera* has been exceptionally prolific in varieties, and numerous forms of this species are grown in many gardens. Some of these are seminal and others vegetative sports and they are perpetuated by cuttings and by grafting. Into Europe the earliest known kinds were introduced in 1861 by John Gould Veitch and into this country in 1862 by Dr. George R. Hall.

JUNIPERUS L.

This genus is widely scattered over the Northern Hemisphere from the Arctic Circle to the highlands of Mexico, Lower California and the West Indies in the New World, and to the Azores and Canary Islands, northern Africa, Abyssinia, the mountains of tropical East Africa, the Himalayas, China and Formosa in the Old World. Some 45 species and several well-marked geographical varieties are recognized. One species (*J. communis* L.) is circumpolar. Seventeen species are indigenous in North America and five species in Japan, of which two are probably endemic.

KEY TO THE JAPANESE SPECIES

Leaves always acicular, spreading in whorls of threes, jointed at the base; fruit smooth or nearly so, marked at the apex by three radiating lines or furrows.
　Leaves with one white stomatic band above.
　　Leaves concave above; branches ascending, ascending-spreading or prostrate.
　　　　　　　　　　　　　　　　　　　　　　　　　　　　J. COMMUNIS.
　　Leaves sulcate above.
　　　Branches ascending or ascending-spreading; fruit from 6 to 8 mm. in diameter.
　　　　　　　　　　　　　　　　　　　　　　　　　　　　J. RIGIDA.
　　　Branches prostrate; fruit from 7 to 12 mm. in diameter . . . . . J. CONFERTA.
　Leaves with two stomatic bands above, lower surface bluish, spotted with white; branchlets glaucous-white on the edges of the pulvini . . . . . J. PROCUMBENS.
Leaves both acicular and scale-like, the acicular in pairs or ternate; branches ascending, ascending-spreading or prostrate; fruit tuberculate, brown; seeds from 1 to 5.
　　　　　　　　　　　　　　　　　　　　　　　　　　　　J. CHINENSIS.

JUNIPERUS COMMUNIS L.

JUNIPERUS COMMUNIS Linnaeus, *Spec.* 1040 (1753). — Pallas, *Fl. Ross.* I. pt. 2, 12, t. 54, fig. b, c (1788). — Ledebour, *Fl. Ross.* III. 684 (1850). — Turczaninow in *Bull. Soc. Nat. Mosc.* XXVII. 417 (1854); *Fl. Baical.-Dahur.* II. 144 (1857). —

Maximowicz in *Mém. Sav. Étr. Acad. Sci. St. Pétersbourg*, IX. 264 (*Prim. Fl. Amur.*) (1859). — Fr. Schmidt in *Mém. Acad. Sci. St. Pétersbourg*, sér. 7, XII. no. 2, 178 (*Reis. Amur. Sachal.*) (1868). — Masters in *Jour. Linn. Soc.* XVIII. 497 (1881). — Hooker f., *Fl. Brit. Ind.* V. 646 (1888). — Miyabe in *Mem. Boston Soc. Nat. Hist.* IV. 260 (*Fl. Kurile Isl.*) (1891). — Sargent, *Silva N. Am.* X. 75, t. 516, fig. 1-11 (1896). — Matsumura, *Ind. Pl. Jap.* II. pt. 1, 10 (1905). — Elwes & Henry, *Trees Gr. Brit. & Irel.* VI. 1400, t. 348 (1912).

Juniperus difformis Gilibert, *Exercit. Phyt.* II. 216 (1792).
Juniperus borealis Salisbury, *Prodr.* 397 (1796).
Juniperus communis, a erecta Pursh, *Fl. Am. Sept.* II. 646 (1814).
Juniperus communis, a vulgaris Endlicher, *Syn. Conif.* 15 (1847).
Juniperus communis, β hispanica Endlicher l. c. (1847).

I did not meet with this Juniper in my travels in the Orient, but have before me two specimens collected in Saghalien by Père Faurie. These have straight or slightly curved, spreading leaves and differ in no particular from material of typical *J. communis* from North America or Europe. Very little is known concerning the distribution of this plant in eastern Asia where apparently it is not common. It is known from Kitami province, Hokkaido, but is unknown in the other islands of Japan and in China. From Korea I have a specimen collected at the foot of Paiktu-san by Dr. T. Nakai in August 1914 and in this Arboretum there are growing shapely plants from 1 to 1.2 m. high raised from seeds sent from that country by T. Uciyama in 1900. A variety of this species is

JUNIPERUS COMMUNIS, var. MONTANA Aiton, *Hort. Kew.* III. 414 (1788). — Spach in *Ann. Sci. Nat.* sér. 2, XVI. 290 (1841). — Rehder in Bailey, *Stand. Cycl. Hort.* III. 1727 (1915).

Juniperus communis, γ Linnaeus, *Spec.* 1040 (1753).
Juniperus communis, β Lamarck, *Encycl. Méth. Bot.* II. 625 (1786).
Juniperus sibirica Burgsdorf, *Anleit.* II. 124 (1787).
Juniperus canadensis Burgsdorf, l. c. (1787).
Juniperus communis, var. Pallas, *Fl. Ross.* I. pt. 2, 12, t. 54, fig. a (1788).
Juniperus nana Willdenow, *Berl. Baumz.* 159 (1796). — Ledebour, *Fl. Ross.* III. 683 (1850). — Turczaninow in *Bull. Soc. Nat. Mosc.* XXVII. 418 (1854); *Fl. Baical.-Dahur.* II. 145 (1857). — Miyabe & Miyake, *Fl. Saghal.* 593 (1915).
Juniperus communis, var. saxatilis Willdenow, *Berl. Baumz.* 159 (as a synonym) (1796).
Juniperus communis, β alpina Wahlenberg, *Fl. Lapp.* 276 (1812).
Juniperus communis, var. nana Baumgarten, *Enum. Stirp. Transsylv.* II. 308 (1819). — Elwes & Henry, *Trees Gr. Brit. & Irel.* VI. 1401 (1912).
Juniperus alpina S. F. Gray, *Nat. Arr. Brit. Pl.* II. 226 (1821).
Juniperus dealbata Hort. ex Gordon in *Gard. Chron.* 1842, 652 (as a synonym, not Loudon).
Juniperus nana, A montana Endlicher, *Syn. Conif.* 14 (1847).
Juniperus nana, B alpina Endlicher, l. c. (1847).
Juniperus pygmaea K. Koch in *Linnaea*, XXII. 302 (1849).
Juniperus communis, var. Sibirica Rydberg in *Contrib. U. S. Nat. Herb.* III. 533 (1896). — Sargent, *Silva N. Am.* X. 76 in a note, t. 516, fig. 12 (1896).

The only specimen of this Juniper from the Japanese Empire that I have seen is Faurie's No. 284, collected at Korsakof, Saghalien, in June 1908. This bears male flowers and the leaves are scarcely as broad as is usual in this variety, but agree exactly with those on specimens in this herbarium from Newfoundland.

Willdenow and many later botanists cite *J. communis*, var. *saxatilis* Pallas as a name for this Juniper, but Pallas did not make the combination attributed to him, and this leaves Aiton's name the oldest. Another variety is

JUNIPERUS COMMUNIS, var. NIPPONICA Wils. n. var.

Juniperus nipponica Maximowicz in *Bull. Acad. Sci. St. Pétersbourg*, XII. sér. 3, 230 (1868); in *Mél. Biol.* VI. 374 (1868). — Franchet & Savatier, *Enum. Pl. Jap.* I. 471 (1875). — Masters in *Jour. Linn. Soc.* XVIII. 496 (1881). — Matsumura, *Ind. Pl. Jap.* II. pt. 1, 10 (1905). — Hayata, *Veget. Mt. Fuji*, 95 (1911). — Elwes & Henry, *Trees Gr. Brit. & Irel.* VI. 1422 (1912). — Clinton-Baker, *Ill. Conif.* III. 20, t. (1913).

There can be no question that this Juniper is a variety of *J. communis* L. and I very much doubt if it is entitled to rank as distinct from the variety *montana* Ait. The upper side of the leaf is normally deeply sulcate and not merely concave as in all recognized forms of *J. communis*. This is the only difference I can find and on specimens I collected on Mt. Ontake some of the leaves are concave above and indistinguishable from those of the variety *montana*. Moreover, on specimens of the latter from Alaska I find an occasional leaf which is sulcate above. The fruit of var. *nipponica* is from 1 to 3 seeded as in the var. *montana* and in the fruits themselves I cannot find the slightest difference. Maximowicz recognized the similarity in appearance of his *J. nipponica* and *J. nana* Willd. (syn. *J. communis*, var. *montana* Ait.), but considered his plant to be more closely related to *J. rigida* S. & Z. of which he suggested it might represent a dwarf form — although he had seen no intermediates. To me this view is untenable. The straight, acicular, triquetrous leaves of *J. rigida* S. & Z. readily distinguish it from *J. communis* L., and any of its forms, while some specimens of Maximowicz's plant are almost identical with *J. communis*, var. *montana* Ait. The Japanese variety is now in cultivation in this Arboretum from seeds I collected and until more is known about it I think it best to retain it as a variety distinct from others of *J. communis*.

This Japanese variety of the Common Juniper is an alpine shrub and is found on many of the high mountains of Hondo from the Shinano province northward, but it has not yet been reported from Hokkaido. I met with it first on Mt. Ontake in Shinano province, between 2800 and 3200 m. altitude, where it grows with *Pinus pumila* Regel and scrubby bushes of *Abies Mariesii* Mast. On Adzuma-san in Uzen province it is common above 1800 m. altitude, and on Chokai-san in Ugo province it is plentiful above the tree limit. The most northerly point I met with it was on Hayachine-san in Rikuchu province, where it is abundant on the upper slopes and summits. Usually the branches of this Juniper are wide-spreading and ascending toward the ends and form a broad shrub from 0.5 to 1.3 m. high; very often, however, the branches are prostrate and form a wide mat. The leaves are curved and point forward and are more or less strongly keeled on the under side. The fruit is globose or slightly longer than broad, more or less glaucous and black or brownish black when ripe and contains from one to three seeds; the summit of the fruit is marked by three short radiating lines and three slight depressions overhung by three minute mucros which indicate the three scales of which the fruit is composed. On ripe fruit these lines, depressions and mucros are often somewhat obscure, but not more so than on similar fruits of *J. communis*.

The Japanese name for this Juniper is Miyama-nezu, and for garden purposes its decorative value should be the same as that of the var. *montana*, but as yet we know nothing of its hardiness and adaptability to cultivation. I did not see this plant in any Japanese gardens, but I have before me a specimen from a garden of the Yore-nezu which, according to Matsumura, is the *J. rigida*, var. *filiformis*[1] of Maximowicz. My specimen represents a mere condition of *J. communis*, var. *nipponica* with weak slender branchlets and is not a form of *J. rigida* S. & Z.

JUNIPERUS RIGIDA S. & Z.

PLATE LVIII

JUNIPERUS RIGIDA Siebold & Zuccarini in *Abh. Akad. Münch.* IV. pt. 3, 233 (*Fl. Jap. Fam. Nat.* II. 109) (1846). — Endlicher, *Syn. Conif.* 17 (1847). — Miquel in *Ann. Mus. Lugd.-Bat.* III. 167 (1867); *Prol. Fl. Jap.* 331 (1867); in Siebold & Zuccarini, *Fl. Jap.* II. 56, t. 125 (1870). — Franchet & Savatier, *Enum. Pl. Jap.* I. 471 (1875). — Franchet in *Nouv. Arch. Mus. Paris*, sér. 2, VII. 102 (*Pl. David.* I. 292) (1884). — Sargent, *Forest Fl. Jap.* 78 (1894). — Palibin in *Act. Hort. Petrop.* XIV. 145 (1895). — Kent in Veitch, *Man. Conif.* ed. 2, 188 (1900). — Shirasawa, *Icon. Ess. For. Jap.* I. 28, t. 12, fig. 1-13 (1900). — Komarov in *Act. Hort. Petrop.* XX. 207 (*Fl. Mandsh.* I.) (1901). — Matsumura, *Ind. Pl. Jap.* II. pt. 1, 11 (1905). — Nakai in *Jour. Coll. Sci. Tokyo*, XXXI. 383 (*Fl. Kor.* pt. 2) (1911). — Elwes & Henry, *Trees Gr. Brit. & Irel.* VI. 1408 (1912). — Clinton-Baker, *Ill. Conif.* III. 12, fig. (1913). — Bean, *Trees & Shrubs Brit. Isl.* I. 674, fig. (1914).

Juniperus communis Thunberg, *Fl. Jap.* 264 (not Linnaeus) (1784).

This Juniper is common on grass- and shrub-clad mountain-slopes from central Hondo southward to Kyushu. The northern limit of its distribution appears to be about the latitude of Tokyo and it is found from sea-level up to 1500 m. above the sea. On the moorland slopes of Yatsuga-dake, on the borders of Kai and Shinano provinces, this Juniper is abundant. It is also plentiful in the vicinity of Akashina in Shinano province and, according to Sargent, it is equally so on barren sandy hills around Gifu in Mino province. On the mainland of eastern Asia, it grows in Korea and in parts of Mandshuria and reaches its western limit on Hsiao-Wutai-shan in the Chili province of northern China. As usually seen *Juniperus rigida* is an upright, columnar bush or small tree from 1 to 6 or 8 m. tall; more rarely is it a tree of medium size. At Miyajima in Aki province I saw the largest trees. These grow in the Pine woods at sea-level and are from 12 to 15 m. tall and from 1.3 to 1.6 m. in girth of trunk. The bark is gray, thin and scaly and furrowed on old trees. On the larger trees the branches are ascending-spreading and spreading and form a narrow pyramidal crown; the lesser branchlets are pendent. The leaves are spreading, in whorls of threes, are from 1.5 to 3 cm. long, acicular, triquetrous and very pungent; the upper surface is deeply channelled and has one narrow median line of stomata. The fruit, which ripens the second year, is globose, about the size of a garden pea, and is composed of three scales separated at the summit by three radiating lines, and is normally three- or sometimes two- or rarely one-seeded by abortion. When ripe the fruit is brownish black and slightly shining, but until then it is more or less glaucous.

This Juniper is cultivated in temple grounds and gardens generally in Japan

---

[1] This name was not published by Maximowicz and the first reference to it I can find is in Bretschneider's *Hist. Europ. Bot. Disc. China*, 610 (1898).

and is known at Muro and Nezu. In eastern North America it thrives and is perfectly hardy as far north as Boston. It grows freely and with its gray-green leaves and columnar habit it is decidedly ornamental. It was discovered by von Siebold and introduced into England in 1861 by John Gould Veitch.

JUNIPERUS CONFERTA Parl.

PLATE LIX

JUNIPERUS CONFERTA Parlatore, *Conif. Nov.* 1 (1863); in De Candolle, *Prodr.* XVI. pt. 2, 481 (1868). — Sargent, *Forest Fl. Jap.* 78 (1894).

Juniperus litoralis Maximowicz in *Bull. Acad. Sci. St. Pétersbourg*, sér. 3. XII. 230 (1868); in *Mél. Biol.* VI. 375 (1868). — Franchet & Savatier, *Enum. Pl. Jap.* I. 471 (1875). — Masters in *Jour. Linn. Soc.* XVIII. 496 (1881). — Matsumura, *Ind. Pl. Jap.* II. pt. 1, 10 (1905). — Elwes & Henry, *Trees Gr. Brit. & Irel.* VI. 1422 (1912). — Clinton-Baker, *Ill. Conif.* III. 18, t. (1913).

This is a littoral species and is widely spread on sandy shores where it forms dense, broad mats. I met with it first on the southern island of Tanega-shima in Osumi province, Kyushu, and the most northerly place I saw it was at Sakaihama in Saghalien on the shores of the Okhotsk Sea. In Hokkaido it is common on sand dunes on the west shores of Hakodate Bay in Oshima province. In Hondo it is plentiful on the sea coast at Nishizaki-mura, Sakai district, in Boshū province and also on the west coast near Akita in Ugo province. Very probably it occurs in many other places on the Japanese coast. The habit is always prostrate; the leaves, which are very densely crowded, are straight, pungent and are concave and often sulcate above with one median stomatic line; the under side is pale green and keeled. The fruit is three-seeded and is produced in great profusion; it is globose and bloomy black when ripe and is very variable in size. On specimens from Tanega-shima the fruit measures 1.3 cm. across and on others from Sakaihama only 0.6 cm. but between these extremes there is every gradation. The Japanese name for this Juniper is Hai-nezu. I secured a plentiful supply of seeds of this species and many young plants raised from them are now growing in this Arboretum. These plants are now a year old and all are strictly erect in habit, about 30 cm. high and very glaucous; in another garden here and raised from my seeds there are plants both upright and prostrate in habit. The species ought to be perfectly hardy in eastern North America and if it thrives should make a good ground cover and be especially valuable for covering sand dunes. *Juniperus conferta* was discovered in 1854, by the American botanist Charles Wright, in the vicinity of Hakodate and later in the same place by C. Maximowicz.

JUNIPERUS PROCUMBENS Sieb.

JUNIPERUS PROCUMBENS Siebold in *Jaarb. Nederl. Maatsch. Aanmoed. Tuinb.* 1844, 31 (*Naaml.*). — Miquel in Siebold & Zuccarini, *Fl. Jap.* II. 59, t. 127, fig. 3 (1870). — Elwes & Henry, *Trees Gr. Brit. & Irel.* VI. 1422 (1912).

Juniperus chinensis, B *procumbens* Endlicher, *Syn. Conif.* 21 (1847). — Matsumura, *Ind. Pl. Jap.* II. pt. 1, 10 (1905). — Beissner, *Handb. Nadelh.* ed. 2, 607 (exclude the synonym *J. japonica*) (1909).

Juniperus japonica Hort. apud Carrière, *Traité Conif.* 33 (as to the synonyms *J. procumbens* and *J. chinensis*, B *procumbens*) (1855).
Juniperus recurvata, var. *squamata* Masters in *Bull. Herb. Boiss.* VI. 274 (not Parlatore) (1898). — Matsumura, *Ind. Pl. Jap.* II. pt. 1, 10 (1905).
Juniperus litoralis Hort. ex Henry in Elwes & Henry, *Trees Gr. Brit. & Irel.* VI. 1422 (as a synonym, not Maximowicz) (1912).

This Juniper, so common in Japanese gardens, I did not see growing wild. As Henry points out it has no connection whatever with *J. chinensis* L. with which it was united by Endlicher as a variety and has been so accepted by many authors. It is certainly most closely related to *J. squamata* Lamb. from which, as Henry points out, it differs "in the branchlets being glaucous-white on the edges of the pulvini." The leaves are homomorphic and ternate, lance-shaped, acuminate, pungent, ascending-spreading, and concave on the upper surface with a very broad stomatic band which is divided except near the apex by a raised, green midrib. The young shoots are glaucous and the appearance of the whole plant is rather glaucous or bluish green. This Juniper is a low, spreading plant with shoots ascending at the ends. The habit is lax and the branches are rather stiff. The fruit is not known. It is perfectly hardy in this Arboretum, but brown dead leaves persist for a long time on the branches and rather disfigure the plant. However, when growing freely in good soil this is one of the handsomest of all the low-growing Junipers. The Japanese names for the plant are Hai-byakushin and Sonare.

It was sent to the Royal Dutch Horticultural Society by Teijsmann from Buitenzorg, Java, in 1843. In 1864 Maximowicz sent living plants from Japan to Petrograd, but it does not appear to have become well known in England until near the close of the nineteenth century. It is much cultivated in this country, especially in California, where there is good reason to believe it was introduced by Dr. George Hall in 1862.

JUNIPERUS CHINENSIS L.

JUNIPERUS CHINENSIS Linnaeus, *Mant.* 127 (1767). — Roxburgh, *Fl. Ind.* ed. 2, III. 838 (1832). — Bunge in *Mém. Sav. Étr. Acad. Sci. St. Pétersbourg*, II. 137 (*Enum. Pl. Chin. Bor.* 63) (1833). — Siebold & Zuccarini in *Abh. Akad. Münch.* IV. pt. 3, 233 (*Fl. Jap. Fam. Nat.* II. 109) (1846). — Miquel in *Ann. Mus. Lugd.-Bat.* III. 167 (1867); *Prol. Fl. Jap.* 331 (1867); in Siebold & Zuccarini, *Fl. Jap.* II. 58, t. 126, 127 exclude fig. 3 (1870). — Franchet & Savatier, *Enum. Pl. Jap.* I. 472 (1875). — Masters in *Jour. Linn. Soc.* XVIII. 497 (1881). — Sargent, *Forest Fl. Jap.* 78 (1894). — Shirasawa, *Icon. Ess. For. Jap.* I. 29, t. 12, fig. 14–27 (1900). — Palibin in *Act. Hort. Petrop.* XIX. 137 (*Consp. Fl. Kor.*) (1901). — Matsumura in *Tokyo Bot. Mag.* XV. 138 (1901); *Ind. Pl. Jap.* II. pt. 1, 10 (in part) (1905). — Matsumura & Hayata in *Jour. Coll. Sci. Tokyo*, XXII. 402 (*Enum. Pl. Formos.*) (1906). — Beissner, *Handb. Nadelh.* ed. 2, 602 (1909). — Elwes & Henry, *Trees Gr. Brit. & Irel.* VI. 1430 (1912). — Rehder & Wilson in Sargent, *Pl. Wilson.* II. 60 (1914).

Juniperus barbadensis Thunberg, *Fl. Jap.* 264 (not Linnaeus) (1784).
Juniperus virginica Thunberg, l. c. (not Linnaeus) (1784).
Juniperus cernua Roxburgh, *Fl. Ind.* ed. 2, III. 839 (1832).
Juniperus dimorpha Roxburgh, l. c. (1832).
Juniperus Thunbergii Hooker & Arnott, *Bot. Voy. Beechey*, 271 (1838?).
Juniperus flagelliformis Hort. apud Loudon, *Encycl. Trees & Shrubs*, 1090 (1842).

Juniperus nepalensis Hort. ex Endlicher, *Syn. Conif.* 21 (as a synonym) (1847).
Cupressus nepalensis Hort. ex Endlicher, l. c. (1847).
Juniperus Reevesiana Hort. ex Endlicher, l. c. 31 (1847).
Juniperus struthiacea Knight & Perry, *Syn. Conif.* 13 (name only) (1850?).
Juniperus sphaerica Lindley & Paxton in *Paxton's Fl. Gard.* I. 58, fig. 35 (1850–51).
Juniperus Cabiancae Visiani in *Mem. Istit. Venet. Sci.* VI. 246, t. 1** (1856).
Sabina sphaerica Antoine, *Cupress.* 52, t. 72 (in part) (1857).
Sabina chinensis Antoine, l. c. 54, t. 75, 76, fig. a, t. 78, fig. 1, u (1857).
Sabina struthiacea Antoine, l. c. 69 (1857).
Sabina dimorpha Antoine, l. c. 70 (1857).
Juniperus Fortunii Van Houtte ex Gordon, *Pinet.* 119 (as synonym) (1858).
Juniperus chinensis, var. *pendula* Franchet in *Nouv. Arch. Mus. Paris*, sér. 2, VII. 101 (*Pl. David.* I. 291) (1884).

I saw in Japan no plants of this Juniper that could be properly regarded as wild, but in the valley of the Otake-gawa in the heart of Shinano province bushes from 1 to 2 m. high with gnarled stems are common in hedgerows. Sargent reports it wild in the western part of the same province and I have wild specimens from Yakushima in Kyushu. Dr. Nakai informed me that this Juniper is spontaneous and a common tree at low level in Korea. It also grows wild in southern Mandshuria and in northeastern China and is planted in gardens and temple grounds in many places in China. As a planted tree I saw it in gardens and temple grounds in Japan from Tanega-shima northward to Tokyo, but it is not common. At the Kasuga shrine in Nara Park there is a fine old specimen of *J. chinensis* about 18 m. tall and 5 m. in girth of trunk but hollow and from it is growing a Cryptomeria tree fully 25 m. tall. The Japanese names for this tree are Byakushin and Ibuki. This Juniper was first introduced to Europe by William Kerr, who sent it from Canton, China, to England in 1804. It is very polymorphic and in Japan the form most usually cultivated has mainly acicular leaves and is a tall columnar bush or small tree. It is the var. *japonica* Vilmorin (*Hort. Vilmorin.* 58 [1906]) and was introduced into this country by Dr. George R. Hall in 1862; though common here, good specimens are rare. The branches die back and it transplants badly. Of this form there are yellow and white variegated sorts less tall than the type and even less satisfactory as garden plants. A well-marked variety of *Juniperus chinensis* is

JUNIPERUS CHINENSIS, var. SARGENTII Henry in Elwes & Henry, *Trees Gr. Brit. & Irel.* VI. 1432 (1912).

Juniperus davurica Fr. Schmidt in *Mém. Acad. Sci. St. Pétersbourg*, sér. 7, XII. no. 2, 178 (*Reis. Amur. Sachal.*) (possibly of Pallas) (1868).
Juniperus chinensis, var. Sargent, *Forest Fl. Jap.* 78 (1894).
Juniperus chinensis Matsumura, *Pl. Nikko*, 9 (not Linnaeus) (1894); *Ind. Pl. Jap.* II. pt. 1, 10 (in part) (1905). — Masters in *Bull. Herb. Boiss.* VI. 274 (1898).
Juniperus procumbens Sargent in *Garden & Forest*, X. 421 (not Siebold) (1897).
Juniperus chinensis, var. *procumbens* Takeda in *Jour. Linn. Soc.* XLII. 486 (not Endlicher) (1914). — Miyabe & Miyake, *Fl. Saghal.* 593 (1915).

This boreal and prostrate variety of the Chinese Juniper is indigenous in northern Hondo but is not common. The southern limit of its range as far as is known is on the lofty Shirane-san in the Nikko region where it grows at 2300 m. altitude. On Hayachine-san in Rikuchu province I found it fairly plentiful on the upper southeast slopes at about 2000 m. altitude, forming dense mats on and among rocks. Faurie collected it on Hakkoda-yama in Mutsu province, but I did not see it there. In Hokkaido this Juniper is more abundant and descends to sea-level near Mororan in Iburi province and elsewhere. In Saghalien it appears to be rare, but on the island of Shikotan, one of the most southern of the Kurile group, Takeda says it is "common on hillsides; replacing *Pinus pumila*, which is unknown on this island." From continental Asia there is no record of this Juniper, but it is possible that it may be the *J. davurica* Pallas (*Fl. Ross.* I. pt. 2, 13, t. 55 [1788]).

In habit this plant is perfectly prostrate and the long spreading stems hug the ground, but when crowded among rocks or bushes the stems are forced upward and form a low hummock-like mass. Normally, however, this plant makes broad mats. The lateral branches are short and point upward and forward. On the fruiting plants the leaves are all, or nearly all, scale-like and imbricated, but on young plants the leaves are all lanceolate, concave and ascending-spreading. According to the age of the plants all intermediate stages can be found. In color the foliage varies from grass-green in young plants to bluish green in adults. The fruit in size and shape is identical with that of the type species and on material before me contains from one to four seeds.

This plant was introduced to this Arboretum by Professor Sargent, who collected seeds near Mororan, Hokkaido, in 1892. It has proved perfectly hardy, grows freely and its stems and branchlets overlap one another in such a manner as to form neat, low, wide-spreading masses of green. As a ground cover this Juniper is among the most valuable of all the known kinds. Henry appears to have been the first to recognize the difference of this Juniper from the other forms of *J. chinensis*. Some Japanese botanists have confused it with the very different *J. procumbens* Sieb. (syn. *J. chinensis*, var. *procumbens* Endl.). On a specimen collected on Shirane-san in the Nikko region by K. Sakurai the vernacular name of Sargent's Juniper is given as Ibuki.

INDEX

INDEX

Abies, 14, 54.
   acicularis, 42.
   ajanensis, 44.
      microsperma, 45.
   ajonensis, 44.
   Alcoquiana, 42, 45.
   araragi, 49.
   bicolor, 42.
   bifida, 55.
   brachyphylla, 57.
   diversifolia, 50.
   Eichleri, 61.
   excelsa, var. *acicularis*, 42.
   Finhonnoskiana, 57.
   firma, 27, 37, 54.
   firma, 57.
      bifida, 55.
   Glehnii, 40.
   Gmelinii, 32.
   homolepis, 54, 57.
      Toknaiae, 62.
      umbellata, 58.
   japonica, 61.
   jezoënsis, 44.
   Kaempferi, 30.
   kamtschatica, 33.
   Khutrow, 36.
   leptolepis, 30.
   Mariesii, 54, 59.
   Maximowiczii, 38.
   Menziesii, 45.
   microcarpa, 45.
   microsperma, 45.
   momi, 55.
   nemorensis, 63.
   obovata, var. *japonica*, 38.
   polita, 36.
   sachalinensis, 54, 62.
      nemorensis, 63.
   Schrenkiana, 45.
   Sitchensis, 45.
   Smithiana, 36.
   spec.nova (Pichtae aff.), 61.
   Thunbergii, 27, 37, 55.
   torano, 36.
   Tschonoskiana, 57.
   Tsuga, 49.
      nana, 50.
   umbellata, 58.
   umbilicata, 58.
   Veitchii, 54, 60.
   Veitchii, 57.
      Nikkoënsis, 61.
      olivacea, 62.

Abies *Veitchii*
      reflexa, 61.
      sachalinensis, 62.
Abieteae, 14.
Abura-gaya, 7.
Agathis Dammara, 5.
Aka-matsu, 25.
Aka-yezo-matsu, 41.
Anatni, 7.
Aomori-todomatsu, 60.
Araragi, 12.
Asuhi, 72.
Asunaro, 72.

Bandaisho, 26.
Bara-momi, 37.
Byakushin, 85.

Caryotaxus nucifera, 9.
Cephalotaxus, 3, 6.
   ? *Buergeri*, 8.
   coriacea, 7.
   drupacea, 6.
      β, 8.
      fastigiata, 8.
      Harringtonia, 8.
      pedunculata, 8.
   foemina, 7.
   Fortunei foemina, 7.
      Harringtonia, 8.
      koraiana, 8.
      pedunculata, 8.
         fastigiata, 8.
   tardiva, 13.
   umbraculifera, 11.
Chamaecyparis, 14, 76.
   obtusa, 76.
      formosana, 77.
      gracilis aurea, 78.
      nana, 78.
      nana aurea, 78.
   pisifera, 76, 78.
      filifera, 79.
      plumosa, 79.
      squarrosa, 79.
Chamaepeuce obtusa, 76.
Chosen-maki, 8.
Chosen-matsu, 17.
Cryptomeria, 14, 66.
   Fortunei, 71.
   japonica, 66.
      araucarioides, 71.
      elegans, 71.
      elegans nana, 71.

Cryptomeria japonica
      Fortunei, 71.
      japonica, 66.
      Lobbii, 66, 71.
      sinensis, 71.
Cupresseae, 14, 71.
Cupressus japonica, 66.
   nepalensis, 85.
   obtusa, 76.
   pisifera, 78

Dake-momi, 58.
Dammara Veitchii, 5.
Dolophyllum sp., 71.

Fœtataxus nucifera, 9.
Fuji-matsu, 31.

Ginkgo, 1.
   biloba, 1.
   macrophylla, 1.
Ginkgoaceae, 1.
Ginnan-no-ki, 2.
Gorō-hiba, 75.
Goyō-matsu, 24.
Goyō-toga, 53.

Hai-byakushin, 84.
Hai-matsu, 19.
Hai-nezu, 83.
Hari-momi, 37.
Hiba, 72.
Hime-bara-momi, 39.
Hime-komatsu, 24.
Hinoki, 77.
Hinoki-asunaro, 74.
Hon-maki, 4.

Ibuki, 85, 86.
Ichii, 12.
Ichō, 2.
Ichō-no-ki, 2.
Inu-gaya, 7.
Inu-maki, 4.
Iramomi, 44.

Juniperus, 14, 79.
   alpina, 80.
   barbadensis, 84.
   borealis, 80.
   Cabiancae, 85.
   canadensis, 80.
   cernua, 84.
   chinensis, 79, 84.
   chinensis, 4, 85.
      japonica, 85.

INDEX

Juniperus *chinensis*
    pendula, 85.
    procumbens, 83, 85.
    Sargentii, 85.
    var., 85.
  communis, 79.
  communis, 82.
    alpina, 80.
    β, 80.
    γ, 80.
    erecta, 80.
    hispanica, 80.
    montana, 80.
    nana, 80.
    nipponica, 81.
    saxatilis, 80.
    Sibirica, 80.
    var., 80.
    vulgaris, 80.
  conferta, 79, 83.
  davurica, 86.
  davurica, 85.
  dealbata, 80.
  difformis, 80.
  dimorpha, 84.
  flagelliformis, 84.
  Fortunii, 85.
  japonica, 84.
  litoralis, 83, 84.
  nana, 80.
    alpina, 80.
    montana, 80.
  nepalensis, 85.
  nipponica, 81.
  procumbens, 79, 83.
  procumbens, 85.
  pygmaea, 80.
  recurvata, var. *squamata*, 84.
  Reevesiana, 85.
  rigida, 79, 82.
    filiformis, 82.
  sibirica, 80.
  sphaerica, 85.
  struthiacea, 85.
  Thunbergii, 84.
  virginica, 84.

Kara-maatz, 31.
Kara-matsu, 30, 31.
Kaya, 9.
Kome-tsuga, 52.
Koya-maki, 64.
Kurobi, 75.
Kuro-matsu, 27.
Kuro-tsuga, 52.
Kusa-maki, 4.

Larix, 14, 29.
  alaskensis, 29.

Larix
  Cajanderi, 32.
  dahurica, 31.
  dahurica, 32, 33.
    chlorocarpa, 34.
    japonica, 30, 33.
      ochrocarpa, 34.
    Kurilensis, 33.
    pubescens, 33.
    typica, 32.
  europaea, var. *dahurica*, 32.
  japonica, 30.
    macrocarpa, 30.
  Kaempferi, 30.
  Kaempferi, 30.
    minor, 30.
  Kamtschatica, 33.
  Kurilensis, 33.
  laricina, 29.
  leptolepis, 30.
    minor, 30.
    Murrayana, 30.
  orientalis, 30.
  pendula, 32.
  sibirica, 33.
Libocedrus Dolobrata, 71.
Lo-han-sung, 5.
Lo-hon-tsong, 5.

Maki, 4.
Me-matsu, 26.
Micropeuce Sieboldii, 49.
Miyama-nezu, 81.
Momi, 55.
Muro, 83.
Myrica nagi, 5.

Nageia japonica, 5.
  Nagi, 5.
Nagi, 6.
Nezu, 83.
Nezuko, 75.

Oba-goyō-matsu, 17.
Oh-shirabiso, 60.
O-matsu, 28.
Onko, 12.

Picea, 14, 35.
  acicularis, 42.
  Ajanensis, 44.
    japonica, 45.
    microsperma, 45.
    subintegerrima, 45.
  Alcockiana, 42.
  bicolor, 36, 42.
    acicularis, 42.
    reflexa, 42.
  brachyphylla, 57.

Picea
  excelsa, var. *obovata japonica*, 38.
  firma, 55.
    A, 57.
    B, 55.
    bifida, 55.
  Glehnii, 35, 40.
  Hondoënsis, 45.
  japonica, 42.
  jezoënsis, 36, 44.
    hondoonsis, 45.
  Khutrow, 36.
  Koyamai, 35, 39.
  Maximowiczii, 35, 38.
  microsperma, 45.
  obovata, 45.
    japonica, 38.
  polita, 27, 35, 36.
  Schrenkiana, 40.
  Torano, 36.
  Tschonoskii, 38.
  Tsuga Sieboldii, 49.
  Veitchii, 61.
Pinaceae, 14.
Pinus, 14.
  Abies, 27, 37, 55.
  Alcoquiana, 42.
  araragi, var. *diversifolia*, 50.
    nana, 50.
  Armandi, 15, 20.
    Mastersiana, 20.
  bifida, 55.
  brachyphylla, 57.
  cembra, 18, 22.
    excelsa, 15.
    Japonica, 22.
    Manchurica, 16.
    pumila, 18.
    pygmaea, 18.
  dahurica, 32.
  densiflora, 15, 25.
    aurea, 26.
    globosa, 26.
    pendula, 26.
    umbraculifera, 26.
  excelsa, var. *chinensis*, 20.
  Finhonnoskiana, 57.
  firma, 55, 57.
  glehnii, 40.
  Harryana, 57.
  homolepis, 57.
  hondoënsis, 45.
  jezoënsis, 44.
    microsperma, 45.
  Kaempferi, 30.
  kamtschatika, 33.
  koraiensis, 15.
  koraiensis, 20, 22.
    variegata, 17.

INDEX

Pinus
  Larix, 30.
  leptolepis, 30.
  levis, 20.
  mandshurica, 15, 18, 20.
  mariesii, 59.
  Massoniana, 25, 27.
    aurea, 26.
  Mastersiana, 20.
  Menziesii, 45.
  momi, 55.
  morrisonicola, 24.
  nephrolepis, var. *veitchii*, 61.
  parviflora, 15, 22.
  parviflora, 18.
    pentaphylla, 22.
    variegata, 24.
  pentaphylla, 22.
  Pinea, 25.
  polita, 36.
  pumila, 15, 17.
  pygmaea, 18.
  quinquefolia, 20.
  rubra, 27.
  sachalinensis, 62.
    nemorensis, 63.
  scipioniformis, 20.
  scopifera, 25.
  selenolepis, 61.
  Sieboldii, 49.
  Strobus, 15.
  sylvestris, 25, 27.
    rubra?, 25.
  Thunbergii, 15, 27.
  Thunbergii, 37, 55.
    monophylla, 28.
    pendula, 28.
    variegata, 28.
  torano, 36.
  Tsuga, 49.
    nana, 50.
  umbilicata, 58.
  Veitchii, 61.
  verticillata, 64.
Platycladus dolabrata, 71.
Podocarpeae, 3.
Podocarpus, 3.
  appressa, 5.
  chinensis, 4.
  coraianus, 8.
  coriacea, 7.
  drupacea, 7.
  japonica, 5.
  koraiana, 8.
  macrophyllus, 3.
    angustifolius, 4.
    appressus, 5.

Podocarpus macrophyllus
    grandifolius, 4.
    maki, 4, 5.
  Makoyi, 5.
  Miquelia, 5.
  Nageia, 5.
  nagi, 3, 5.
  nucifera, 9.
  Sciadopitys, 8.
  Vrieseana, 5.
Pseudolarix Kaempferi, 30.
Pseudotsuga, 14, 52.
  japonica, 52.
  Wilsoniana, 53.
Pterophyllus Salisburiensis, 1.

Rakuyōshō, 31.
Retinispora obtusa, 76.
  pisifera, 78.
Retinospora obtusa, 76.
  pisifera, 78.

Sabina chinensis, 85.
  dimorpha, 85.
  sphaerica, 85.
  struthiacea, 85.
Salisburia adiantifolia, 1.
Sawara, 78.
Sciadopitys, 14, 64.
  verticillata, 64.
    pendula, 65.
Sekkwa-maki, 5.
Shan-sha, 6.
Sha-shan, 6.
Shirabe-momi, 62.
Shirabiso, 62.
Shira-tsuga, 62.
Sonare, 84.
Sugi, 69.
Sūo-no-ki, 12.

Tanyosho, 26.
Taxaceae, 3.
Taxeae, 3, 6.
Taxodieae, 14, 64.
Taxodium japonicum, 66.
Taxus, 3, 10.
  adpressa, 13.
  baccata, 11.
    adpressa, 13.
    cuspidata, 11.
      latifolia, 11.
    globosa, f. tardiva, 13.
    microcarpa, 11.
    tardiva, 13.
  brevifolia, 13.
  chinensis, 4.

Taxus
  coriacea, 7.
  cuspidata, 11.
    densa, 13.
    nana, 13.
  Harringtonia, 8.
  Inukaja, 8.
  Japonica, 7, 8.
  macrophylla, 3.
  Makoya, 4.
  nucifera, 9.
  Sinensis, 8.
    tardiva, 13.
  tardiva, 13.
  verticillata, 64.
Thuiopsis? Standishi, 74.
Thuja, 14, 74.
  dolabrata, 71.
  japonica, 74.
  Standishii, 74.
Thujopsis, 14, 71.
  dolabrata, 71.
  dolabrata, 73.
    australis, 71.
    Hondai, 72.
    nana, 72.
  Hondai, 73.
  laetevirens, 71.
Thuya gigantea, 75.
  Japonica, 75.
  obtusa, 76.
  pisifera, 78.
Todo-matsu, 63.
Toga-matsu, 50.
Toga-suwara, 53.
Tōhi, 48.
Toranoo-momi, 37.
Torreya, 3, 9.
  nucifera, 9.
Tsuga, 14, 48, 50.
  Ajanensis, 45.
  Araragi, 49.
    nana, 50.
  diversifolia, 48, 50.
  japonica, 52.
  Pseudo-tsuga japonica, 52.
  Sieboldii, 37, 48.
    nana, 50.
  Tsuja, 49.
Tumion nuciferum, 9.

Urajiro-momi, 58.

Veitchia japonica, 45.

Yatsuga-dake-tōhi, 40.
Yezo-matsu, 41, 48.
Yin-kuo, 2.

ILLUSTRATIONS

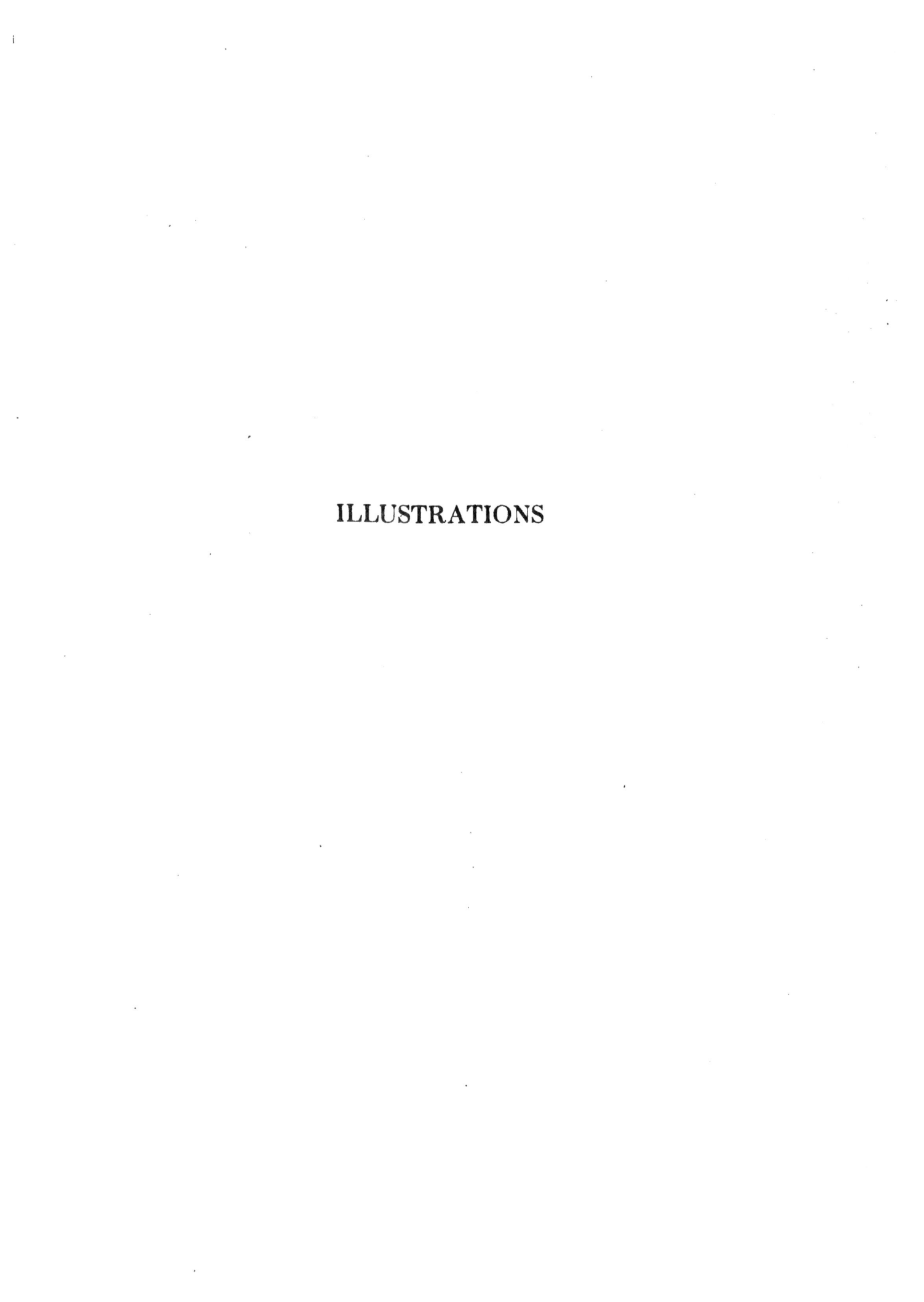

PLATE I

PODOCARPUS NAGI Zoll. & Moritz.

PLATE II

PODOCARPUS NAGI Zoll. & Moritz.

PLATE III

TORREYA NUCIFERA S. & Z.

PLATE IV

TORREYA NUCIFERA S. & Z.

PLATE V

TAXUS CUSPIDATA S. & Z.

PLATE VI

PINUS KORAIENSIS S. & Z.

PLATE VII

PINUS KORAIENSIS S. & Z.

PLATE VIII

PINUS PUMILA Regel

PLATE IX

PINUS PARVIFLORA S. & Z.

PLATE X

PINUS PARVIFLORA S. & Z.

PLATE XI

PINUS DENSIFLORA S. & Z.

PLATE XII

PINUS DENSIFLORA, var. UMBRACULIFERA Mayr

PLATE XIII

PINUS THUNBERGII Parl.

PLATE XIV

PINUS THUNBERGII Parl.

PLATE XV

LARIX KAEMPFERI Sarg.

PLATE XVI

LARIX KAEMPFERI Sarg.

PLATE XVII

LARIX DAHURICA, var. JAPONICA Maxim.

PLATE XVIII

LARIX DAHURICA, var. JAPONICA Maxim.

Plate XIX

PICEA POLITA Carr.

PLATE XX

PICEA POLITA Carr.

PLATE XXI

PICEA MAXIMOWICZII Regel

PLATE XXII

PICEA MAXIMOWICZII Regel

PLATE XXIII

PICEA KOYAMAI Shiras.

PLATE XXIV

PICEA KOYAMAI Shiras.

PLATE XXV

PICEA GLEHNII Mast.

PLATE XXVI

PICEA GLEHNII Mast.

PLATE XXVII

PICEA JEZOËNSIS Carr.

PLATE XXVIII

PICEA JEZOËNSIS Carr.

PLATE XXIX

TSUGA SIEBOLDII Carr.

PLATE XXX

TSUGA SIEBOLDII Carr.

PLATE XXXI

TSUGA DIVERSIFOLIA Mast.

PLATE XXXII

TSUGA DIVERSIFOLIA Mast.

PLATE XXXIII

PSEUDOTSUGA JAPONICA Beissn.

PLATE XXXIV

PSEUDOTSUGA JAPONICA Beissn.

PLATE XXXV

ABIES FIRMA S. & Z.

PLATE XXXVI

ABIES FIRMA S. & Z.

PLATE XXXVII

ABIES HOMOLEPIS S. & Z.

PLATE XXXVIII

ABIES HOMOLEPIS S. & Z.

ABIES HOMOLEPIS, var. UMBELLATA Wils.

Plate XL

ABIES MARIESII Mast.

PLATE XLI

ABIES MARIESII Mast.

PLATE XLII

ABIES VEITCHII Lindl.

PLATE XLIII

ABIES VEITCHII Lindl.

PLATE XLIV

ABIES SACHALINENSIS Mast.

PLATE XLV

ABIES SACHALINENSIS Mast.

PLATE XLVI

SCIADOPITYS VERTICILLATA S. & Z.

PLATE XLVII

SCIADOPITYS VERTICILLATA S. & Z.

PLATE XLVIII

CRYPTOMERIA JAPONICA D. Don

PLATE XLIX

CRYPTOMERIA JAPONICA D. Don

PLATE L

THUJOPSIS DOLABRATA, var. HONDAI Mak.

THUJOPSIS DOLABRATA, var. HONDAI Mak.

PLATE LII

THUJA STANDISHII Carr.

THUJA STANDISHII Carr.

PLATE LIV

CHAMAECYPARIS OBTUSA S. & Z.

CHAMAECYPARIS OBTUSA S. & Z.

Plate LVI

CHAMAECYPARIS PISIFERA S. & Z.

PLATE LVII

CHAMAECYPARIS PISIFERA S. & Z.

PLATE LVIII

JUNIPERUS RIGIDA S. & Z.

PLATE LIX

JUNIPERUS CONFERTA Parl.

Printed by BoD in Norderstedt, Germany